Quintet

FIVE JOURNEYS TOWARD MUSICAL FULFILLMENT

DAVID BLUM

FOREWORD BY

ARNOLD STEINHARDT

CORNELL UNIVERSITY PRESS

ITHACA AND LONDON

First Published 1999 by Cornell University Press

Chapters 1, 2, 3, and 4 originally appeared in *The New Yorker*. An abridged version of chapter 5 appeared in *The New York Times* on 23 July 1995.

Printed in the United States of America

Library of Congress Cataloging-in-Publication Data
Blum, David, 1935–1998.
Quintet : five journeys toward musical fulfillment / David Blum;
with a foreword by Arnold Steinhardt.
p. cm.
Articles originally published in The New Yorker and the New Tork Times.
Includes bibliographical references and index.
ISBN 0-8014-3731-8 (cloth)
1. Musicians—Biography.   2. Ma, Yo-Yo, 1955–   3. Tate, Jeffrey.   4. Gingold, Josef.
5. Goode, Richard.   6. Nilsson, Birgit.   I. Title.
ML394.B66 1999
780'.92'2—dc21
[B]
99-047562

Cornell University Press strives to use enviornmentally responsible suppliers and materials to the fullest extent possible in the publishing of its books. Such materials include vegatable-based, low-VOC inks, and acid-free papers that are recycled, totally chlorine-free, or partially composed of nonwood fibers. Books that bear the logo of the FSC (Forest Stewardship Council) use paper taken from forests that have been inspected and certified as meeting the highest standards for enviornmental and social responsibility. For futher information, visit our website at www.cornellpress.cornell.edu.

Cloth printing   10 9 8 7 6 5 4 3 2 1

FSC   FSC Trademark © 1996 Forest Stewardship Council A.C.
SW-COC-098

For the formation of the artist, the first prerequisite

should be the development of the human being.

—Franz Liszt

Each of the stories of these five remarkable musicians traces a journey in which musical and personal development are inseparable. A struggle is waged that eventually leads, often in unforseen ways, to greater human and artistic fulfillment. In every case, success is measured in terms that are internal as well as external.

—David Blum

CONTENTS

FOREWORD

Rereading these five portraits, brought together in the present collection for the first time since their original appearance in the *New Yorker* and the *New York Times*, I am all the more taken with their breadth, detail, and honesty. Yo-Yo Ma, Jeffrey Tate, Josef Gingold, Richard Goode, and Birgit Nilsson appear to have overcome the obstacles of shyness, privacy, and career management and allowed David Blum unreservedly into their lives. I was informed, stimulated, entertained, and moved—sometimes to the point of outright laughter and, yes, even to tears. Having known and worked with all these musicians except Nilsson, I could hear their individual voices lifting off the printed page. Blum captures their inimitable self-expression, their turn of mind and fine shading of wit. And more significantly, he accompanies his subjects into the mysteries of the creative process, uncovering hidden connections and latent meaning for reader and subject alike. Jeffrey Tate commented: "David's deeply original and inspiring relationship to music gave me so much insight into what I was doing, why I was doing it, and its place in the nature of things."

Those of us destined to appear in print tend, instinctively, to adopt a defensive stance. Musicians are no exception to the rule, sometimes doling out bits and pieces of their thoughts and lives that serve their public and privately held images. I have often sensed an unspoken conflict of goals lurking behind the smiles and good cheer when "note-makers" meet "wordsmiths." The writer seeks truth, even if unflattering and painful to the subject. The musician also values truth, but preferably an alluring and glamorous version so that he or she might be bathed in a more favorable light. Even for those musicians who earnestly want to tell their whole story, warts and all, crucial elements may never see the light of day. There are writers who seek to dramatize or sensationalize for effect, and there are those who are unwilling or simply incapable of sallying forth into deep waters. Often we are left with the superficial, the banal. *Quintet*'s profiles stand in marked contrast.

As I ask myself how David Blum managed to create studies of such depth and scope, the intense, rather awkward adolescent I knew nearly half a century ago spontaneously comes to mind. By the time I met David he was a seventeen-year-old composer with a considerable body of work already behind him. Among his works are a ballet score to *Cyrano de Bergerac*, two operas, symphonic works, tone poems, and several books of songs. In the dual legacy he left, those principles so critical to composing—originality, clarity, proportion, and expressive nuance—imprinted themselves on both his writing and music-making.

Our first musical encounter took place in his parents' living room where David somehow cajoled several young musicians into rehearsing works for chamber orchestra. His face flushed and uplifted with the discovery of new treasures, David led us for the first time through a host of works from Mozart's *Eine Kleine Nachtmusik* to Wagner's *Siegfried Idyll*. Looking back on that experience, I see that the ardor, the urgency that we all shared might have evoked patronizing smiles from any adults present. "Teenagers!" they probably muttered with the knowledge that youthful excess would give way to a reasonable and predictable existence. Most of the youngsters in that living room undoubtedly did settle down quietly. But David never seemed to acquire the calluses that time and repetition bring to the senses. His response to things of beauty and meaning—the engines that seem to have driven his life—remained fresh and charged.

From those embryonic living room rehearsals evolved a series of live television performances. David made his conducting debut in 1952 with his Youth Orchestra. A decade later, he founded the Esterhazy Orchestra with Pablo Casals as honorary president. This orchestra became one of New York's finest chamber ensembles. The Blum-Esterhazy Orchestra recordings made more than twenty-five years ago are treasured by many for their Haydn interpretations.

Among the seminal influences in David's musical life, one figure towers above the rest. David first heard Casals conduct at the Prades Festival. It was a transformative experience. Subsequently, his warm friendship with the maestro took him on numerous occasions to Puerto Rico where they had probing and far-ranging conversations. In the early 1960s David attended a series of master classes in Zermatt, Berkeley, and the Marlboro Music Festival, observing and notetaking for his own sake to learn from this great artist and teacher. The conversations, observations, and—perhaps most important of all—Casals's profound influence on David's actual music-making, became the incisive analytical groundwork for David's first book, *Casals and the Art of Interpretation*, a distillation of Casals's musical legacy. This work launched David into a major writing career.

The relationship between performer and music was central to Blum's thinking. He refined his craft over the years, interviewing and writing profiles for the *Strad, BBC Magazine*, and the *New York Times* about artists with whom he felt a keen affinity—including Igor Oistrakh, Kyung-Wha Chung, Felix Galimir, Bernard Greenhouse, Bruno Giuranna, Richard Stolzman, Michael Tree, and Dawn Upshaw. He went on to write two more books: a biography, *Paul Tortelier*, and *The Art of Quartet Playing: The Guarneri Quartet in Conversation with David Blum*.

When one spends a lifetime in a career that demands facing interviewers of every description, a David Blum encounter stands out with a rare and provocative glow. I know this from the direct experience of thoughtful and searching conversations we held in preparation for the Guarneri Quartet book and later for a *Strad* article about my reflections on Schubert. David had a way of getting at the elusive beauty of a work, often asking not just one but a series of interrelated questions to probe beyond the expected. Absent were mechanical questions. A more typical query might lead into the architecture of music: What made the wild "Great Fugue" at the end of Beethoven's String Quartet Opus 130 so structurally important, and why, under pressure from his publisher, was he so willing to replace it with a lighter weight movement? Or, why did Schubert feel compelled to alter his song, "Sei mir gegrüsst," when it appears in his *Fantasy for Vio-*

lin and Piano as the theme for a series of variations? David's knowledge, involvement, humor, and, I might add, good will made productive conversation inevitable.

Diagnosed with inoperable cancer in 1996, David, true to his nature, chose to meet the threat of terminal illness honestly and openly with family, friends, and the public. In an article unprecedented for the *BBC Magazine*, "The Healing Power Of Music," David shared how music helped to deliver him from his fears as he dealt with the challenges of cancer. An astonishing legacy of his inner journey is the moving documentary film he made in the last year of his life. Never having taken an art lesson, David created a series of oil-based drawings depicting his dreams throughout his struggle with cancer. Those dreams were of radiant landscapes, sustaining feminine figures, a dachshund quartet, and the music of Mozart and Beethoven. The film is an incandescent expression of David's creative imagination and spiritual powers.

Substance and depth are what animated David. It would have been out of character to write about a glib virtuoso or a fashionable new diva. David searched for musical personalities who inspired him, and although he became a prolific writer he never wrote about anyone who didn't arouse a deep-rooted empathy. David was drawn to the towering works of music in the canon and to performers who could crawl inside a composer's skin, inhabit one of his creations, and convey to the listener its radiance and mystery.

The challenges and discoveries of *Quintet*'s five artists provide fascinating and valuable information. Yo-Yo Ma's frank disclosures about his youthful excesses might be invaluable for parents with a gifted child on their hands; Birgit Nilsson's confession of her early vocal problems is a lesson for any young hopeful; Richard Goode's confrontation with concert nerves gives courage to those of us who are performers; Josef Gingold's example of what it means to be a concert master—the ideal conduit between orchestra and conductor—is instructive to audiences as well as to orchestra players. And Jeffrey Tate's transition from opera coach to world class conductor, while transcending his disability, is nothing less than inspiring to all.

David focuses on the organic whole, the musician inseparable from the human being, and the personal journey each artist has undertaken to create the alchemy of performance. It is a process of musical study, self-awareness, and recognition of one's limitations that every musician must undergo privately. To be rounded, whole, and truthful, these journeys require an exploration of the lesser known side of our natures—a terrain to which David felt deeply connected and compelled to visit. He invited his subjects into that subterranean place where a high degree of insight is possible; and as acts of trust and integrity they responded publicly. Our group of five speak unflinchingly about what music they excel least in, stage fright and how to deal with it, career mistakes, dead ends and their causes, and the very essence of music itself. Writing about the distinguished singer, Lotte Lehmann, David observed, "She never backed away from the living flame." It was this living flame he sought out in his subjects, and undoubtedly his own life credo, one that was severely put to the test in those last years of illness when a variety of forces—pain, doubt, fear, hope, serenity, and joy—fought for dominance.

In the course of these portraits, David makes several references to chamber music—the interplay between soloist and conductor, for example. It strikes me that the candid disclosures, the rich detail, the moving personal stories make such a powerful impression in part because David has woven himself into the interviews. His own observations about music and the resonance of his fertile mind allow the profiles to feel like music themselves as they develop and evolve. David is playing chamber music with his subjects—perhaps a duo with each, a sextet with them all. The interaction draws us to the ongoing struggle, experimentation, and fantasy of their music making. *Quintet* takes us into the living workshop of the creative artist.

—ARNOLD STEINHARDT

QUINTET

CHAPTER ONE

A Process Larger than Oneself

T he rehearsal in Monte Carlo had just ended. Yo-Yo Ma had
flown in from Lisbon that morning, and had just worked intensively on the Schumann Cello Concerto. Rehearsal time had
been short, and L'Orchestre Philharmonique de Monte Carlo, though
playing attentively, had not yet been able to get fully into the spirit of
things. "The Schumann Concerto presents difficulties for every orchestra," Ma said to me. "One needs time to warm up to it, to respond
to its very particular expressive character. Take the beginning of the
concerto. I can't be complacent when playing this melody. It took me
a number of years to learn to interpret this eloquent, this sorrowful
theme—to address all the issues of the slurs, the syncopations, the accents. Why is there an accent in the second and then in the fourth bar?
And Schumann says something special in the orchestral accompaniment: for several bars there are no notes on the first beats, only on off-
beats; one has a sense of agitation, of breathlessness. If the musicians
realize this, they'll sense the music's fear and trembling. They'll sit up
in their chairs. Suddenly the notes will mean something far beyond
what they are on the paper. When your brain and heart are engaged,
you can't go wrong."

Like many of Schumann's late works, the Cello Concerto is a problematic piece, challenging the interpreter on many levels. The composer, who was becoming increasingly subject to fits of depression,
corrected the manuscript to allay tormenting visions of angels and
demons. Much of the material—the opening theme, for instance—is
magnificent. Compositionally, some developmental passages are relatively weak and repetitious; atmospherically, they are haunting and

Yo-Yo Ma. Photograph copyright © Dorothea von Haeften. Reproduced with the permission of the photographer.

disturbing. The finale is based largely upon a short motif, an idée fixe, that flits before one like a spectre. If monotony is not to set in, the repetitions of this motif must be tempered by variety of nuance. "If the Dvořák Concerto is a heroic piece, the Schumann is a psychological one," Ma said. "In a traditional concerto you have a drama of some sort between a protagonist and an antagonist, set forth in a fairly clear-cut musical form. But the drama in Schumann is expressed in a more complex way. For instance, in the first movement a falling two-note fragment appears time and again, in different guises. If you follow its development, you can see that it has deep emotional significance. You have tremendously quick changes. The music may be following its course persistently in one mood, and then it's suddenly distracted, or panicked into something else. You have to dare to express these contrasts. All these opposing forces can't be categorized in normal sequences of time, action, and place, but they can occur in someone's mind. It's all a kind of daydream."

It is the evening of the concert, and before the performance Ma goes over some details in the Schumann score with Lawrence Foster, the conductor. There is agreement on every point. Ma, as is his custom, tunes offstage. He bounds out from the wings and greets audience and orchestra with an unassuming, boyish smile. The warmth is virtually tangible. "When I give a concert, I like to think that I'm welcoming someone to my home," he said earlier. "I've lived with the music for a long time; it's an old friend, and I want to say, 'Let's all participate.' " The greeting is genuine, but the extroversion is transitory. Taking up his cello, he embarks on an inner venture that allows no distraction of any kind; he is telling a story in sound.

In Ma's hands, the dramaturgy of the Schumann Cello Concerto emerges in an unbroken line. The opening theme is set forth feverishly, valiantly. As the movement progresses, the cello traverses pathways and byways of darkness and light. The orchestra grows increasingly responsive. Ma shapes the cantilena of the slow movement with tender restraint. To my taste, the tempo is a little too drawn out—a small matter in this context; the sense of intimacy and of fragility is deeply poignant. During bars where the cello is silent, and in orchestral transitions between movements, Ma's concentration remains uninterrupted. The finale is charged with élan. No sequence seems repetitive. Virtuosity is at the service of fantasy. The cadenza speaks of disconsolation in tones that are almost ghostlike, the bow barely touching the string. The concerto ends ebulliently: hope is renewed. And Yo-Yo Ma, smiling, accessible, is with us again.

"Some people don't consider the Schumann a 'successful' concerto," he told me. "The piece is misunderstood as a vehicle for a cello soloist, as if one were to say, 'I'm going to play the Schumann Concerto and wow the audience.' The interpreters should draw the audience into Schumann's inner world—and the audience should leave moved, perhaps fulfilled, but certainly not wowed."

Visually, Yo-Yo Ma's playing cannot be judged by traditional standards. He often departs from a consistent, classic beauty of form that one associates with such artists as Leonard Rose and Bernard Greenhouse. His playing defies the conventional wisdom that preordained orderliness of movement and position is essential to producing a beautiful tone. The cello itself appears to be almost inconsequential, no more than the most convenient conduit for his musical thought and feeling. He cradles it and rocks it from side to side, depending on which string he wishes to favor; it seems an extension of his body. No matter how impetuous his movements, no matter how awkward they may sometimes appear, his bow retains its telling contact with the string. There is no loss of tonal beauty or of accuracy of intonation. Isaac Stern praises Ma's "tremendous mastery of the instrument," and says, "He's more serious about the cello than his carefree appearance conveys. He's very conscious of what is going on, and is thinking all the time. There can be problems, as there always are, but he makes it all seem ridiculously easy. And that's the sign of a great artist."

Ma developed the extraordinary fluency and accuracy of his left hand when he was still a child. He approaches the upper and lower registers with equal surety, and the cello seems considerably reduced in size; one has the impression that he is playing a violin. He hardly ever looks at the fingerboard. This can be credited, in part, to his confidence in his technique, but, above all, he *listens* rather than looks. Curiously, many musicians don't actually listen while they play. In sustained expressive passages he closes his eyes and thrusts his head back, as if he were trying to separate himself as far as possible from the cello. In this way, paradoxically, he is able to hear the instrument better—to concentrate more closely on its sound. At the same time, he gains a wider musical perspective. His friend David Zinman, the conductor of the Baltimore Symphony, describes such moments: "Yo-Yo's whole physical presence seems to change. He breathes with the contour of the phrases. His face grows wider; the changing moods of the music are written on his features. He becomes a different person."

If one puts aside preconceptions and enters into Ma's musical mind, one finds that his movements when he is playing have a logic and a beauty of their own. Some concertgoers who initially found Ma's gestures excessive and off-putting have been increasingly drawn to him. Ma's untraditional approach is not just a question of temperament. "I have built-in problems with the left hand," he explains. "My fingers are too long and thin for the cello. If I want to widen my vibrato in order to get a warmer and richer sound, I have to do crazy things to get enough flesh on the string, such as placing my fingers at very strange angles, or even using two fingers at once. I've also had problems with my bow arm. For years—until I was well into my twenties—it wasn't relaxed enough. I not only had to restudy the physical basis of my bowing but also felt a need to increase my palette of sound. I started listening to great orchestras: to the Berlin Philharmonic, with its enormous repertoire of tone color. I listened to great singers, and was struck by the way some voices seem to pierce through a wall of sound while others seem to float on top of a body of sound. I asked myself how I could find these textures of sound on the cello. How do you match a particular amplitude of vibrato with a particular speed or weight of bow? I added or subtracted components and tried them out in different permutations. I learned—I stole—from my colleagues. For instance, when I began playing chamber music with Gidon Kremer I had to find a way to match his sound. Even when he plays at a low decibel level, he uses very fast bow strokes, which convey a lot of energy; he puts a spin on the sound like putting a spin on a ball. The sonority doesn't project in beam-like fashion, but—to use microphone terminology—it's omnidirectional, going off at very wide angles. When I see Rostropovich play, with his bent end pin that makes the cello more nearly parallel to the floor, I study how he hangs his bow on the string and gets such a marvellous tone. I've tried to find a way of benefiting from this bowing technique while still using my own straight end pin."

The bow is the primary shaping force in interpretation, and Ma's bow arm is formidable. Like a major-league hitter, he prepares his strokes; his arm traces an arc greater than the length needed for a given note. The bow draws out the sound, instead of pressing it out. He can attain fullest strength of tone without distortion. In quiet passages, his bow control is absolute. The violinist Lynn Chang, who often plays chamber music with Ma, remarks on his rare artistry in finding variety of nuance: "Within the range of *piano*, he covers the entire gamut of human emotion—intensity and relaxation, passion and delicacy, and anything in between. When he plays quietly and purely, the sound projects: there's a shimmer to it." No less remarkable is Ma's articulation: fast notes, short notes, short notes after long notes—all speak with immediacy and clarity.

"I've never been able to learn in smooth transitions," Ma says. "I've found that to go from one level to another you often have to destroy some knowledge in order to gain other knowledge. You realize after a while that you're not happy with what you're doing; you're at a standstill. Then, from the various ideas you've collected, you find one little piece of information that helps. It brings about a chemical reaction, and—ZOOM!—things finally fall into place. What excites me most is not the cello but interpretation—when an idea clicks and for the first time a piece of music truly makes sense. Then you're at the next level, awaiting further answers."

With Ma, as with all outstanding artists, one finds oneself listening to the music rather than to the instrument. "You're always trying to transcend the technical limitations," Ma says. "It's the same in every field. If it's a language, you try to express the content of something with whatever words you have at your disposal. Before I began to play the cello, I saw a double bass, but since it was too big for me I had to settle for second best. So there are no profound spiritual reasons that led me to the cello. I understand Casals' feeling. He saw himself not primarily as a cellist but as a musician, and even more as a member of the human race. Actually, I think very few people are interested in the cello as such. For instance, I love the piano—but what's the piano? It's a *means* of expressing music. I've tried it the other way also; I've tried to play a 'perfect' concert. I was nineteen, and performing at the Ninety-second Street Y. I had worked my butt off, practicing four hours a day—a lot for me—and knew the music inside out. While sitting there at the concert, playing all the notes correctly, I started to wonder, 'Why am I here? I'm doing everything as planned.

So what's at stake? Nothing. Not only is the audience bored but I myself am bored.' Perfection is not very communicative. However, when you subordinate your technique to the musical message you get really involved. Then you can take risks. It doesn't matter if you fail. What does matter is that you tried."

According to ancient Chinese custom, every family keeps a book in which the names for many generations ahead are planned. All family members from a particular generation will share a single written character. *Yo*, which in Chinese means "friendship," is the generational character for Ma and his sister, Yeou-Cheng. "With me they seem to have got lazy and been unable to think of anything else, so they added another Yo," he said one day as we talked in Zurich. "In China, as in Hungary, a person is addressed by the last name first; I would be called Ma Yo-Yo. (Incidentally, *Ma* means 'horse.') It means something philosophically, doesn't it, when you state your family name as your primary identity? Throughout the Orient, the family is the basic unit, and the society as a whole is a larger family. The Japanese have a word, *amae*, which is the feeling a baby gets when it's being breast-fed—the feeling of being totally loved, enveloped, and nurtured. This is how the individual feels in Oriental society. The Orient is based less on dialogue than on monologue. In the Confucian hierarchy, you're always placing somebody above or below you. The role of every family member is defined. For instance, my sister loves her little brother, and will do everything for me. She does this of her own free will, but it's also culturally expected. If the youngster goes significantly against the system he brings shame on the family." Ma's parents adhered to these traditions.

Ma's father, Hiao-Tsiun Ma, was born into a landowning family in Ningbo, a city south of Shanghai. He decided to devote his life to music, learned to play the violin, and eventually became a professor at Nanjing University. Education was highly prized in Chinese society; the small scholar-gentry class was accorded the greatest respect. But after the emergence of Sun Yat-sen, in 1911, China entered into a prolonged period of cultural and political instability, and the structure of life changed rapidly; conditions were often chaotic. Educated Chinese increasingly gravitated to the West. In 1936, Hiao-Tsiun left for Paris to further his musical studies. Ma's mother, Marina, was born in Hong Kong. ("The southerners are generally warm and temperamental," Ma says.) Gifted with a beautiful voice, she first met Hiao-Tsiun at Nanjing, as a student in his music-theory class. In 1949, she, too, moved to Paris. There they were married, and there Yo-Yo was born, on October 7, 1955, four years after the birth of his sister.

"My father was a born pedagogue," Ma told me. "He wanted not only to advance himself through learning but to share that learning. He wanted to teach everybody; it was a way of life. He taught languages and music to his brother and his two sisters, and even claimed that he had taught a dog how to sing." Hiao-Tsiun tutored his children in French history, Chinese history, mythology, and calligraphy. Yeou-Cheng studied the violin with Arthur Grumiaux, and Yo-Yo took up the piano and the cello. His cello teacher, Michelle Lepinte, was astonished when the four-year-old, under his father's guidance, began to play a Bach suite. Hiao-Tsiun had developed a method of teaching young children how to concentrate intensively. No more than a short assignment was given daily, but this was to be thoroughly assimilated. He proceeded systematically and patiently. Each day, Yo-Yo was expected to memorize two measures of Bach; the following day, two more measures. He learned to recognize patterns—their similarities and their differences—and soon developed a feeling for musical structure. By the time he was five, he had learned three Bach suites. The same technique was applied to a host of études. "I found this method ideal, because I didn't like to work hard," Ma recalled. "When problems in cello technique arose, my father would apply the principle '*Coupez la difficulté en quatre.*' This helped me to avoid the kind of strain young cellists often experience. When a problem is complex, you become tense, but when you break it down into basic components you can approach each element without stress. Then, when you put it all together, you do something that seems externally complex, but you don't feel it that way. You know it from several different angles."

Chinese calligraphy was taught by the same method. Hiao-Tsiun prepared several hundred cards, each one marked with a character and an explanation of it in French. Yo-Yo was required to learn two characters a day, and to keep a diary in Chinese. He says that he still knows French because his father gave him a paragraph to memorize every morning before going to school. These French studies included formal écriture. "If you've noticed my penmanship, you'll see how I've since rebelled," he said. "However, my father's pedagogical techniques have proved invaluable. When I was twelve, Leonard Rose" — with whom Ma studied at the Juilliard School—"assigned me the Dvořák Concerto. I was unbelievably excited. When I got home, my father said, 'Let's get down to work.' At the end of six hours, I had memorized the whole first movement. Last year, I gave myself ten days to learn two major works, by Barber and Britten, both for cello and orchestra. I had looked at the scores but had never played them on the cello. It was irresponsible of me. They were a horrible ten days—but I succeeded."

Ma's musical studies progressed so rapidly that he was able at the age of five to give a concert at the University of Paris, playing both the cello and the piano. But his life was soon to change radically. In 1962, Hiao-Tsiun received news that his brother, who had recently emigrated to America, was discouraged and was thinking of returning to China. Gathering up his life savings, Hiao-Tsiun hurried his family to New York and managed to persuade his brother to stay on. Hiao-Tsiun had planned to visit for six months; he remained for sixteen years. Once he was established in the New World, he formed the Children's Orchestra of New York, and a generation of youngsters benefitted from his exceptional gifts as a teacher. Yo-Yo began lessons with Janos Scholz, the distinguished cellist, who is also noted for his collection of Italian Master drawings. Scholz remembers Ma as "the most natural and eager boy you could imagine," and says, "He was adored by my whole family. We went through a mountain of repertoire in two years. He learned with lightning speed. He was everything one could wish for as a student, and the last I ever took."

Ma is loath to admit that as a child he actually enjoyed playing the cello. He remembers chiefly the rigors of memorization, the absorption of endless bits and pieces of information. Despite all, he performed with a freshness and an enthusiasm that captivated his listeners. Isaac Stern is a witness. "I first heard Yo-Yo play in Paris when he was five or six years old," he says. "The cello was literally larger than he was. I could sense then, as has now been confirmed, that he has one of the most extraordinary talents of this generation. I was so taken by him that when he was nine I arranged for him to study with Leonard Rose. Lenny told me that, unlike any other student he could remember, Yo-Yo would come to every lesson perfectly prepared. It's not just that he had practiced. He played every piece from memory and had obviously worked constantly on everything he had been assigned. He bloomed under Lenny."

"At some level, I must have liked playing," Ma told me. "But, more important, I loved music. I adored certain pieces—for instance, the Schubert E-Flat-Major Trio in the recording by Casals, Schneider, and Horszowski. And my love of music kept me going." Rose took on a paternal role and nourished what needed to be nourished. "I was a pipsqueak of a kid, and overwhelmingly shy," Ma said. "I was afraid to speak to Mr. Rose above a whisper. I'd try to hide behind the cello. He was always calm, soothing, and gentle. He tried to get me to overcome my timidity by constantly urging me to sing out on the instrument. I was amazed to hear phrases coming from a fifty-year-old man such as 'Sock it to me, baby!' or, to my dismay, 'Thrill me, thrill me—like my wife did this morning.' "

If the move to America opened new horizons for the Ma family, it posed problems as well. "America was my father's third culture, and it was hard for him to adjust," Ma said. "One of the duties of an Oriental child is unquestioning obedience to the parents; this is supposed to continue throughout one's life. It goes beyond obedience; the parents identify completely with the child. When I got into trouble, it was not considered my fault; it was somebody else's fault. I couldn't have deliberately done anything wrong, because I was, after all, an extension of my parents. As soon as we moved to America I had to deal with two contradictory worlds. At home, I was to submerge my identity. You can't talk back to your parents—period. At school, I was expected to answer back, to reveal my individuality. At home, we spoke only Chinese; we were taken to Chinese movies to remind us of our traditional values. But I was also American, growing up with American values. I became aware that if I was to be a cellist playing concertos I would have to have ideas of my own; that's one of the great things about being a musician. My conflict was apparent to Pablo Casals, to whom I was presented when I was seven. I don't remember what he said about my cello playing, but he did suggest that I should be given more time to go out and play in the street.

"My home life was totally structured. Because I couldn't rebel there, I did so at school. In the fifth grade, I began to cut classes, and I continued doing so through high school. I spent a lot of time wandering through the streets, mainly because I just wanted to be alone." Eventually, in 1968, Ma entered the Professional Children's School, in New York, but he missed so many classes that his teachers concluded that he was bored and would be better off in an accelerated program. That program enabled him to graduate from high school when he was fifteen. He spent the following summer at Ivan Galamian's camp for string players, at Meadowmount, in the Adirondacks. It was his first experience on his own, away from home.

"Suddenly, I was free," Ma told me. "I had always kept my emotions bottled up, but at Meadowmount I just ran wild, as if I'd been let out of a ghetto. The whole structure of discipline collapsed. I exploded into bad taste at every level. Mr. Galamian was concerned that the boys and girls maintain a certain decorum. He would say, 'They shouldn't go into the bushes together.' I took some white paint and decorated the stone walls with graffiti on the subject. When Galamian found out, he was horrified. I knew I had gone too far, and spent a whole day washing the walls. I would leave my cello outside, not worrying if it might rain, and run off to play Ping-Pong. That summer, I played the Schubert Arpeggione Sonata and the Franck Sonata with uninhibited freedom—just letting go, in a way that had never happened before." Lynn Chang, who was then also studying at Meadowmount, remembers these performances as "*appassionato*, full of abandon, tremendously impressive." Ma's playing leapt startlingly into another dimension, bursting not only with virtuosity but with imagination, irritating those who admire restraint in youth, and gratifying those who share Blake's view that "Exuberance is Beauty."

In the fall, Ma surprised Leonard Rose by arriving for his lesson wearing a leather jacket and uttering a string of swear words. "I'm embarrassed when I think of the language I used," Ma says. "But Mr. Rose took it in his stride and saw me through this phase. At some level, he must have been very happy to find me opening up in that way. And, for some reason, he kept his faith in me. In the early years of our lessons, he would explain every piece in advance and demonstrate his interpretation. But as time went on he gave me leeway to experiment for myself. When I was fifteen, after I had given a concert in Carnegie Recital Hall, he said, 'Well done. Now I'm going to give you a piece—Beethoven's C-Major Sonata—to work on entirely by yourself. I'm not going to suggest bowings, fingerings, or anything. You just go ahead, learn it, and play it for me.' One of the hardest things a teacher can do is to give a student permission to go his own way. I'll always be grateful to Mr. Rose for that."

Emanuel Ax, who is now Ma's sonata partner, attended that first New York recital. "It was the most incredible exhibition of string playing I've ever heard from such a young player," he said recently. "I was twenty-one at the time, and I vividly remember thinking that I'd like to work with him one day."

Ma had begun playing concertos at the age of twelve, with the Doctors' Orchestra of New York; and at fifteen he played the Saint-Saëns Concerto with the San Francisco Symphony. He sometimes performed with orchestras of modest quality, and found that experience valuable. "There you are, playing in Venezuela with a seventy-year-old conductor who's starting the Schumann Concerto at a tempo three times as slow as you've practiced it," he said. "You don't speak Spanish, and the orchestra is very basic. So you have to dig deep down to figure out how to make the performance work. This is a terribly important component of experience that you can't get if you play only with the best orchestras. And if you really screw up it's better to do so where everyone isn't looking at you and thinking, This kid is supposed to be fantastic, but he's not living up to his billing. One good thing is that as a child I didn't perform much. It's risky to create careers for 'geniuses' at age nine. The tendency is to make do with your technical limitations in order to get through your performances. The weaknesses then easily become ingrained."

Yeou-Cheng was now at Radcliffe; Yo-Yo had been tempted to apply to Harvard, but after his experience at Meadowmount his instinct told him that he was too young to take that step. He entered Columbia University, meanwhile continuing his lessons with Leonard Rose, at Juilliard. It seemed an ideal way to combine music with academics, but difficulties arose. "I was still living at home and trying to do a lot of things," Ma said. "I still felt as if I were going to high school." He eventually dropped out of Columbia, without telling his parents.

Ma then spent his days hanging about at Juilliard, trying to act older than he was. He acquired a fake I.D. card so that he could drink. During breaks in orchestra rehearsals, he would run to the liquor store and buy a bottle of Scotch to hand around when playing resumed. "One day, I passed out in a practice room, having thrown up all over the place. They thought I had O.D.'d on drugs. So they carted me off by ambulance to Roosevelt Hospital, where they recognized that I was suffering from the effects of alcohol. As I was a minor, my parents were sent for. A moment of deep shame in the Ma household. My father thought that if his son had become an alcoholic he himself should set an example through self-denial. He had always reserved for himself one special treat: a glass of wine before dinner. So he gave up this glass for four years. The other repercussions were enormous. I was called into the dean's office. Leonard Rose was informed, and, concerned that I was under too much pressure, arranged for me to see a psychiatrist. The news of my drinking spread to friends in France. All I was trying to do was to be accepted as one of the guys, and not be considered a freak. But for the next five years everywhere I went people would look at me and think, This guy is trouble. When I'd arrive late at a rehearsal, or entirely forget to come, everybody thought the worst." Even today, Ma is slightly abashed to recall his teen-age misconduct. From the American point of view, such episodes were typical adolescent behavior; from the Chinese point of view, they were grave transgressions.

"In college, even until I was in my twenties, I fought against the whole principle of discipline," Ma went on. "I was meshuga. I didn't know when to go to sleep or when to do my laundry. I learned to drive in three days, and had a couple of car crashes that people knew about and a couple that no one ever found out about."

Ma was nearly seventeen and had reached a crossroads: Should he pursue a full-time musical career or go to Harvard? Isaac Stern recalls, "During those growing years—whatever growing pains there were—Yo-Yo made a decision rather remarkable for a talented young man of his age, and that was to try to get an education. He could have devoted all his time to preparing pieces for concerts and competitions, but he took the unusual step of deciding to become a person. He may have been influenced by his Chinese background, with its tremendous respect for the value of learning. In any event, he went through Harvard, keeping his music up while taking a full course of studies. Those two things don't ordinarily go together." In four years at Harvard, in addition to studying music, he took courses in the rise and fall of civilizations, Chinese and Japanese history, anthropology, French civilization, fine arts, modern Chinese literature, German literature, Dostoyevski, astronomy, math, sociology, and natural sciences. When I asked how he had found time to combine such studies with his career as a cellist, he said, "I was able to manage because I was unbelievably lazy in everything. I had very low standards—I didn't feel compelled to get high grades, or to practice many hours every day. I worked in spurts. If I could no longer put off writing a paper, I studied into the night. And when I had a concert to give and didn't want to make an absolute fool of myself I'd put in a few more hours of practice. Once, when I hadn't listened to the works assigned for a music exam, I jimmied the lock of the music library and heard a semester's worth of music in one night. In my freshman year, I overslept and missed an exam and was put on probation. That was a bad moment. But my generally undisciplined approach to life offers me the possibility of doing many things. I didn't apply myself sufficiently in high school to learn how to do research or how to write papers. Yet I was curious about things. I wanted to try to tie together the various threads of my life—my Chinese upbringing, the atmosphere of Paris, my totally different experience in America. Studying history was a way of putting these diverse cultures in perspective, and studying anthropology—the !Kung people of the Kalahari desert, the Yanomamö of Venezuela—helped me to understand better the tremendous variety of values in all of humanity."

An old French saying has it that "painters are dirty, architects are wicked, and musicians are ignorant." If Ma can give this adage the lie as far as musicians are concerned, one must credit his encounter with the Harvard music faculty when he was seventeen. "Much of music deals with emotions, and musicians tend to be suspicious of an intellectual approach," he told me. "They will say, 'I don't feel it that way.' But when you can combine thought and feeling your intuition becomes more acute." Ma found studying chamber music with Leon Kirchner revelatory, for Kirchner explained the pieces from a composer's point of view. "He's passionate about music and tells stories to make you think about why a phrase turns in a certain way, or why a particular note has infinite meanings," Ma said. "I owe a lot, too, to Luise Vosgerchian. Luise had studied composition with Nadia Boulanger and was the pianist of the Boston Symphony. She helped me turn a corner, by giving me the courage to look at a musical score analytically, to ask my own questions, and to begin to find answers. Why is this piece boring or exciting or amusing? I gained the confidence to study a piece not just as a cellist but as a musician. I also worked with Patricia Zander. Patricia, a Boulanger student herself and a superb pianist, had called me after a concert and implied very nicely that I really didn't know what I was doing. We started playing music a couple of hours a week, and that eventually led to our performing together."

Patricia Zander recalls, "In the initial stages of our music-making, it's possible that I helped Yo-Yo to gain more courage to do what he was capable of. I noticed that he'd sometimes accept a comfortable instrumental solution—for instance, by restraining his tone when going to a risky high note. I'd challenge him: 'Aren't you backing away from that?' He was put on alert as to where he must stretch his technique to fulfill his musical ideal. He'd never say, 'I can't do it'; occasionally, he'd draw in his breath and say, 'That's difficult.' But as soon as he understood the idea he'd find the physical wherewithal to bring it to realization. Sometimes we'd work on the day of a performance. I remember making some fairly radical suggestions about Bach's Sixth Suite. I went to the concert thinking that maybe, with time, he'd be able to absorb the ideas. But as soon as he began to play, there they were—already assimilated."

"While I was at Harvard, I gained a new vocabulary for understanding music: linear polyphony, harmonic rhythm, hidden scale relationships," Ma told me. "I was fascinated to realize how a composer can create interest in his musical line by varying the lengths of phrases. Bach, for instance, may write several successive phrases of uneven length—say, of five or seven measures—which provide a lot of surprises and interruptions. He may follow these with eight-measure phrases, which offer a sense of relief and allow the music to flow with an easier continuity. Such numbers mean nothing in themselves, but in the hands of a great composer they have expressive impact. The interpreter always has to be aware of questions of shape and structure. It takes much experience to be able to sustain the listener's attention over a span of twenty or thirty minutes. My tendency was to maximize every individual moment without taking into consideration the over-all musical architecture. When I performed with Karajan in 1978, I understood how an artist can envision a work in its largest perspective. One has to find a way of giving expression to single events without upsetting the balance of the whole; one must think big and small at the same time."

It's particularly difficult for string and wind players to envision their individual parts in terms of the surrounding harmony or counterpoint. Ma advises all musicians to begin learning a new piece by studying the whole score. "Before you bring the piece to your instrument, you should know what it's all about," he has said. "Typically, the order is reversed: one just picks up the cello part and decides on bowings and fingerings. But this is looking at a piece from an ant's view rather than from an eagle's."

Ma hopes that music schools will develop curricula to educate the whole musician, so that to some degree the performer becomes a composer and the composer a performer—a state of affairs that was normal in the eighteenth century. Instrumentalists would be required to write short compositions of their own. "It's not the quality but the process that counts," he said. They would also be asked to perform recently written works and to discuss them with the composers. Composers would be required to show some proficiency as instrumentalists. "Not only would all this help the individual musician develop," Ma said. "There would be an explosion of connections, with ramifications throughout the music profession. Orchestras have started doing this sort of thing, by having composers-in-residence. Through membership in the Massachusetts Council on the Arts and Humanities, I myself have made a bridge to the community of composers, and have begun to commission works."

While Yo-Yo and Lynn Chang were in Leon Kirchner's class, they formed a trio with the pianist Richard Kogan. "We were doing this not for a grade, a review, or a fee, but because we wanted to make music in as interesting a way as possible," Ma told me. "I was totally obnoxious—always complaining that this or that passage sounded terrible. They still kid me about it. We'd work at all kinds of pieces, always looking for a more convincing interpretation. That was as important an experience as any I've ever had."

Another major influence on Ma was his sister. "In some ways, Yeou-Cheng is more musically gifted than I am," he said. "It's only that I'm less inhibited as a performer—I'm the brash one of the family. She's an excellent pianist as well as a violinist, and has a prodigious musical memory and fine taste; her sense of aesthetics has had a strong effect upon me. She has a true thirst for knowledge. She combined her musical studies with biochemistry, and then went to Harvard Medical School and became a pediatrician."

During his Harvard years, Ma made his London début, performing the Elgar Concerto with the Royal Philharmonic Orchestra, conducted by Yehudi Menuhin. The concerts started accumulating, and Ma felt that it would be possible for him to make a living as a musician. In fact, he was so inundated with concerts that his academic work suffered. "I even thought of leaving school, but my father insisted that I stay, and limit my concerts to one a month," he said. "In retrospect, I'm happy I followed his advice." Isaac Stern says of Ma's experience at Harvard, "He learned musical analysis and a good deal about life in general. But, above all, he learned how to learn—something that may be the most important thing a young person can do in any profession. He learned how to apply himself in the best possible way to everything he needed for his artistic development."

At sixteen, Ma spent the first of four summers at the Marlboro Festival, in Vermont. He felt privileged to perform with such artists as Felix Galimir, Isidore Cohen, and Sandor Végh. "I learned enormously from more experienced players, and when things didn't sound right I learned by thinking about why that was so," he told me. Pablo Casals, then in his mid-nineties, was visiting Marlboro, and Ma played in the orchestra under his direction. "I'll never forget the way his mind and body would radiate vitality the moment he raised his baton. That was an inspiration for a lifetime."

The first summer at Marlboro proved important to Ma in another way. He struck up an acquaintance with Jill Hornor, who was working as a festival administrator. He had met Jill briefly the previous spring, when he was giving a concert at Mount Holyoke and she was a sophomore there. By the end of the festival, he had overcome an attack of shyness, and told her, "I think I've fallen in love with you." She had thought of him as a little brother, and was touched and amused. Later that summer, they met in Boston and cycled back and forth between Cambridge and Jill's apartment, in Brookline. "At that time, I was putting out a lot of bullshit," Ma says. "The nice way of saying it is that I liked to fantasize. When people would ask me what my parents did, I'd make up a different story every time. I was unsure where I was in life—I was absolutely swimming. Jill was the first person to cut through all that. She would ask me questions and expect serious answers."

That fall, Ma entered Harvard as a freshman, and Jill went to Paris for her junior year. Correspondence intensified the relationship. Ma could commit to paper everything he had felt unable to say in person, and Jill began to take him more seriously. Soon each was writing a letter a day, and Ma was running up astronomical telephone bills. After Jill finished at Mount Holyoke, she did graduate work in German literature at Cornell, in Ithaca, while Ma was completing his studies at Harvard. "Paradoxically, the fact that we had rarely been in the same city at the same time allowed us to get to know each other better," he said. "The breathing space also permitted us to develop on our own."

In the spring of 1977, Heiichiro Ohyama, now the principal violist of the Los Angeles Philharmonic, who was a friend of Ma's, gave him some common-sense advice about Jill: "If you don't do something, fish swim away." He then worked out a scenario, and Ma followed it to the letter. Ma called Jill from New York City and told her to be sure to be home that evening at seven. He then bought a wedding ring and a pair of plane tickets to Cleveland, where Jill's parents were living. Putting on his best suit and tie, he took a bus to Ithaca and telephoned

Jill from a corner laundromat on the dot of seven, asking her if she missed him. "Of course I do," she said. Thirty seconds later, he rang her doorbell, went down on his knees, and asked, "Will you marry me?"

"I can't believe this!" she shrieked. "Yes, sure!"

Ma then said, "Good. Here's the ring and here are the tickets. We're going to see your parents."

With his marriage, Ma made his boldest departure from traditional Chinese culture. Predictably, it created strong tensions within the Ma family. The root of the difficulty was cultural rather than personal. When a Chinese marries a Westerner, the family structure is threatened. There is no guarantee of strict obedience to the in-laws, no guarantee that a newborn child will adhere to Chinese traditions. It took some time for Ma's father to come to terms with the situation—at first, there was a painful separation—but he eventually accepted Jill as his daughter-in-law, and when grandchildren were born he went as far as to give them Chinese names. Ma's parents, who now live part of the time in Taiwan, returned to America to celebrate Yo-Yo and Jill's tenth wedding anniversary with them.

After spending three years at Harvard's Leverett House, where Yo-Yo was artist-in-residence and Jill was a tutor in German, the Mas bought a house in Winchester, Massachusetts. They now have two children—Nicholas, aged six, and Emily, aged three. "My daughter is like me, at least as I'm told I was as a child—strong-willed and a bit rebellious," Ma told me. And Nicholas is not unlike his father, in that part of his charm resides in a rich imagination and a quiet mischievousness.

Charles Beare, the internationally renowned expert on stringed instruments, knows the Mas well. "Jill is a very lovely, very New Englandy, very American lady," he says. "They're well suited to each other. She's a good mother and a wonderful ground base for a musician to have. It has not always been easy for Jill to have a husband who arrives after three weeks with a suitcase full of music and then leaves the next day. And it has not been easy for Yo-Yo to come crashing in on his family for such short periods. They've taken tremendous steps to eliminate the tensions of that sort of life."

"When we married, we never imagined how busy my career would become," Ma told me. "We had visions of an equal relationship, where we would share the cooking, share taking out the garbage—share everything. To make matters worse, I've proved horrible at all domestic chores. During my first years of performing, all the travelling and concertizing seemed terribly exciting. My management would call and ask if I'd like to give a certain series of concerts two years later. I'd be in the middle of dinner, and I'd say, 'Fine, sure'—but eventually I'd be faced with actually having to play those concerts. I'd end up with as many as a hundred and fifty concerts a season. I was always flirting with getting burned out from exhaustion. When I returned from a concert tour, I'd have to come down from hyperactivity to being nobody. If I took a month off, I'd be depressed for the first two weeks. By the third week, things would be back to normal, but during the last week the tension would mount as I got ready to go on the road again. Then Nicholas was born. When you have your first child, everything changes. You realize that life is finite, and that you absolutely have a limit to your energy. You give, you love, you care, and it's all different.

"So I finally sat down and wrote out a list of the things I care most about. First of all, I promised myself that if I ever felt really burned out and lost enthusiasm for giving concerts I'd be responsible enough to quit. After all, if I lose interest in what I'm doing how can anyone else be interested? Second, I decided that every concert I played—no matter where, no matter if the city was big or small—was going to be special. Third, I accepted the fact that only one person is responsible for what's going on, and that person is me. Fame and success are always being dangled before you. You can easily become a slave to your desire, become an addict. But you have to choose your drugs carefully. I have yet to find something that beats the power of being in love, or the power of music at its most magical. So if someone suggests adding just one more concert at the end of a tour—it's always just one more—you just have to say no. Itzhak Perlman, who is dedicated to his family, showed me how to take a good, hard look at a schedule and protect time for my family. I reserve the dates of the kids' birthdays, and keep the month of July exclusively for the family. I'm taking more short respites from touring, and learning not to get as hyped up as before. Finally, I decided that it's not enough just to make time to be at home; I have to preserve the quality of that time. So, aside from practicing, I don't let professional obligations encroach upon my family life."

In April of 1980, when Ma was twenty-four, he had an operation for scoliosis, a curvature of the spine. His condition may have been accentuated by his cello playing. A curve exceeding thirty degrees tends to worsen, causing the spine to impinge on one organ or another. Ma had an S curve of sixty-three and sixty-seven degrees. After one's mid-twenties, one's bones tend to harden; in a sense, Ma had the operation at the last moment. "My friend Mark Ptashne, a professor of biochemistry and molecular biology at Harvard, found the very best people for me to consult," Ma said. "I shall be eternally grateful to him. My doctor was John Hall, the eminent orthopedic surgeon. They stretch your spine by means of small steel rods held fast by rivets. Then they take a graft from your pelvic bone and sprinkle it on your spine; this fuses with the spine and regenerates it." The operation posed a risk that nerves could be damaged in such a way as to prevent Ma from playing the cello. "Jill knew of the risk before we were married, and she had faith in me even if it turned out that I couldn't continue playing," he said. "I remember saying on the eve of the operation, 'Look, if I come out of this alive but not able to have total control of my fingers I will have had a very fulfilling life in music.' "

Jill says that Ma is a true performer, because when he awakened after the operation the first question he asked was "How many inches did I grow?" He learned that he had gained two inches. He could announce with pride that he had "grown in stature." Afterward, to keep the spine absolutely rigid, he was put in an upper-body cast for six months. Jill brought the cello to the hospital, and the cast was cut in such a way that Ma would be able to practice. "With my cast on, I felt like a football player," he told me. "I had broad shoulders, a fabulous physique. I thought I could walk through the most dangerous slum of any city and nobody would dare attack me. It was a very exciting summer, because it was the first time in years that I didn't play concerts. That's not quite true: I did play one concert, of Bach suites. But I went hiking in Maine, picking cranberries.

"Long before the operation, I was prepared for the possibility that it might not turn out successfully," Ma said. "I had decided that there's more to life than the cello. There are so many things that I would find enormously exciting. I love people; perhaps I'd do social work, or become a teacher, although I can't say in what field. It would be wonderful to have the luxury of going back to school. I'd consult the catalogue; I'd go to lectures until a subject clicked, and then I'd say, 'Wow, this is what I'd like to do.' Then I'd find out after eighteen years that I can't do it. But at least I'd have pursued a passion."

The operation proved a total success. Ma's cello playing was unimpaired and he had to resign himself to doing gladly what he must do. In recent years, he has been able to reconcile elements that had once seemed irreconcilable. "For a long time, I fretted over the conflicting messages coming from within, from parents, from school, from career," Ma said. "I disliked myself intensely. I felt as though I were living someone else's life, someone else's dream. I felt that I should be doing almost anything other than playing the cello. Friends such as Manny Ax and Mark Ptashne would tell me to stop pretending that my career in music only interfered with what would otherwise be an ideal life. It's only recently that I've begun to take hold of my energy and commitments and say to myself, 'Wait a minute, this is actually my own life.' I've come to accept many things, above all that I'm really happy to be a cellist."

A person with artistic gifts will usually develop in one of two ways: as an artist at the expense of others, or as a human being at the expense of art. One of Ma's close friends ribs him for his "persistent striving after normalcy." But Ma follows his calling in his own way. Jung wrote, "Great gifts are the fairest, and often the most dangerous, fruits on the tree of humanity. They hang on the weakest branches, which easily break. In most cases . . . the gift develops in inverse ratio to the maturation of the personality as a whole. . . . A gift is not an absolute value, or rather, it is such a value only when the rest of the personality keeps pace with it." Ma is dedicated to the principle of keeping pace. He maintains that his creativity is nourished by the stream of everyday life. "I can be playing with my kids and a thought related to music will come to me," he said. "Inspiration is an intuitive process and often comes from chance encounters. A conversation with a cabdriver can become extremely meaningful. I have friends who are visually oriented; I go for a walk with them and they say, 'Look at that tree,' or, 'Look at that building,' and suddenly a world of perception opens for me. I see parallels between sculpture and music. When I look at Michelangelo's statues—carved with tremendous strength of line, and not necessarily smooth—I'm reminded of Casals' playing. His phrasing had depth and density; each note was etched with absolute authority, as if in marble. In cinema you see how the director uses the art of montage, cutting abruptly from one image to another, from one mood to another, and you realize that some composers use a similar technique. A crescendo to a sudden *piano* is a favorite device of Beethoven's. Schumann uses it with really terrifying effect in the Cello Concerto.

"I'm just a performing musician," Ma continued. "It's true that the act of creating, as compared to re-creating, may take you into a darker realm, a path not travelled before. Some composers, like Schumann, have strayed beyond the limits of survival. Part of Beethoven's greatness is that he really went beyond what most people could bear and still survived and created. He's like the man who went to the very edge and returned to tell about it. The gift of an interpreter lies in the quality of his imagination. Some people maintain that no one can understand the Holocaust who hasn't gone through it. But reading Primo Levi or Elie Wiesel can go a long way toward helping you understand something even so inconceivable. One must go out of oneself, finding empathy for another's experience, forming another world. I feel that when a composer writes a piece of music he's translating a human experience into sound. I know that some people see music as merely sound for sound's sake. I disagree. There can be moments when you are in contact with the experience from which the music came. And there are audiences who listen at that level. They're not listening to say that this guy has a fantastic technique or fantastic sound—they're really getting the message of the music. When that happens, the ritual of concert-giving is at its highest. And a composer's ideas from two hundred years ago find absolute contact in their purest form with people living now. That's quite amazing."

No document brings one closer to the inner experience of a composer than the Heiligenstadt Testament, which Beethoven wrote when he was thirty-one, and which was found among his papers after his death. It reads, in part:

O my fellow men, who consider me, or describe me as, unfriendly, peevish or even misanthropic, how greatly do you wrong me. For you do not know the secret reason why I appear to you to be so. Ever since my childhood my heart and soul have been imbued with the tender feeling of goodwill; and I have always been ready to perform even great actions. But just think, for the last six years I have been afflicted with an incurable complaint which has been made worse by incompetent doctors. From year to year my hopes of being cured have gradually been shattered and finally I have been forced to accept the prospect of a *permanent infirmity* (the curing of which may perhaps take years or may even prove to be impossible). Though endowed with a passionate and lively temperament and even fond of the distractions offered by society I was soon obliged to seclude myself and live in solitude. If at times I decided just to ignore my infirmity, alas! how cruelly was I then driven back by the intensified sad experience of my poor hearing. Yet I could not bring myself to say to people: "Speak up, shout, for I am deaf." . . . How humiliated I have felt if somebody standing beside me heard the sound of a flute in the distance and *I heard nothing*, or if somebody heard *a shepherd sing* and again I heard nothing—Such experiences almost made me despair, and I was on the point of putting an end to my life— The only thing that held me back was *my art*. For indeed it seemed to me impossible to leave this world before I had produced all the works that I felt the urge to compose. . . . I hope that I shall persist in my resolve to endure to the end, until it pleases the inexorable Parcae to cut the thread.

When I discussed this document with Ma, he said, "I had known that Beethoven was a difficult man—impossible in many ways. But reading the Heiligenstadt Testament and his letters brought me close to him. I understood his idealism. Beethoven thought that through his music he could change the world. Today, rock musicians are virtually the only ones who think that. Beethoven believed that there is a soul.

Today, most people don't believe that there is a soul. Although he wasn't religious in a traditional sense, Beethoven believed in God. Today, most people don't believe in God. When you perform Beethoven, you have to transform yourself and commit yourself. You have to believe that God exists, that there's a soul, and that you can change the world."

Beethoven's five sonatas for cello and piano were composed over a space of nineteen years, and they trace a spiritual odyssey. "The first two sonatas have a bold design," Ma said. "Long, dramatic first movements are followed by short finales that provide a sense of release. Extremely innovative—and this is only Opus 5. One of the striking features of the Second Sonata is the series of extraordinarily long rests at the end of the introduction. You wonder what the hell is going on. The answer comes in the allegro theme, which grows out of the introduction with a certain dreamlike quality; it has harmonic ambivalence. There's a sense of confusion. For a moment, you feel lost.

"The Fourth Sonata also has a slow introduction. Here, harmonically, the phrases seem suspended; they are yearning, questioning. It took me a while to get into the world of Beethoven's imagination in his late period. I would listen to recordings of Schnabel, Kempff, and Serkin playing the last piano sonatas, and would be struck by many things—for instance, by the trills. These are no ordinary trills; they are searching, reaching out toward the ideal. I also began to see that early Beethoven has a lot to do with late Beethoven. The harmonic daring, the otherworldliness of his late works are to some extent apparent in his earlier works. His striving, as Goethe puts it, moves in a spiral; his evolution builds on his own experience. The musical language of the last two cello sonatas is terse. At one moment, it's turbulent and assertive; then he interjects something that's just heaven, and you get a glimpse of a better world. That's where you find the cinemalike montage. But even when the music is fierce it's not just violent. He's doing more than shaking his fist at destiny; there's nobility, there's heroism within the drama—a sense of exaltation. He has not negated the Heiligenstadt Testament; he's still holding on. The slow movements of both sonatas are intensely introspective. After that, you've earned your freedom. The finales have to do with a divine comedy; they are a celestial play, not in the realm of human endeavor. The gods are sporting among themselves."

Ma paused, and then said, "It may seem irreverent if I compare Beethoven to a great comedian, but they share something in common: superb timing. Beethoven likes to fool you. He'll take your mind in a certain direction by doing something three times, and then he'll suddenly do something else. On occasion, he'll do everything possible to deny you one chord. Wordplay, musical play—they use the same kinds of techniques. Beethoven is a very physical composer; you have to struggle for the interpretation. The notes look easy, but every note has its place. You must have absolute conviction in your musical ideas, and fulfill them to the nth degree. You have to concentrate fiercely; to judge the timing, the character, the density of the sound with absolute precision. To get into Beethoven's creative process, the player must almost become the creator himself."

Just as the Beethoven sonatas evolve in expression, so do the six Bach solo suites. And, just as Beethoven strove to overcome the limitations of the piano, Bach explored and expanded the potential of the cello. These works of Bach stand at the pinnacle of the cellist's repertoire. From internal evidence we can surmise that they were conceived not merely as a collection of separate pieces but in a progressive relationship. They become increasingly adventurous in technical complexity, imagination, and intensity. "When I was first given a cello, I began by playing Bach," Ma said. "This music has accompanied me for twenty-nine years, and will continue to do so for as long as I can play. It grows with you and constantly enriches you; you can never do it full justice. Each suite has its own distinctive character. The First is the simplest of the set, the most open, the most innocent. I feel that I'm out in nature; the prelude evolves like light becoming stronger. If the First Suite is sunrise, the Second, in D minor, is sombre—defiant. The Third Suite is noble and exuberant; it's so human and accessible that it has become the most popular of all. The prelude of the Fourth Suite is a tremendous leap in imagination. The different lines strive in opposite directions and seem to cover a space far exceeding the actual range of the notes. When I am playing this, I feel that the cello becomes an orchestra or an organ. The Fifth Suite, in C minor, is the big brother of the Second. The music struggles with grandeur and resignation. This is more than sadness. It's the process you go through when you know you have to give up what's most precious; it's the courage, the will to accept what must be endured. In this way, it's the most profound of all the suites. Casals' performance of the saraband from this suite will always stay with me. He captured its simplicity, its complexity, and its depth all at once. It's astonishing how much Bach has conveyed here in just over a hundred notes. The last suite, written for an instrument of five strings, is equally great, but in another way; it is exalted, and celebrates the glory of life. One of the main challenges in playing this music is to do justice to the illusion of polyphony which Bach so miraculously achieves while writing for a single-line instrument. Say that the bass establishes a stepwise progression at the rate of one note per bar. Each bass note may last only a second. You have to play it with sufficient conviction so that it will impinge on the ear of the listener and seem to be connected to the subsequent bass note. Much of Bach's writing is based on this kind of harmonic movement, and if you get it right everything else falls into place. If you only emphasize the more obvious melodic element, everything else falls apart.

"During the German occupation of Paris, my father lived by himself in a garret. He would memorize violin pieces by Bach and play them in the dark. He eventually advised me to follow his example and play through a Bach suite from memory every night before going to bed. This isn't 'practicing'; it's contemplating. You're alone with your soul. It was a strong image—total concentration, total dedication. Although I can't actually do this now at bedtime, because I give so many concerts, the image remains with me. This helped me understand the continuity of feeling within all music—how all the movements are related and shouldn't be disturbed by tuning or other distractions. I know my greatest joy as a musician when I am playing a concert dedicated exclusively to Bach. Then for a whole evening I'm living in one man's mind—and a great man's mind. That's how I can justify being a performer. One is involved in a process that is larger than oneself."

As a partisan of the Elgar Cello Concerto, and of Ma's performance in particular, I asked for his comments on it. "The Cello Concerto was Elgar's last major piece," he said. "I feel that it tells a story of the past, recounts things that are gone. Some people even find in it a nostalgia at the passing of the pre-First World War era. If the main melody of the first movement is played with a lush tone, it can sound like an awful piece of music. It's poignant and wistful, and should have a somewhat veiled quality. The last movement deals with pomposity. It parodies society; it needs swagger and lilt. Then, in the coda, Elgar suddenly tells us what it's all about: *Vanitas vanitatum*; the illusions of the past are gone. He's now exposing his true feelings. It's the heartbreak in the present time. This is at least my subjective imagery. For me, any interpretation has to become personal—but that's for the enjoyment of anything. If you can't connect to it, it has no value. For instance, it took me some time to get into the First Shostakovich Concerto. The music seemed like not much more than social realism—Workers of the World, Unite! But then I read 'Testimony,' Shostakovich's autobiography as told to Volkov. It tells of the world he came from—of the Stalin era, of friends disappearing, of feeling guilt in being a survivor, of the musical posing that was required, of the compromises one had to make to stay alive. I understood the first movement in a new light. Yes, it's social realism, but viewed ironically. The slow movement exposes the Russian soul that is behind all this; you sense vastness of land, of history. In the finale you're catapulted into a crazed state. It's like an individual who, having been through absolute hell, goes to a carnival where everyone is rushing about madly and telling him, 'Smile, smile, smile.' Now I love playing Shostakovich—the two concertos, the Cello Sonata, the Piano Trio. We have Rostropovich to think for all of these works."

Ma is set on expanding the cellist's repertoire. He plays a lot of twentieth-century music: Barber, Britten, Walton, Penderecki, Lutoslawski, Kirchner, Carter, Henze, Dutilleux, and also new American works. Ma disavows a holier-than-holy attitude, and has no hesitation in making transcriptions. (Bach set a precedent in this regard.) With considerable daring, he has borrowed Brahms' D-Minor Sonata from the violinists, and he has taken at will from the viola repertoire, the plum of these pickings being Mozart's Sinfonia Concertante for Violin and Viola.

For an artist, too much public adulation can be as risky as too little. Chekhov once commiserated with a friend for having "suffered a success." Ma is one of the few cellists who have been hoisted onto a public pedestal and labelled with the epithet "superstar." He remains remarkably unscathed. "My own goal is simple," Ma said. "I hope that people will want to come to concerts, and that those who already do will continue to be excited by the music they hear. So I try to use in a creative way whatever success I have had. You can build trust with a community if you return to it often enough; you can gradually develop a relationship that deepens over time. Whether you're a jazz, rock, or classical musician, as long as you're absolutely sincere about it the passion transmits itself. Music should be part of everybody's experience. It's not that I'm in favor of 'popularizing' fine art, in the sense of lowering its quality—only that I want it to be accessible without the stigma of social barriers. Classical music shouldn't be reserved for the élitists."

One sometimes reads that So-and-So is the "greatest" performer in a given field. But when it comes to artistic excellence there is no greatest performer, only a great performance, and that can occur unexpectedly. I've seen an English secondary-school production of Farquhar's "The Beaux' Stratagem" that ran rings around the National Theatre for sheer acting skill and Restoration high spirits. A "great" violinist may possess genuine sensibility and enchanting beauty of tone, but does the enchantment cut through to the essence of the composer? Some of the truest performances—Szigeti playing Bach, Furtwängler conducting Beethoven—distinctly lack the typical superstar's sense of ease and protective sheen. "The concept of superstardom can, in fact, lessen the experience for the listener," Ma told me. "If someone goes to a concert only for the name of the performer, he may be less aware of the music itself, and not trust himself to open up to the real musical experience, on whatever level it may be. The listener should develop a personal relationship to the music. He or she should say, 'I'm going to *react*, no matter what anyone thinks. I may hate it or love it, but the reaction is mine.'

"Sometimes I feel guilty about the degree of success that's come to me. This is a cruel profession. The ones who are out there performing aren't invariably the best musicians, but they have what's called fire in the belly. There are artists who may be more gifted but are more fragile. I wish the system were devised so that there was space enough for everybody. When I give master classes, I discover so many interesting young players. Are they going to have their rightful opportunity to perform, to make their own contributions? I wonder, Who am I to take someone else's place if he or she is deserving? I feel a sense of responsibility. I can't abuse my success; I can't take advantage of the system by doing less work or playing less well. Rather, I have to do more, to care more.

"If anything should put the 'superstar' in his place, it's the fact that an interpreter's fame is ephemeral. Casals, above all, should live on through the centuries; but, sadly, even now many young cellists haven't heard his recordings and don't know what his contribution was. That's going to happen to all of us. Not so long from now people will say, 'What's that name again—Yo-Yo Who?' " Ma is right. How many concertgoers of today know the name of Servais, the most celebrated cello virtuoso of the mid-nineteenth century; of Romberg, who proudly trampled upon the cello part of Beethoven's first Razumovsky Quartet; or of Duport, who elicited from Voltaire the comment "Monsieur, you make me believe in miracles: you've turned an ox into a nightingale!" Ma says, "The main thing is that the composers will live on. And they can only do so through the interpreter and the listener at a given moment. *That* becomes the value of my point in time.

"What I like about my profession is that it's the most important thing you can do and at the same time it's not at all important. Of course, when you're involved with your chosen activity you have to feel that what you're doing makes a difference. Yet it would be terrible if you couldn't switch off, and began to think, Worship me, I'm Bach's chosen representative. That would be ludicrous. One has to be like an actor in the best sense. He lives the part every evening; afterward, he returns to his normal life. It's insufferable to be with people who take themselves seriously all the time. Nobody is that important. I used to get nervous when I played in certain cities—particularly Salzburg, New York, and London. But I've now learned to treat the 'important' concerts no differently from any other. I have to accept that I played in a certain way in 1978, say, and perhaps in a different way in 1988. You can't suddenly play better just because you say that you want to, or by desperately practicing for another few hours. What you can do is care about your performance *every* time you play, so that when you return a year later you're in a general sense a better musician. I've learned to treat performing as a natural process, like breathing and eating."

Concerto playing is, of course, only one part of Ma's musical activity. For him, a fulfilled life as a cellist means finding a balance between solo playing, recitals with piano, chamber music, and teaching. "I used to devote my summers, in Marlboro, to chamber music and my winters to solo playing," he said. "At first, I found this terribly confusing. I thought there was a real difference between playing chamber music and playing concertos. As a soloist, I wanted to be sure that my tone would carry to the last row, and I'd usually end up playing quite loudly. But when I started to sneak a tape recorder into the back of the hall I became conscious that my problems were really questions of articulation and of focus—quality—of sound. The more you learn about projection, the more you gain confidence that you needn't overdo the volume. Eventually, you develop a kind of third ear; you hear your playing as if you were outside yourself. When you're a soloist with an orchestra, you think you have to go great guns all the time. That's not true. Often you may be playing with only a couple of wind instruments. In chamber music as well, you have to know when to project and when to blend into the texture. The more aware I became of what's in the score, the more the differences between solo and chamber-music playing diminished. When I play a concerto, I try to listen to the orchestra part as carefully as I listen to my own. Then you're playing everybody's part. But it's everybody's job to play everybody's part. In some exceptional orchestras, this is understood. Sometimes I'll join the orchestra for the second half of the concert, sitting at the back of the cello section. To do this with a great orchestra—the Cleveland, the Chicago, the Philadelphia—is a fascinating experience, because these orchestras are truly playing chamber music."

Patricia Zander says, "As with other great artists, Yo-Yo can be simultaneously aware at many levels: of the note he's playing, of the note within the phrase, of his partner or of the conductor, of the orchestra, of the acoustics, of the sensibility of the audience. I know how aware he is because if, while performing with him, I make a small error—I miss a beat, say—he's right there and, as it were, makes the error with me. His reflexes are remarkable, especially considering that he's often playing from memory."

Ma met Emanuel Ax at Marlboro in 1973, and they became good friends. They began to perform together in 1979, and their duo has turned into a lasting partnership. Their rehearsals are revelatory but also relaxed, with plenty of amusing banter. There is much spontaneity, but also a framework. Both come to rehearsals prepared with mental notes they have taken of points of dissatisfaction in their last performance of the work in question; there are certain goals to be agreed upon and aimed at. They give close attention to the balance of inner voices, and question aspects of interpretation as though for the first time. They approach the score with fidelity to the letter as well as to the spirit. Minor discrepancies in Beethoven's way of notating similar passages may be mere oversights; yet these are in the hand of the Master and to be observed scrupulously. A deep mutual respect allows Ma and Ax to take a risk that few musicians' egos could withstand: they cross over into each other's instrumental province. Ma will comment on the nuances of a solo-piano variation; Ax will suggest a more floating tone quality when the cello takes over the melody. They listen to each other caringly, almost maternally. "Manny is a very honest, truthful companion," Ma said to me. "He'll tell me, 'Look, Yo-Yo, this is just not good enough.' "

"When we began working together, the biggest problem was finding a common language," Ax says. "We both love to expound at length and to use imagery. So if one of us suggested a 'sunrise,' we had to learn to define what we meant in precise musical terms. Sometimes chamber music can be a kind of polite quadrille where one person says, 'I'll give you liberty here if you'll give me liberty there.' That's of no interest to us. If I ask to take more time, Yo-Yo won't just say, 'O.K., I'll give you more time.' He'll do everything in his power to understand why I want it. Of course, I'll reciprocate in the same spirit."

Both feel that they've grown as a result of their partnership. "Manny has a very solid sense of rhythm; that helps me enormously," Ma said. "His musical culture is much broader than mine, in the sense that he has a vast knowledge of the whole repertoire, including opera.

Over the years, I've learned from his seriousness of purpose. He believes that if you're going to play a great piece of music you owe that work serious preparation on the day of performance, even if you've played it two hundred times. This can be done in any way—practicing, thinking, looking over the score—but you have to spend time in that world."

"We always assume that a performer either has it or doesn't have it," Ax says. "But I've learned from Yo-Yo that there are things you can study about performing, just as there are things you can study about harmony. You're relating to the audience from the moment you step onstage; you're not there in the abstract. There may be features in the music that, although they are apparent and dear to you, are not actually getting across to the audience. You have to learn how to heighten the expression to just that point where those ideas communicate. You give up something important if you say to yourself that an audience is distracted and you don't care. Because of my work with Yo-Yo, I generally feel more liberated onstage. He's able to turn the nervous tension of a performance into something very positive—into an extra kind of freedom."

Ma and Ax are frequently joined by Young Uck Kim to play piano trios. "We three are completely different, but somehow our music-making truly comes together," Ma said. And it is a special moment for Ma when he can perform with Isaac Stern. "I've known him since I was a child, and now I'm close to his children," Ma told me. "When I was young, he took me under his wing and helped me when basically there was no need for another cellist. I have to try to rise to the level of matching his purity of intention for each note. He has a breadth of conception, where—if we talk of detail versus structure—the detail is so large because the structure is so much larger. When we travel together, he sometimes shares his early memories, as Rubinstein did, and you have a link with a past culture. Even though Manny and I kid him, we treat him with a lot of respect; he's Mr. Stern to us."

Ma enjoys teaching. Wherever he travels, he is willing, when time permits, to give a master class. Many musicians are intolerant of technical or intepretative approaches other than their own. Ma feels otherwise. "I'm the listener who wants to be pleased, and I can be pleased in many ways," he said. "There are as many ways to play the cello as there are different bodies, hands, and minds. But certain components have to be there. If I feel uncomfortable or if I'm bored, I'll let the student know. It's not my view versus someone else's view; it's whether the other view is convincing. I know that the student can find a lesson terrifying. You're playing a piece for someone who's taking it apart, and you have to try to put it back together without sufficient distance and time. This basic process, however, is what performance is made of. A performance is like a sandcastle, which has to be built anew every time. The idea of a 'definitive' interpretation is stupid. All performers know the truth that if you are able to give an exceptionally good performance one night you may be able to do the same thing the next night. The magic moments are never going to be the same. All you can do is store away the previous performance somewhere in your mind, and rethink the piece in the hope that you can play it well again, even if in a different way." Ma never puts any markings in his music—not a single indication of bowing or fingering; that is a testament to his sense of spontaneity. He feels no need to buttress his sandcastles against change.

Before Leonard Rose died, in 1984, he expressed the wish that Ma teach his gifted student Matt Haimovitz, who was then only fourteen. Ma has enthusiastically fulfilled that obligation. "The next five years are going to be crucial to the kind of musician, the kind of person Matt wants to be," he said. "He will have to go through the process of discovery. I hope that he will dare to take chances—to try new approaches in interpretation and technique. These are the years when one develops resources to draw upon for the rest of one's life."

Ma has been fortunate in that since the age of sixteen he has been able to play in turn on three superb instruments. Two are Venetian: a Goffriller of 1722, which had belonged to Pierre Fournier, and a Montagnana of 1733. The third—a renowned Stradivari of 1712 once owned by the nineteenth-century cellist Davidoff, and more recently by Jacqueline du Pré—has been made available to Ma for his lifetime. He alternates between the Strad and the Montagnana. Charles Beare, the instrument expert, knows these cellos well. "The quality of the Montagnana is very fine, but it's not the ultimate warm, natural cello poetry," he said. "I never thought of Yo-Yo as being anything other than a Strad player. Only a Stradivari could express his range of sensibility. What distinguishes Strads from ordinary great cellos is their warmth of tone quality and immediacy of response. This combination gives the player a vast palette of tone color. Almost before the bow touches the string, the instrument begins to resonate. There are modern instruments that have fine tone quality, but the player's variety of nuance filters out to some extent as the sound travels. The volume remains, but not the quality, whereas the tone of a Strad keeps all its complexity right to the back of the hall."

Ma can't resist an enological comparison. "With wine, you talk about flavor, body, finish, and the subtle balance of various elements," he said. "While in the bottle, it remains highly concentrated; when let out, it interacts with the air, it breathes, it opens up, you savor its bouquet. That's just like a cello tone. The Strad has a tenor quality; it's a Bordeaux, while the Montagnana—big, full, and massive—is a Burgundy. Just as a fine wine leaves a distinctive aftertaste, the Strad leaves a reverberation; its overtones linger for a moment after the bow leaves the string."

One thing the illustrious Italian stringed-instrument makers didn't have to worry about was air travel—a mode of transport that is becoming increasingly difficult, especially if you play the cello. "I can't risk putting the Strad or the Montagnana in the hold," Ma said. "I'm always told I can't take the cello on board. I then explain patiently that I've paid a full extra fare for the privilege of having it with me. Once, they couldn't find the reservation at all, and, as the plane was full, insisted that the Strad be put in the hold. In desperation, I asked for the flight list and scrutinized it. There it was at last: 'Mr. Cabinba,' short for 'cabin baggage.' When I'm asked, 'Are you going to entertain us on board?,' I say, 'Sure. If you circle for more than forty-five minutes, I'll take requests.' In fact, I've practiced in airports, on trains, on ships, and on the Autobahn when my car broke down—I believe in popularizing art—but not yet in an airplane."

"Travelling with Yo-Yo is such a riot—no holds barred," Patricia Zander says. "Under the duress of travel, I'd sometimes get quite tense. I remember walking down airport corridors, and Yo-Yo making funny noises, trying to embarrass me in order to cheer me up. There were pillow fights in airplanes. We were once in a taxi going to a concert, and shivering with anxiety because the luggage hadn't shown up. But Yo-Yo said, 'Never mind, don't worry; it always makes such a great story afterward.' He gave that concert in a brown suit."

Charles Beare recently accompanied Ma and Emanuel Ax on one of their American tours. "To say that they're energetic travellers is an understatement," he told me. "After playing a concert in San Francisco, they go to a reception till two in the morning. At half past seven, a car picks us up at the hotel and takes us to the airport. We get to Salt Lake City just before noon. Yo-Yo gives two interviews. After a very quick lunch, he goes with me to a violin-makers' school and sits down with a brand-new cello—unplayed and almost unplayable—and with breath-taking aplomb launches into the Prelude to Bach's Third Suite. Then he pulls out his Strad, shows the students how it differs from the modern instrument, and fields questions for forty minutes. He is utterly informal and approachable. One would never know that he has a 'great name.' Back to the hotel to practice and to snatch a fifteen-minute nap, then to the hall to set the balance and play the concert. After the concert, Yo-Yo and Manny invite me to share a quiet dinner. Tears run down my face—these two are so funny. Yo-Yo is a born storyteller; he mimics with incredible accuracy. We get to bed at half past twelve. The next morning, a flight back to the West Coast: Portland, Seattle, Vancouver, Los Angeles. On a free day, we go up to the Napa Valley and sample the wines. The schedule is a killer, and yet the remarkable thing about Yo-Yo is that each performance is completely fresh. A routine concert would be unthinkable for him. This boils down to the integrity that runs right through his music and his life."

Ma's travels have brought him to China on two occasions, at the invitation of the Ministry of Culture: in 1986, for thirty-six hours, and in 1987, for five days. "These were memorable visits, but hectic," Ma told me. "Extra concerts were added at the last moment. I had to play three concertos in one evening, almost without rehearsal. I met some of my father's colleagues from forty years ago, including three former presidents of the Shanghai Conservatory. The Shanghai Symphony is of fine quality and is well disciplined. They rehearse every day, and managed to do so even during the Cultural Revolution. At the conservatory—which, by the way, manufactures its own instruments—I was made an honorary professor and gave a master class. I was impressed by the talent and willingness of the students. You sense a vitality in the air. People are ready to do things. That's very exciting. After those five days, it took me a month to decompress."

To what extent does Ma feel himself to be Chinese? "In recent years, I've become increasingly identified with my Chinese origins," he says. "I'm fascinated by Chinese history and the complexities of Chinese culture. I love Chinese art, especially the landscape painting, and want to learn more about it. I understand the Confucian ethic, although I don't abide by it all the time, and I value the traditional Chinese veneration of wisdom and learning. But it's hard for me to say just who or what I am. I'm a person of various influences; sometimes they connect, sometimes they don't."

"When I know that Yo-Yo is coming to perform with the Baltimore Symphony, my first thought is not that I'll have the joy of making music with him, wonderful though that is, but that I'll have the joy of seeing him," David Zinman, the symphony's conductor, said recently. "When I have problems, I call him up and unburden myself. I think he would have made a fine psychiatrist, because he's the ideal listener and always has something perceptive to say—and it's not a cloying sympathy. He's much younger than I am, but he's not a young person; he's an older person. He has always been that way."

Emanuel Ax says, "You know the well-worn saw 'Familiarity breeds contempt.' Yo-Yo is the opposite. With him, familiarity breeds more respect and affection."

"On the personal side, he's incredibly generous," Charles Beare says. "When you go to a restaurant with him, he manages to get his credit card into the manager's hands before anybody else can get through the door. He pays for everything and for absolutely everybody. You have to plan in advance how you're going to outwit him. If he's asked to do a charity concert in Anchorage, Alaska, in February, his instant reaction will be to say, 'Yes, I'll be delighted.' There ought to be a rule against asking him to do this sort of thing."

"Not only does Yo-Yo have abundant good will but it's informed by a deep sense of relationship," Patricia Zander says. "He has a phenomenal memory for what you've said ten years ago. When we travel, he'll greet someone whom he might not have seen in ages by asking, 'Did your son decide to go to Stanford or Columbia?' His sense of things shared is intensively programmed, and that's one reason people trust him. In an apparently light way, he has an ability to connect. He's always *there* with you."

Ma is now thirty-three. He stands again at a crossroads, one that is more subtle and less appreciated by modern society than the crossroads he faced at seventeen. Given his distinguished career, achieved in such an exceptionally short period of time, one would assume that he could ask for nothing more, and that his problems are solved. But there are still major issues facing him, and he's aware of this. How will he challenge himself? What inner callings must he heed? Are there sacrifices to be made? In the glare of the public spotlight, might he lose the often lonely, often out-of-the-way path that can lead to further development? Isaac Stern has said of him, "Yo-Yo has reached extraordinary heights, but he still has to realize his full potential. He has the greatest success today, but there's more to be looked for. I'm speaking of musical accomplishment over decades. How far he goes depends entirely upon him, and I have enormous faith in his good sense. His potential is limitless."

To understand Ma's artistry, one must hear him play a major work that challenges the interpreter's power of sustained expression. In Zurich in June of 1988, I heard Ma and Ax in two concerts devoted to Beethoven's complete works for cello and piano. The ensemble fulfilled the players' ideal that "no one follows, but both come together as equal partners in a unified conception." From the first note, these artists set forth unhesitatingly on an audacious journey. They revelled in the composer's gigantic temperament: tempestuous, serene, joyful, painful, vulgar, sublime, strange, and willful—all forged into daring musical architecture, as modern today as when it was conceived. If one considers the cello apart from the music, I have on occasion heard a more beautiful cello sound. But what is the Beethoven sound? Not voluptuous or highly sensual but chaste and noble. Casals had a purity of tone that enabled one, forced one, to focus on the music rather than on the cello. Ma is moving toward a similar goal in his own way, and is willing to sacrifice a too easily obtained beauty for a harder to obtain truth. While listening to these Zurich performances, I was less than ever interested in brilliant instrumental execution or in what is commonly termed "good musicianship" —often used as a euphemism for playing it safe and neutral; least of all was I interested in superstardom. There was only one superstar, and that was Beethoven.

No music is more profoundly human than the slow movement of the last cello sonata. It begins funereally; then it changes to the major key, and a quiet melody, taken up in turn by the piano and the cello, seems to share with us a secret yearning such as that hidden in the postscript to the Heiligenstadt Testament:

> Oh Providence—do but grant me one day *of pure joy*—For so long now the inner echo of real joy has been unknown to me—Oh when—oh when, Almighty God—shall I be able to hear and feel this echo again in the temple of Nature and in contact with humanity—Never?—No!— Oh, that would be too hard.

As Ma and Ax play, this melody embraces them in its gentle folds of purity and devotion. They are eavesdropping on the soul of the composer. Time and space lose their particularity. A spirit, set free from the past, tends us with its power of consolation.

After the concert, Ma and Ax host a dinner party for a few close friends at the Hôtel Baur au Lac. The food, delicious but outrageously expensive, is accompanied by endless jokes, mostly Jewish, some Chinese—all outrageously bad. The dinner ends at one in the morning. In the darkened lobby, Ma embraces everyone in farewell. He must be up at seven to catch a plane to Paris, where Jill, Nicholas, and Emily are awaiting him. There, later in the week, the Beethoven performances will be repeated—not repeated, but renewed.

This interview, conducted in Zurich, Switzerland, first appeared in *The New Yorker*, 1 May 1989.

CHAPTER TWO

Walking to the Pavilion

One afternoon in the fall of 1988, Jeffrey Tate, on holiday in France after a year of non-stop opera and symphony conducting, visited Amiens Cathedral. Renowned for its vastness and its perfect proportions, Amiens is one of the glories of Christendom. "I had never been there before," Tate told me when I met him a month later in London. "When I entered, I had the most extraordinary sensation. For about two minutes I couldn't speak. It seemed more like a stone bubble than like a building. One soared inside there; one felt as if one could float. I had been a little tired—and suddenly I felt enormously young."

By the age of twenty-five, Jeffrey Tate had become a doctor, by thirty-five he had become a conductor, and by forty-five—the time of his visit to Amiens—he had been appointed principal conductor of the Royal Opera in London, and the special quality of his music-making had been recognized in Europe and America. By any standard this is an unusual success story. But the success has another dimension: Tate has had to cope with being severely handicapped.

"I'm immensely aware of my physical imperfection," Tate said. "And that may be one of the reasons I'm intrigued by structural balance wherever I find it. I'm especially attracted to Romanesque churches—Vézelay, Autun, Tournus. There's intense concentration in their structure; it's revealing to see the degree to which drama can be obtained by following through with a single idea." Tate's feeling about architecture carries over to music. "Music has a remarkable capacity, in an abstract way, for mirroring an ideal equilibrium," he said. "That's why I'm particularly drawn to the great Classical com-

Jeffrey Tate and David Blum. Photograph by Sarah Blum, London, November 1992.

posers. The sense of an ordered creation is inherent not only in music itself but also in the very nature of music-making. If you like, the most perfect expression of human behavior is a string quartet—where the four individual lines blend into a unity. Our world is a chaotic place, with potential for destruction as well as creation. I feel that there are positive, unifying forces, which can bring us a sense of wholeness, of well-being—which can counteract the forces of destruction. Music is one of those unifying forces."

Jeffrey Tate was born on April 28, 1943, in Salisbury, England, near where his father, Harry Tate, who was then an officer in the Royal Air Force, was stationed. Harry Tate, a handsome man, is an outdoorsman and was an excellent cricket player. After the war, he took up a position in the postal service. His son was a robust fellow, to all appearances physically normal except for flat feet. The family doctor suggested that Jeffrey be fitted with wedge shoes, but they had no effect. When Jeffrey was three, his mother, Ivy, took him to a specialist. The diagnosis was that Jeffrey did indeed have flat feet, and also a serious malformation of the spine.

"One always expects one's child to be perfect," Ivy told me as she served tea in her present home, in Farnham, Surrey. "Jeffrey was such a lovely boy. Seeing him running about, you'd think he was like any other child. When you're told such a thing, you're so shocked—I went almost numb." The malformation particularly affected Jeffrey's left leg, and to insure that it would grow straight he had to wear a leg iron that immobilized it from the hip to the ankle for two years. "They don't recommend that treatment anymore, but at the time it seemed the wisest course," she went on. "I was told not to coddle him. He'd often fall over and cry, but I had to let him pick himself up, and offer him no comfort. This was very difficult for me to do."

Jeffrey was nevertheless a cheerful boy. He was good with his hands, and enjoyed sketching and drawing. He also seemed to have an ear for music. His maternal grandfather was an opera lover, and his mother played the piano and sang for her own pleasure. Jeffrey began piano lessons when he was five; soon he was able to play the popular songs he found among his mother's sheet music. When he was seven, the family moved to Farnham, and he became a choirboy at the chapel of St. Thomas, in Bourne. Gifted with a beautiful soprano voice, he eventually became head chorister.

As Jeffrey grew, his physical problem worsened. Tate now describes it by saying, "There were two separate elements in my disability; both were congenital. One was a deformation of the spine. The spine can be deformed in two ways: it can bend, and it can twist. Mine did both. It bent laterally, which is called scoliosis, and twisted backward, which is called kyphosis. Put them together, and you have kyphoscoliosis. Generally, you won't notice this deformity in a baby, but it will become increasingly apparent during the growth period of the spine, which occurs between the ages of five and fourteen. The other element in my disability was spina bifida in the lumbar region. This is a failure in the completion of the spinal structure. In a normal child, the bones of the spinal column close around the spinal cord, forming a canal. As the spinal column grows, the cord, which grows more slowly, is drawn up into it; nerves serving the lower limbs are pulled up through the spaces between the vertebrae. In my case, however, some of these nerves became tethered. Tension damaged them and impaired their function. The damage was on the left side, affecting my left leg. If I could have rested in a position where there was no gravity—hanging by my arms, or sleeping for seven years—the deformity might have been arrested. In the event, the doctors did as much as they could. There have been some extraordinary developments in medicine since then. Nowadays, if they detect scoliosis early enough they can often correct it."

Jeffrey had two operations, both carried out by a noted orthopedic surgeon, A. Graham Apley. "He is a wonderful man and was tremendously supportive," Tate told me. The first operation, which was performed when Jeffrey was eight, was primarily neurological. The object was to relieve the tension on the nerves and prevent paralysis. Jeffrey was in Rowley Bristow Orthopedic Hospital, in Surrey, for six months, and during the first three months he had to lie in a plaster bed, without moving at all. "That was rotten—really rotten," Tate recalls. "You can't lie still in a plaster bed without getting sores, and, of course, I couldn't get up to go to the toilet. It was profoundly degrading. But children somehow cope with that sort of thing. The greatest pain came when, after three months, I was finally allowed to leave the bed. I had literally to be taught again how to walk."

Tate's mother remembers his being "marvellously patient"; Tate says, "I can be impatient about minor things, but in major situations I have some reserve of calm, which stands me in good stead as a conductor. Some problems have to be faced, and there is no point in complaining. I was always, thank God, able to think like that."

Although Jeffrey had been visiting hospitals and seeing surgeons for some time, the operation and its aftermath came as a sudden revelation. "It was a profoundly disruptive time in my life," Tate says. "The children in the ward weren't very nice to each other. It opened my eyes as an eight-year-old to the fact that the world isn't quite as straightforward as I had thought it was. In those days, it was believed that fresh air was good for everything. We were pushed out into the bitter cold whenever possible. The food was disgusting—my gourmet tastes were forming even then. I used to secrete this sometimes inedible substance in a tin can, hide it in my locker, and, when we were taken outside, wait for a suitable moment to empty it into a hedge. For the first time in my life I became deceitful. Being underhanded was a way of coping. And when I eventually returned home I was a far more introverted, secretive child than before. As the months in the hospital wore on, my patience did gradually wear thin. I felt as though I were in a prison. There was a pavilion, a hundred and fifty yards across a playing field, that seemed like a promised land. I had been told that I'd eventually be able to walk that far. And I remember, one rainy day, finally managing to get there on my crutches. It gave me an unforgettable sense of achievement. The whole of the six months was a very strange and out-of-time experience."

Music manifested itself even under such conditions. Reaching out to the piano through the bars of his bed, Tate made his broadcast début, playing "The Mountains of Mourne" for the hospital's radio station.

When Jeffrey was twelve, he returned to Rowley Bristow for the second operation, which was exclusively orthepedic—an attempt to limit the already considerable spinal curvature and save him from life in a wheelchair. One of his ribs was removed and grafted on to the spine, in the hope that it would hold the spine in place and help straighten it. This was a drastic intervention, rarely performed at that time, and it posed considerable risks. The second operation, however, proved somewhat less of a psychological ordeal than the first. This stay in the hospital was only two and a half months, and now Jeffrey was just old enough to be placed in the adolescent ward, where, being the youngest, he was treated as a mascot. He spent his time reading books on mountaineering, and in his imagination scaled peaks he would never climb in reality. "I can still rattle off the relative heights of most of the Alps," he says. A mountain-climbing enthusiast recently told Tate about having made an ascent of the Whymper Ridge, on the Breithorn. Tate asked "From which hut?" and "How many hours did you manage it in?"

The operations had preserved Jeffrey's ability to walk and had stabilized the spinal curvature, but he was nonetheless left with a crippling malformation. Tate summarizes: "My left leg is almost useless below the knee, and is six inches shorter than the right. As ill luck would have it, my spinal curvature twisted me in such a way that the pelvis on the left side tilts upward and comes a little higher than the lower end of the rib cage; meanwhile, my left shoulder pushes downward. The effect is that the left side is crushed together. The upward tilt of the pelvis makes my left leg seem even shorter than it actually is. Therefore, I have both real and apparent shortening of the leg. My spine is in an extenuated S. The exaggerated spinal curve throws everything over to the right and gives the impression of a hunchback. Through growth in this funny position, the left lung and rib cage are smaller than the right, and my lung capacity is limited." Without his deformity Tate would have stood six feet four; with it he stands five feet nine.

Tate knew that he owed his mobility to the staff at Rowley Bristow, and gladly returned there several times to allow students taking courses in surgery to examine him. After the second operation, his doctors told him that he must thenceforth wear a plastic brace. It was a rigid corset, fitted with leather straps. Its purpose was to help solidify the spinal fusion and to support the weakened back muscles. "Every morning I dutifully strapped myself in," Tate says. "The brace proved quite unpleasant. It rubbed against the armpits and the thighs. I always had to wear an undershirt beneath it, and in hot weather it became almost unbearable. Of course it smelled, so I had to wash it all the time. In a romantic situation, anyone whom I would embrace would suddenly come up against this plastic cage. All the possibilities for farce were there."

Jeffrey was also fitted with a built-up surgical shoe. "The brace was one thing," he says. "People didn't really see it when I wore a jacket; it was my own personal affliction. But the shoe looked awful—its sole was nearly six inches thick—and it felt like a ball and chain." Sometimes its weight would carry his foot in unexpected directions. The shoe twice destroyed a friend's sewing box set on a coffee table.

When Jeffrey returned home from the hospital, he acquired his first gramophone and went through a popular-music period. He remembers donning a floral dress and an enormous hat, and doing a "terrible mime" under a willow tree to Ruth Etting's recording of "Smoke Gets in Your Eyes." Jeffrey got on better with adults than with children. After school, he would visit the family's friends for a chat, and would nearly always play the piano for them. "Above all, he was never resentful that he was handicapped," his mother recalls. "He was always busy doing something he wanted to do."

Practical plans had to be made for Jeffrey's future. He was enthusiastic about music, but his parents weren't well-to-do, and had no guarantee that he had any special musical gifts. They believed that, given his disability, he would have little chance to support himself in that field. For his part, Jeffrey felt that he owed a debt of gratitude to the medical profession and that he might repay it by becoming a doctor himself. He was bright academically, and his parents encouraged him along those lines. They reluctantly decided to discontinue his piano lessons. "I then began to play the piano even more," Tate recalls. "I began to experiment, to search in my own way for the sounds and colors I wanted."

When Jeffrey was eleven, he had been accepted by the Farnham Grammar School, where he studied until he was eighteen. He thus came under the influence of the school's director of music, Alan Fluck. "All of my slightly mad musical education came from Alan's class," Tate now says. "His great belief was that youngsters should make music as much as possible. He conveyed his love, whether for Mozart or for Hindemith, Britten, or Schoenberg. I learned from him how to understand and appreciate music." Tate tried his hand at the cello; he remembers the results as "appalling." The piano became the vehicle for his musical explorations. He would borrow piano-vocal scores of operas from the school library—"Der Rosenkavalier" and Britten's "A Midsummer Night's Dream" —and teach himself to play them. Tate's piano playing is still unorthodox, but it is expressive and conceptual. He manages to find sonorities on the piano which somehow match the textures of an orchestra.

In 1956, thanks to Fluck's enterprising spirit, the school gave the first performance outside America of Gian Carlo Menotti's "Amahl and the Night Visitors." Menotti came over to attend the performance. Jeffrey was at the piano; it was his first experience as a coach for opera singers. Menotti was impressed by the boy's talent. When Jeffrey told him that he planned to become a doctor, Menotti commented, "You can heal souls by being a musician." Later that year,

Jeffrey sang one of the prima donnas in Fluck's production of Mozart's comic opera "The Impresario." In true prima-donna fashion, he came down with a bad cold for the first performance, but nothing could deter him from getting onstage. He ingeniously arranged to mouth the part while a soprano stationed in the orchestra pit sang the actual notes. By the third performance, he couldn't resist croaking out some notes himself. His mother remembers that he got so excited that—unknown to him—his wig slid partway off, his bustle came around to the front, and his false bosom began to droop. The audience was in hysterics.

Fluck, as idealistic as ever, is now the director of Youth & Music, an international organization, based in London, that is dedicated to building young audiences and helping young musicians. He works out of a small office on Charing Cross Road. "Jeffrey and I had more than a teacher-student relationship; it was a musician-musician relationship," he told me. "Even then, Jeffrey was a great talker, with a sharp sense of humor. He was also a very sensitive boy—so sensitive, in fact, that once, when we disagreed and I got the upper hand, he burst into tears. But since then he's learned to be both sensitive and tough—like so many outstanding musicians. I know now that I helped Jeffrey along toward music, but I feel that sooner or later talent will out."

Jeffrey also appeared in the school's theatrical productions. At thirteen, he portrayed Lady Bracknell in the handbag scene from "The Importance of Being Earnest." "My other great female role was Lady Macbeth," Tate says. "That caused infinite mirth among my schoolmates. Interestingly enough, despite my disability, I enjoyed acting. Maybe I favored women's roles because I could conceal my shape under long dresses."

In his early teens, Jeffrey went on a holiday to Switzerland with a group of youngsters. When he returned, his mother found him exceptionally quiet. She eventually learned that he had been razzed. "The children around me were sometimes not very nice," Tate told me. "It was just fear of the unknown. A deformed child was something to be suspicious of, to be slightly rejected. The problems of a disabled child begin to ease when you're about sixteen or seventeen. But early adolescence and early sexuality—I obviously wasn't going to be included in that element of life as far as people of my age were concerned."

In Laurens van der Post's novella "The Seed and the Sower," an exceptionally handsome officer named Celliers describes the pity he felt as a child for a neighbor who was born deformed. "Yet today I am not sure that I should not have envied him," Celliers reflects. "I simply do not know which constitutes the greatest danger to the integrity of being: to attract or to repel; to incur the dislikes or likes of one's fellow men. . . . I know now that from my earliest age the effect I had on those about me enticed me away from myself, drew me out of my own inner focus of being." Whatever limitations and suffering Tate's disability visited upon him, he was not drawn out of his own inner focus of being. "I was thrust in upon myself," Tate says. "I entered into an artistic realm which fascinated me, where I could hold my own, where I could make my mark in things of a nonphysical nature." Jeffrey eventually became head boy of the school, a position usually held by a boy who excels in sports. "Jeffrey wasn't going to be left behind," Alan Fluck recalls. "He wasn't fragile at all. He had a driving force and excelled through his strength of character."

Jeffrey loved to read; he would spend hours in the local secondhand bookshop. "The Mill on the Floss" and "Adam Bede" affected him deeply. But the book that had the most impact upon him was Alain-Fournier's "Le Grand Meaulness." "I read it for the first time in my adolescence and was profoundly moved," Tate told me. "It's beautifully written, with immense restraint, and has a bittersweet quality that I associate with certain French music—for instance, the second movement of the Ravel Piano Concerto. The story deals with loneliness and isolation. The narrator, a boy named François, is crippled, which is perhaps why I identified with him. He suffers from a weakness of the knee and has to hop about on one leg. He joins his audacious friend Meaulnes, another outsider, in a search for a lost domain, in which lives an elusive and beautiful girl. The dream atmosphere is reminiscent of 'Pelléas et Mélisande' but has more of a sense of reality than Maeterlinck's play. The story appears to veer between the real and the unreal, and has a strong symbolic element. But it seemed very real to me. It's about a dream that we once had, and attempt to recapture all the rest of our lives."

Midway in his narrative François tells us:

> For the first time I too am on the path of adventure. For once it is not for shells left stranded by the tide that I am prospecting. . . . I am looking for something still more mysterious: for the path you read about in books, the old lane choked with undergrowth whose entrance the weary prince could not discover. You'll only come upon it at some lost moment of the morning when you've long since forgotten that it will soon be eleven, or twelve. . . . Then, as you are awkwardly brushing aside a tangle of branches, your arms at the same time trying to protect your face, you suddenly catch a glimpse of a dark tunnel of green at the far end of which there is a tiny aperture of light. . . . But I hadn't found anything.
>
> My weak leg was beginning to bother me.

In 1961, when Tate was eighteen, he won a scholarship that allowed him to study medicine at Cambridge; his career now seemed determined. Yet he was beginning to have doubts. During the three years he spent at Christ's College, his enthusiasm for theatre continued unabated. He directed various Cambridge dramatic societies in works by Shakespeare and Ibsen. One day he announced to his mother that he had written a letter declaring his interest in acting which he intended to send to Peter Hall, then the director of the Royal Shakespeare Company. His mother dissuaded him from taking such a step until he had finished his medical studies. The letter remained unposted.

At fourteen, Tate had been taken to a dull performance of Wagner's "Tristan und Isolde" and had fallen asleep. "It nearly put me off opera for life," he says. Yet he decided to give opera another chance, and joined a group of Cambridge students who would go down to London and queue for tickets to the Royal Opera House, Convent Garden. He once spent a weekend on the pavement waiting for a ticket for a Callas performance that the diva eventually cancelled. "In general, I was upset by the rather impoverished production values in opera compared with what one could see on the straight stage," he told me. "I was also then discovering masterpieces of chamber music, such as the last Beethoven quartets. In the opera house, one rarely heard the finesse of phrasing that's typical of good string-quarters players. I didn't approve of opera, but I forgave it. There were, however, bright moments. When Giulini conducted 'Il Trovatore,' I truly enjoyed Verdi for the first time. Every accompaniment figure had a life of its own. I realized that opera is a very difficult art form, and I began to see that when it does work it can be deeply satisfying."

When Tate was twenty-one, his parents divorced. "This was a traumatic event for me," he said. "Unexpectedly, it brought me closer to my father. For the first time, he needed support from me. I had always had the impression that because he was a fine sportsman and I had become a creature of the arts and mind I had little in common with him. I discovered that he had always been, underneath, as warm and supportive as my mother was." The divorce had another effect: with the breaking up of the family, Tate felt somewhat less obliged to carry out the career plans that had been made for him, less constrained in terms of his future.

After his three years at Cambridge, Tate entered St. Thomas's Hospital in London for three more years of medical studies. Music continued to vie for a place in his life. He soon organized a choir, which he called the St. Thomas Hospital Music Society. Medical students who had known him at Cambridge came from hospitals all over London to sing under his direction. He presented such works as Bach's motets and Purcell's "Dido and Aeneas" in a series of concerts in Southwark Cathedral. He also led a madrigal group on Saturday afternoons. One of its members recalls that Tate would often arrive so out of breath after climbing the stairs that he could hardly speak. But the music of Monteverdi or Gesualdo would soon revive him.

Shortly after Tate began his studies at St. Thomas's, he met John Kentish, a much admired lyric tenor who sang at Sadler's Wells and at Glyndebourne. The occasion was a New Year's Eve party, during which Tate volunteered to accompany the tenor at the piano. Kentish recalls the occasion vividly: "We did Schubert songs together, and I was greatly impressed by Jeffrey's sensitivity. Everybody was completely silenced by the pianist and singer, who seemed entirely at one with each other without having ever rehearsed together." John and his wife, Leigh, suggested that Tate come along to coach young singers at the Meyer-Lismann Opera Workshop, in Kensington, where Leigh taught drama. Three months later, Tate said that he was willing to give it a try.

Leigh Kentish said to me, "It's often the case that those who have a gift are mysteriously helped along by people who suddenly seem to be there to guide them." Soon Tate moved into the Kentish home, and he remained there for eighteen months, while he was working toward his medical degree. He found the Kentish household happily bohemian. Leigh Kentish recalls, "Our house was so disordered that—knowing Jeffrey's sense of order—I think it's a miracle he survived. Our children would sometimes watch Jeffrey strap on his pink brace; they were vastly amused by it. He didn't have a trace of embarrassment, and he never admitted to any pain. But once he was fitted with a new corset, made by a Polish doctor—an invention that was absolutely rigid. He could hardly move at all and was in agony. That proved too much even for him, and it went into the dustbin the next day." The Kentishes remain his close friends to this day.

A primary revelation in opera presented itself in the form of a "Die Meistersinger" at Sadler's Wells Theatre which was conducted by Sir Reginald Goodall, whose Wagner performances have become legendary. An artist of uncommon integrity, Goodall demanded rehearsal time that exceeded the possibilities of most opera houses. Blessed with little personal ambition, he never sought an international career. Tate recalls, "I had found the orchestral playing elicited by most Wagner conductors to be intensely ugly and totally unsatisfactory. Then I heard Goodall's performance: there was such lyricism, such attention to phrasing, such space, such beauty of sound! There were no world-class singers in the production, but because of the way he conducted the orchestra none of the singers had to shout—everyone sang beautifully. All the diverse musical elements flowed together seamlessly. The third act expanded in such a way that the final, great chord of C major seemed related to the chord that ends the Prelude, as if the whole work were hung between two distant but distinct pillars. The opera was produced in a correctly old-fashioned way, so that every character became a real person. When the curtain came down after six hours, I was almost in tears. I had come to identify so totally with those people onstage that I wanted to go on being with them." He saw the production thirteen times.

Then an inconceivable event occurred: Tate failed his medical exams. "I was mortified," he recalls. "My state scholarship vanished. Music had made a mess of it. Shortly afterward, I visited Scotland and took the ferry to the Isle of Arran. I stood by the railing, looked out to the sea, and thought that everything had come to an end. Where was I to turn? It was a low ebb in my life."

John Kentish describes Tate during his early twenties: "One sensed something quite exceptional about him. One couldn't quite define this quality. He just seemed to be somebody one had to get to know. There was something stirring within. He was sitting on a volcano, and that volcano proved to be music."

Tate recalls, "While I was waiting to retake my exams, John and Leigh, perhaps feeling a little guilty for having encouraged me to give so much time to music, suggested that I audition to study coaching at the London Opera Centre, an institute which offered training in every aspect of operatic performance. I did win a place there. Then—it's the kind of thing that usually happens—I succeeded in passing my medical exams." Tate decided that it was only sensible to complete his medical studies, and he spent a year as an interne in a hospital—six months in general medicine, six months in eye surgery. "The hours were long," he says. "I shut myself off from the world." He would often be on duty for thirty-six hours at a time, and occasionally from Friday morning straight through until Monday morning, during which he was lucky if he could catch five hours' sleep. "My interest in medicine was, as with a lot of things I do, very emotional," Tate told me. "The fascination with diagnosis, so essential to medicine, was actually slightly missing in me. I noticed, to my chagrin, that a lot of my fellow medical students were getting enormous stimulus from the intellectual study of disease. But when I got to the actual practice I realized that the only thing I really cared about was my patients and my ability to make them feel better."

Upon completing his year's interneship, in 1969, Tate was registered as a doctor. He then decided to put off practicing medicine for a year while he took up the place he had been offered at the London

Opera Centre, realizing that this was his last opportunity to find out whether it would be feasible for him to devote his life to music.

Tate was thus able to begin studying the repertoire under the guidance of conductors from Covent Garden. An opera coach—known in the trade as a *répétiteur*—makes an essential contribution to every production but gets little public recognition. A *répétiteur* must have a complete musical culture, including a knowledge of the style and the traditions associated with every period of operatic composition; an understanding of vocal technique; a feeling for dramatic expression; a proficiency in languages, especially Italian, German, and French; and an ear for diction. Though Tate was unaware of it, he was laying the groundwork for a career as an opera conductor.

While visiting the canteen on his first day at the Centre, Tate met the soprano Teresa Cahill, then a student. She says, "It was the beginning of a long-lasting musical love affair. I adopted Jeffrey as my only musical coach. We became great friends, had meals together, went to the cinema, enjoyed painting and architecture. He knew he could share his deepest feelings with me. We worked together on everything I had to prepare—even Gershwin and Cole Porter, which we performed at parties." (Tate's own singing of Noël Coward songs— all the verses from memory—is renowned among his friends.)

Tate recalls, "When I met Tess, it was a chance finding of like souls when I really needed it. We had a close artistic empathy. I learned a lot from her—what worked and what didn't work with singers. We experimented—poor Tess—and evolved things together. I felt alone and lacked confidence, but she had faith in me. When she discovered that there was a place free for a *répétiteur* at Covent Garden, she told me that I should damn well go and take the audition. To my immense astonishment, I found myself invited to join the staff of the Royal Opera House. But I was worried. There I was on a precipice, as it were—ready to give up the honorable profession of medicine that I had worked so hard for. And what were my qualifications in music? I had been the lowest of the low, an amateur teaching singers for a year, and now I was suddenly called upon to teach professionals. I had misgivings—but I knew that I had to do it."

Sir Georg Solti, then the music director of the Royal Opera, was less worried. He appreciated Tate's qualities as a *répétiteur:* his flexibility, which allowed him to follow the beat of any conductor; his ability, when he transcribed orchestra scores for the piano, to disregard non-essential musical details and go right to "the essence, the bone of the score." In 1973, Solti invited Tate to come to Vienna to assist him in his recording of "Parsifal." I have been one of Jeffrey Tate's greatest supporters ever since our first meeting, he says. "We worked together on a great many opera productions. In all of them he displayed the innate musicianship and talent which have made him the success he is today. This confirms what I've always said: only a good *répétiteur* can be a good opera conductor."

Tate learned much from his mentor. "I saw how meticulously Georg works with singers on matters of articulation, phrasing, text, and rhythm," he told me. "He has an uncanny sense of dramatic tension and timing. He builds up performances of tremendous intensity." Tate also gained invaluable experience assisting such conductors as Sir Colin Davis, Rudolf Kempe, and Carlos Kleiber.

Teresa Cahill was accepted at Covent Garden and continued working with Tate. "When Jeffrey coached singers, he always insisted on beautiful phrasing," she recalls. "He took care with short notes that shouldn't be hurried over, and with upbeats, which can sometimes be more important than the downbeats—all the things that magic is made of. His ear is fabulous; he knows instantly when a singer is not producing a note in the best way, when the sound remains in the back of the throat. He was always interested in the historical background of a role. When I learned Elvira in 'Don Giovanni,' he gave me a book about women in relation to the Catholic Church. He examines a score in the manner of Sherlock Holmes, and tries to get to the meaning of every marking, and even to the meaning of why certain marks were omitted."

"I used to make pottery on the wheel," Tate said. "When you conduct a vocal line, it's somewhat like having wet clay in your hands. One can virtually feel the texture of the voice as you guide it over the top of a phrase. There is a moment—an exquisite moment—when a voice will possess the right amount of overtones, when it will have a beauty of vibration, and will need just one mini-second more to expand and blossom. If you skate over that moment, the beauty of the line is lost. You can't teach that to a conductor; you can only gain it by listening and having much experience. Of course, one must always consider the text as well. There's a mistaken idea about bel canto. It's not a monotonous legato line, with never a rise and fall. Without sacrificing the musical phrase in any way, the singer must feel the inflections of the language. Listen to recordings of Caruso, Gigli, or Lotte Lehmann."

Tate's talents were soon appreciated by virtually every singer at Covent Garden. He was also sought after in the capacity of Dr. Tate, although he feels that in his dealings with singers his medical background proved more helpful psychologically than physically. "A good doctor will be able to assess the real severity of a symptom through having an acute sense of the whole person," he told me. "By the same token, while working with a musician you have to know what he or she is as a person—to know what quirks in the singers' personalities will enable you to get the best out of them. That goes for working with orchestras, too."

Tate's presence in the theatre was rendered all the more striking by the way he dressed. He recalls, "Everyone about me was so horribly conventionally dressed that I decided to rebel, and attire myself in the fashion of the day, which was determined by Carnaby Street." When he appeared at a rehearsal sporting black-and-white checked trousers, a yellow shirt, and a black leather jacket, Solti took one look at him and said dryly, "Very colorful." Tate had a great, dark, motheaten, ankle-length fur coat that became something of a legend. He acquired a velvet cloak, which he wore with flair; a colleague remembers him as resembling an Aubrey Beardsley drawing. "One of the strange advantages in having a disability is that you can get away with such things," Tate says. "People don't dare make any comment. It's rather naughty, but you can slightly play on their embarrassment. It sounds terribly arrogant when I confess that. Now I don't pay too much attention to my dress. I've only had to get used to formal clothing when conducting."

When Tate was thirty, he decided that something must finally be done about the built-up shoe that was a constant burden to him. He recounts, "First, I visited a distinguished doctor who specialized in artificial limbs, and he advised me, quite seriously, and even rather persuasively, to have my left leg amputated below the knee. I agreed with him that the leg was practically useless, but explained that I didn't want to wake up in the middle of the night and regret not having it. Then I had good luck. The technician at the surgical-appliances department at St. Thomas's Hospital was able to fit my leg into a device called an O'Connor extension. This is laced on well above the ankle and extends almost six inches beyond the toes, which I point downward, like a ballet dancer. It then attaches to a perfectly normal shoe, giving the impression that my leg is of normal length. Perversely, in order to wear this device you have to be badly disabled, with a very short leg. I became straighter as a result, and I looked infinitely better. My improved appearance gave me a new psychological lease on life. More important, in 1975, when I was thirty-two, I got rid of the brace I had worn since I was twelve. I had never questioned the necessity of wearing it, but now the friction it produced caused a superficial thrombosis of a vein in the thigh. When I recovered, I was very suspicious of the brace. I cherish my own suspicions. It was extremely hot, so I decided to experiment by removing the wretched thing. At first, I had little strength in my back muscles, but I managed to do without the brace for increasingly long periods every day. After a week, I realized, to my infinite joy, that I could do without it entirely." Tate's doctors cautiously agreed.

"It was interestingly symbolic that I finally gained the courage at that moment to throw the brace away," Tate says. "There followed an expansion of my musical life. Which factor is cause and which is effect I don't know. But I feel that if I hadn't got rid of the brace I would certainly never have been able to become a conductor." Tate spent the following summer in Bayreuth as Pierre Boulez's assistant for his production of "The Ring." He felt so much freer physically that he was able, when called upon, to stand in for Boulez and conduct the singers in rehearsals, rather than confine himself to the piano. "I had occasionally conducted before—for instance, in choral concerts," Tate says. "But I now discovered that I was physically capable of conducting over a fairly extended period. I tried to convey Pierre's musical intentions, and I felt that I contributed a lot to the performances."

"Jeffrey and I had an exceptional collaboration," Boulez recalls.

"He proved to be invaluable to me, through the initiative he took with the singers and the amazing results he achieved with them."

After six years at Covent Garden, Tate sensed that it was time to spread his wings. His greatest love was German opera, and he felt that he needed experience working in a German theatre. In 1977, he accepted a position at the Cologne Opera as assistant to its director, Sir John Pritchard. At the time of his death, last December, Pritchard was the music director of the San Francisco Opera and of the BBC Symphony Orchestra. When I spoke with him last fall, he told me, "I first met Jeffrey when I was regularly conducting at Covent Garden. There was an interesting aura about him. I think people do have an aura sometimes. One felt within him a human and musical potential that wasn't entirely realized. When he came to Cologne, we had a wonderful artistic collaboration—his musical scope was so wide, and his personality was so attractive."

"John was not only a fine musician but a very practical musician," Tate says. "He was a man of the theatre, and in the theatre, you have to be creatively practical. He had a remarkable ear for balance. I learned an enormous amount from him. His death was a great personal loss for me, and, of course, a great loss for the music world."

Six months after Tate arrived in Cologne, the course of his life changed dramatically. "One day, I was chatting with two singers, Ragnar Ulfung and Donald McIntyre," he says. "Ragnar, who was the director of the Göteborg Opera, in Sweden, was looking for a conductor for 'Carmen,' and I was scratching my brains to think of someone. Donald then said, 'Why don't *you* do it, Jeffrey?' I thought it absolute nonsense. After all, I had never conducted a professional orchestra before, much less an opera, nor had I received any specific training in conducting technique; furthermore, I doubted whether I'd have enough physical stamina to see through a whole performance. However, without my knowing it, Ragnar went the next morning to the administration of the Cologne Opera and arranged for me to take a leave of absence so that I'd be free to go to Göteborg. Faced with a virtual fait accompli, I found myself, against my better judgment, signing a contract to conduct 'Carmen.' I insisted on a clause allowing me to withdraw if after the second orchestral rehearsal I felt uncomfortable with the project. The first rehearsal was, in fact, a nightmare. But

I persevered, and I got through all the rehearsals. When the performance came, I walked into the pit with no fear at all, as though it were the most natural thing in the world. As the music moved under my hands, I suddenly felt that I was doing something I had been waiting to do all my life." Afterward, when Tate came onstage to accept an ovation, his shoe fell off the O'Connor extension and slithered to the footlights. He hopped forward without embarrassment to retrieve it.

There followed "Die Zauberflöte" in Göteborg and, at Pritchard's request, "Les Contes d'Hoffmann" in Cologne. "It was inevitable that Jeffrey's talents should lead him toward conducting," Sir John told me. "I usually mistrust people who come out of conducting schools. The really good conductor never sets out to be one. I watched with great delight when Jeffrey first conducted in Cologne. I sometimes thought—and this is not disloyalty to him—that perhaps he had a baptism of fire. Jeffrey was a natural musician in every way, but the craft of conducting needs experience—it's not an entirely natural thing. If in those days he didn't always manage to give a perfectly clear beat, the orchestra nonetheless respected him and understood his musical intentions. By now, of course, he has become wonderfully expert in opera." At his Cologne début, Tate misjudged the steps to the podium, lost his balance, and fell backward into the viola section. "It wasn't a very auspicious way for me to begin the evening," he recalls.

"I got into conducting by chance," Tate says. "I never consciously sought it out as a means of self-fulfillment. I was amazed when I realized that I could do it, and I began to welcome the opportunities when they came, which means that something inside me was waiting to receive them. My career has gone on like that. People have taken me up and used me, despite the fact that I say, 'Do you really want me?' I'm as astonished as everybody else in that it's gone so very rapidly."

It was no easy matter for Tate to begin a career as a conductor at thirty-five—or, for that matter, to conduct at all. "A conductor, of course, needs good lungs—he relies on good breathing to support his physical effort," Sir John told me. "And Jeffrey has less lung capacity than you or I; he has always had to cope with that impossible situation. I think also that he has felt some of the same pressures that I felt early in my career. When you're much taken up as a young conductor, you have to get through an enormous volume of work in a very short time. You have to learn in detail scores that you've never conducted before, yet every time you come before an orchestra you have to be fully prepared."

"I've had to run like hell to stay where I am," Tate told me. "Sometimes I begin to study a piece only three months before performing it. I still have moments when I feel that my career is built on sand. That's the negative side of my success story. I've fulfilled something without necessarily wanting it, and achieved something without being trained for it. I fear that the sand will dissolve one day and the whole structure will collapse. As a child, I often took the train from Farnham up to London and would look out at the slums on the outskirts of the great city. I had a recurrent fantasy that nothing would work out for me and I would end my life as a lonely old man in one of those slums. I was aware of the lower depths when I was very young, and that thought still comes back to me."

While Tate was in Cologne, he met Klaus Kuhlemann, who has since shared his life. Kuhlemann, who is a geomorphologist by training, is a perceptive music lover. A man of warmth and refinement, he is soft-spoken and has a fine sense of humor. "I don't know how I could have coped during the last thirteen years without Klaus," Tate told me. "I was basically a loner with a few close friends, but none who could really help in my most difficult moments. The blackness is now a little less black, because I can share it with somebody. Klaus is what I'm not—a true optimist—which is immensely helpful for me. As a geologist, he has a relation to practical things, and that implies a response to the visual. We share an appreciation of art and architecture. He is the least self-centered person I know—and is a good example for me. I'm taken out of my self-centeredness."

"Klaus's presence has been extremely beneficial to Jeffrey," Tate's mother told me. "He is completely devoted to Jeffrey and is a calming influence. In an unobtrusive way he irons out all the creases in Jeffrey's complicated existence. Jeffrey doesn't have to do the worrying, and that gives him the time he so much needs. Before performances you have to get by Klaus to bother Jeffrey, and that's not easy. Without Klaus, Jeffrey just couldn't do what he does."

After two years in Cologne, Tate began doing free-lance work. "I became a peripatetic *répétiteur*-cum-embryonic conductor," he says. In 1979, he assisted Boulez in Paris in the first complete performance of Berg's "Lulu," and the following year he worked under Herbert von Karajan in Salzburg. For seven years, starting in 1978, Tate spent part of each season at the Metropolitan Opera, first as a coach, then as a conductor. "Jimmy Levine took a risk by giving me so many opportunities," Tate says. "He had no reason to do so; he had no more than a hunch that it would work out." "Così Fan Tutte," which was to be Tate's Metropolitan conducting début, had to be cancelled owing to a strike. Tate's début thus came when, in December, 1980, he took over a performance of "Lulu" without rehearsal. Although he knew the difficult work thoroughly, he had never actually conducted it. "Solti advised me that I would be mad to conduct 'Lulu' under these circumstances," Tate recalls. "But I decided to go through with it. It was a terrifying four hours. By conquering an extreme fear, and by dint of sheer will power, I actually managed to pull it off." To compound the difficulty, Tate's spectacles flew off during the performance; he couldn't read the score at all for a few minutes, until a player handed them back to him from the orchestra pit.

While Tate was at the Met, he found himself virtually making a specialty of conducting the most difficult works without rehearsal. They included an all-Stravinsky evening and Berg's "Wozzeck." "Somewhere I must enjoy taking risks," Tate acknowledges. "It's part of the darker side of my being. I need to challenge fate—perhaps as a compensation for my limitations." After the "Wozzeck" performance, in 1985, Leonard Bernstein came backstage. Learning that Tate not only had never conducted the opera before but had not had a rehearsal, he fell to his knees and exclaimed "Maestro!"

Tate made his Covent Garden début in June, 1982, with Mozart's "La Clemenza di Tito." Leigh Kentish says, "Certain people had reservations and were embarrassed about the idea of a disabled person conducting. They were amazed when Jeffrey achieved such outstanding musical results and, incidentally, got marvellous notices. It serves them right." Tate has since conducted operas in Geneva, Hamburg, Munich, Salzburg, Paris, San Francisco, Aix-en-Provence—

thirty-two different works. In 1987, he was appointed principal conductor at the Royal Opera House, where Bernard Haitink, the music director, and he now share artistic responsibility.

When we contemplate Tate's success, we cannot forget the other dimension. On the floors of dining rooms in Pompeii one finds mosaics of human skeletons, placed there by those who, while living well, wished to be conscious of the fragility of life. Such reminders are now out of fashion. For Tate they are inescapable. An insurance company once set his life expectancy at forty-eight. "In my twenties and early thirties, I feared that my physical strength might soon give out," Tate told me. "I could see my life coming to a blank-wall end. In a way, this fear had a positive effect. I tended almost to grab at life. I had a frenetic desire to experience things, and thus learned much about life more quickly than many people of my age. But since I discovered conducting as a means of self-expression I've found a sense of fulfillment. It's as though I've managed again to walk that hundred and fifty yards to the pavilion. I feel that my life can last longer than I had anticipated; I even feel physically better."

After spending a quarter of an hour in Jeffrey Tate's company, one ceases to notice that he has any disability. What one remembers is the remarkable, full head; the dark hair that falls over his forehead in a sweep; the eyes that, from behind wide glasses, regard the world with quiet irony, occasionally betraying a tender vulnerability; the commanding voice; the large, expressive hands; the exuberant flow of conversation, urged on by a compelling need to give articulate shape to his thoughts and feelings. Tate moves surprisingly quickly and conveys an unusual sense of physical vitality. Though he walks with a cane, his friends have to adopt a little trot to keep up with him. He used to ride a bicycle—"wobbling like hell, at breakneck speed," he confesses, with a certain mischievous glee—until Kuhlemann persuaded him to give it up. Frances Graham, a friend of Tate's, who studied medicine with him at Cambridge, once tried to teach him to swim. "Jeff is very top-heavy," she told me. "We tried to get his legs to work—there's not much strength in his left leg. We should have encouraged him to swim with his arms. He held on to a rubber dinghy, but it turned over and nearly drowned the Maestro. He hadn't much liked disappearing underwater, and the experience didn't leave him in the best of tempers."

When Tate comes to the podium, he strides with his customary rapidity, the awkward pitch of his body tempered by his determination. He lays down his cane and hoists himself up onto a stool. He normally remains seated during a performance, but when he gets excited he stands up, more often than he himself realizes. Tate's medical friends concur that conducting offers him the best possible form of physiotherapy. Conducting has not only increased his stamina but also pushed his lung expansion to its limit. "It's extraordinary what music can do," Tate said as we talked one afternoon in a rehearsal room at Covent Garden. "Once, I had an attack of gout and was in such pain that I thought that there was no way in which I could conduct 'The Magic Flute' that night. But when the music began I absolutely forgot my pain. Given the weakness in my back muscles, I never imagined that I could conduct an opera as long as 'Parsifal,' but I did give a performance of 'Parsifal,' in Nice, as a fortieth-birthday present to myself. It was a milestone for me to conduct this work, which I enormously admire and love and had always wanted to feel under my fingertips. Although 'Parsifal' is a chaste piece, it's also a sensual piece; even in moments of supreme chastity, it's profoundly sensual. When I finished the performance, I not only was gratified that I'd been able to do it but felt that I could almost do it again straightaway.

"I remember when Otto Klemperer returned to conduct in London after the accident in which he nearly incinerated himself. We all stood up as a tribute to the fact that he had survived, and we wondered if he'd be able to conduct at all. Then came the most galvanic performance of Mahler's Ninth. There was something raging in him. He demonstrated that the flesh had no power over him. What he portrayed, with far more conviction than most conductors, was the blackness in the music. He didn't seek to alleviate its extremely tortured nature; it was unconsoling and vehement. I feel a kinship with Klemperer's vision. I call myself a positive pessimist. There's a side of me that takes a very black view of things. This is curious, coming from someone who is known to his friends and relatives as a positive sort of person, but I think the world is a deep and dark and dangerous place as well as a very beautiful place. We are living in a society whose existence relies on destruction of the environment, and which may very well prove lethal to itself. I've become a committed environmentalist. My negative thoughts may be related to the fact that I've always been very frightened of dying. This may have had something to do with my hospital experiences. I remember lying in bed at night when I was about eight and suddenly realizing that someday I wasn't going to exist, and that therefore nothing would exist. I cried out in terror. Even now this deep fear of nonexistence comes back to me from time to time. A word, a sentence, a moment in music can trigger it off. As I talk about it, it seems absurd. But when that blackness comes it's as black as the sensation I had as a child."

One of the reasons Tate is fascinated with opera is that it deals with what he calls the baroque elements in life—the extreme, the fantastic. "Opera depicts the forces of danger and chaos," he says. "But it expresses them in defined forms and brings them under artistic control, and this control maximizes the experience. I once had tea with E. M. Forster. I dared to tell him that I found it improbable that in 'Howards End' the bookcase should fall over and kill the clerk. He said, 'You're quite right. But improbability is what life is all about.' He told me of a young professor who, while cleaning his car, lit a match without noticing that his gasoline tank was open, and burned to death. 'If I had put that in one of my stories, you wouldn't believe it,' he said. 'These strange things—bolts of fate—do happen.' We can laugh at the improbability of, say, 'Il Trovatore,' but life is in fact not comfortable. Verdi has made all those characters *live*; they are totally palpable human beings—metaphors of our own lives. We say that the plot is absurd because we want to protect ourselves, and not have these characters and their fate intrude upon us. We are frightened, ashamed to be moved."

Tate conducted his first symphony concert in 1983, in the full glare of the public spotlight, when he gave an all-Beethoven program with the London Symphony Orchestra at the Barbican Hall. He has since appeared as guest conductor with major orchestras on both sides of the Atlantic. On nearly every program there is at least one piece that he is conducting for the first time. He studies scores in the morning before getting out of bed, and then steals an hour for them whenever he can, even while carrying on a conversation. He says, "Although as a doctor

I had little interest in the scientific part of medicine, as a conductor I like to unlock secrets concealed in the score—to search out musical lines which have an importance that isn't obvious at first glance."

In 1985, Tate was named principal conductor of the English Chamber Orchestra, and with that group he is currently recording the complete Mozart symphonies and piano concertos, the latter with Mitsuko Uchida as soloist. Ms. Uchida lives happily ensconced among her books and scores in a London-mews flat. Her eyes sparkle when she speaks of Tate. "When Jeffrey and I first performed together, I thought, My God, I've met someone who may become one of the most important musicians in my life! And I was damned right. He's intellectually precise and vigorous, and never lets anything get past him. He understands the chamber-music partnership between piano and orchestra. His knowledge of Mozart's operas gives him the sense for the dramatic characterization which is so important in the instrumental works."

"In Mozart, everything stems from a vocal source," Tate says. "I care that every single part sings—not only the main voices but the inner voices as well. I'm looking not for a composite sound but for as transparent a sound as possible; no part should be regarded as mere padding. I'll rehearse an instrumental ensemble with the same care that I would give to a vocal ensemble from 'Figaro.' "

Tate's delight in unlocking secrets is evident in his recordings. A bassoon line will be lifted out of obscurity to reveal a passage in a new light. A viola line—typically neglected by Mozart interpreters—will emerge to add depth and tenderness. Tate's tempi can occasionally be daring, as when he takes certain allegro movements at an unusually moderate pace to insure textural clarity. One may not always agree with what he does. The important thing is that Tate has a dynamic approach to interpretation; he expresses something of interest. "There's never only one way of looking at a piece," he says. "I think one has a right to focus on especially interesting aspects of a work, particularly of a well-known work. One is obliged not to seek the absolute truth but to show *a* truth."

What makes a good conductor? Technique? Almost all the great conductors have had an unorthodox technique. Academic conducting diagrams are useless when it comes to delineating the living shape of music. (Tate says of Wilhelm Furtwängler, "He was not a technician but a poet.") Emotive gesticulation? It can either inspire an orchestra or disturb it. Some conductors achieve intensity through restraint. Think of Hans Knappertsbusch (whom I have seen conduct an all-Wagner concert while resting his left hand on the rail of the podium throughout), or Richard Strauss, who said that the audience should perspire, not the conductor. Charisma? Fine, if you have it, but it can be as easily misused as used well. Anything may help, but there is one essential ingredient, and that is the conductor's *mind*. The orchestra must know that the conductor knows what he wants; if it respects his intentions, it will play well.

Tate has shaped a sure technique for himself, and music has, in turn, shaped him. His broad gestures express the plasticity of the musical line, even if they don't invariably convey the finest nuances of shading he envisions. His appearance obviously defies the conventional image. In his frankness of manner there is no pretension, but his integrity casts a spell of its own. Yet if there is a secret to his rise toward fame, achieved without the ambition and the methodical planning that usually accompany such a progression, it lies in the unrelenting excellence of his mind, in his sensibility, taste, perception, and commitment, which vitalize musicians who come into contact with him, onstage or off.

Tate prefers to work with orchestras with which he has a long-standing relationship. "Players who know me well get used to my idiosyncrasies," he says. "They intuitively understand my intentions, and will follow me through thick and thin. I don't have to indicate everything with my hands with such ferocity. In opera this is terribly important, because there's so much expression that lies between the beats—the rhythmic flexibility, the sensitivity to singers. Rehearsing with a new orchestra can be emotionally exhausting. I tend to look for deficiencies first in myself rather than in the players. There are conductors who manage to subdue their human tendencies and convey authority by stern discipline. I have the disadvantage of being a nice Englishman. But I have to be what I am. I may shout occasionally, but basically I try to seduce my orchestras by stealth and sloth. I'm reliant on the chemistry between the musicians and me. There's a risk involved. When the chemistry doesn't work, I'm somewhat at a loss to know what to do. But when it does work—when you achieve something through an empathy with the musicians—it's wonderful."

"Some conductors try to terrify you, but Jeffrey knows that the better you respond to people the better they make music," the singer Anne Howells told me. "If he trusts your talent, he lets you bring something of yourself to it. Many conductors mistake humility for weakness. Jeffrey would never do that."

Tate's benevolence is married rather uneasily to his perfectionism. He is not a person to suffer fools. He has a definite standard, and he's not prepared to fall short of it himself or to allow anyone else to diminish it in any way. When rehearsing, whether for a concert, an opera, or a recording, he's exacting and organized, and speaks directly to the musical point, without indulging in extraneous philosophizing. He expects everyone else to be fully prepared, at least the second time a piece is played through. He once dismissed an inattentive percussionist during a rehearsal of "Lulu." One musician who has played under his direction told me, "Jeffrey couldn't get on with all orchestras. His perfectionism can even bring on a slight sense of stress. Perhaps for this reason I feel that his performances occasionally lack a certain dimension of relaxation, especially in quiet passages. But, all told, it's a great pleasure to make music with him; he rehearses in such depth that one feels one has experienced the whole piece."

As an opera conductor, Tate has a special affinity with Mozart, Wagner, and Strauss. He feels less at ease with the Italian repertoire, although in recent years he has gradually come closer to Verdi. Hugues Gall, the director of Geneva's Grand Théâtre, remembers Tate's début there, in 1983, when he conducted "The Marriage of Figaro," produced by Sir Peter Hall. "Peter and I had heard good things about Tate and decided to give him a chance," he told me. "From the first rehearsal he surpassed our expectations and proved himself to be a true Mozartian. Some conductors just conduct, take their money, and leave—and some of these are nevertheless fine musicians. But, more rarely, others, like Tate, take an interest in all aspects of the production—the dramatic side as well as the musical."

"You can't just sit in the pit and conduct," Tate says. "Opera is total theatre, and the conductor is part of that. You're fortunate if you work with understanding directors, who are respectful of the music. But some don't understand—or willfully misunderstand. This can be intensely frustrating, and you have a struggle on your hands."

Tate is at odds with the extremist trend among opera directors to interpret Mozart "in terms of our age" while neglecting to interpret him in terms of his own age. Historical perception does not decrease human relevance. The plot of "The Marriage of Figaro," for instance, plays against the social conditions and the sensibilities of the eighteenth century; the relationships are largely divested of tension if the portrayal of the Count is not sufficiently aristocratic. When I brought this point up with Tate, he agreed wholeheartedly. "Tito Gobbi was one of the few singers who understood this," he said excitedly. "When he played the Count, one felt that the man's social station gave him permission to kill. When he went, sword in hand, to see if anyone was hiding in the Countess's closet, you really believed he would run through any man he found there.

"I never cease to be amazed at the scope of Mozart's imagination. Throughout 'Figaro' he reveals his profound understanding of ordinary human beings. In 'Don Giovanni' he presents us with a wholly different world, in which southern passions are let loose to an extraordinary degree. In 'Così Fan Tutte' he combines irony with deep compassion. This work is often mistreated either as a farce or as cold, inhuman symmetry. Actually, in 'Così' one begins to cry more than one laughs. For me Mozart is the ultimate romantic dramatist. The world of sound he created for 'The Magic Flute' is more imaginative and fantastic than in almost any other opera ever written."

In the operatic masterpieces, drama and music emanate from a single source and flow together in a single stream. The conductor must, by dint of insight and sympathetic imagination, enter into this stream, and insure that the continuity of meaning remains unbroken as it evolves through an entire work. An audience must never be left with notes that are mere patterns of sound, bereft of spirit. "I remember Karajan rehearsing 'Tosca,' " Tate told me. "In a quiet passage—a psychological moment, having to do with the evil character of Scarpia—he asked the strings to make an instantaneous contrast between a warm and a 'glacial' sound. Every response from the orchestra had to be relevant to the drama."

Opera conducting poses a number of special problems that are not found in symphonic conducting. "It's hard for the orchestra in the pit to hear the singers—and the singers, being at a distance from the orchestra, tend to respond late," Tate said. "The conductor is supposed to be the intermediary between orchestra and singer, but sometimes his presence is more harmful than helpful. If the singers are confronted with a continual barrage of sound, they can never sing softer than mezzo forte, and half their range of expression is sacrificed. You have to develop the orchestra's sensitivity. In rehearsal, Karajan would sometimes stop conducting while the orchestra continued playing, and say, 'Please, just listen to the singers.'

"Balance is usually thought of in terms of dynamics, but it's also a question of opacity. I ask the players to think of the music not as harmony but as counterpoint, to tend to their own lines with care, and to enjoy listening to the other parts in the orchestra. This sort of transparency is particularly difficult to attain in 'Tristan' and 'The Ring.' But if you achieve it Wagner's operas can be sung as lyrically as Bellini's— which is what Wagner wanted. That's the orchestral key to Wagner.

"Then comes the crucial question of tempo. Reginald Goodall stressed two principles that may seem to contradict each other: first, that you must actually give enough time to hear all the notes; second, that you don't conduct the music, you conduct the text. The text is where the drama lies. To complicate matters, Wagner sometimes gives us meanings on more than one level, as in 'Das Rheingold,' where he depicts comic irony together with an underlying tragic irony. The challenge—and it's a great challenge—is to find the tempo *juste:* to conduct the text at its real pace while allowing time for the music to speak fully. Verdi is no less problematic. You have to have a knife-edge sense of pause, tension, comma, and breathing point in relation to the drama to weld an entire act together. Pace is everything. That's why I won't conduct translations. I'm a partisan of supertitles, projected above the proscenium, which allow the audience to follow the text without disturbing the relationship of the words to the music.

"Opera conducting is a difficult business. It's rare when all the musical and dramatic considerations come together. Out of every three opera productions you do, one will be satisfying, the second will be acceptable, the third could well be disastrous. It's only one in twelve that will be a triumph."

In the summer of 1987, Alan Fluck reappeared in Tate's musical life. Fluck was organizing performances of Britten's "War Requiem" to be given in both East and West Berlin in celebration of the seven-hundred-and-fiftieth anniversary of the city's founding. Fluck explains, "These concerts were more than a political gesture; they were a human gesture. Three hundred youngsters—including the Boys Choir of Harlem—came from all over the world to assemble in the world's most divided city. We wanted Jeffrey to conduct, so we moved heaven and earth for him to be able to do it. That meant flying him several times in and out of Salzburg. After the first performance, which was a tremendously moving experience for all concerned, when Jeffrey and I were finally free of the crowds of people we just looked at one another and burst into tears. When Jeffrey left Farnham, I had thought he'd be doing medicine. Farewell, Jeffrey, see you around sometime. I never dreamed he'd be doing the 'War Requiem' with me over a quarter of a century later." Tate says that had he never conducted anything other than those two performances all his efforts in music would have been justified.

Not surprisingly, Tate has acquired an antipathy to going to see doctors. Klaus Kuhlemann says, "Jeffrey has accepted a certain level of pain, especially in his lower back, and if he mentions it at all one knows that it's severe. He is most uncomfortable when he's in a confined space: sitting in a chair—he has learned to shift back and forth—or lying down. Travel can be problematic. If the mattress is too soft, he must change hotels."

There have been difficult moments on the podium. "Sometimes in the earlier years of my conducting I'd find that toward the end of a great climax I wasn't able to breathe," Tate told me. "On one occasion I felt as though I might keel over. The harpist, not having anything to do at that moment, realized that I had gone terribly white; she thought that I was going to expire on the podium. In fact, I got off-stage and came back to conduct for an hour and a half longer. In Munich, in the summer of 1987, I actually did collapse during the dress rehearsal of 'Salomé,' but I managed to recover and go on. The doctors examined me and concluded that it was a case of complete physical exhaustion. I cancelled some performances at Covent Garden and gave myself a true vacation for the first time in years."

Tate's mother had become increasingly concerned that, although her son was getting more and more tired, he seemed unwilling to let go of any part of his musical life. "I read Jeffrey the riot act," she says. "I told him, 'If they want you to conduct, they'll wait for you.' Jeffrey finally did take notice, and began to slow his pace. Recently, he's become more serene, more settled in himself. He used to worry about reviews, about his career. Now all that matters to him is whether he himself is happy with a performance. Given his nomadic kind of existence, it means something to him to come out to the countryside and be at home with his family and friends."

"There was a time when Jeffrey used to go a little over the top," one of his friends told me. "A touch of the Maestro would slip in. He'd be a bit flip and scratchy, and a little unhappy if the attention wasn't on him. This isn't uncommon among conductors. But that period has passed. It's nice to see a good friend back again and to know that Jeffrey as a human being is still very much there." Tate seems never to forget anyone. He can pick up with someone exactly where he left off, even if years have gone by. His friends are legion. When you walk through London with him, big as the city is, wherever you go people hail him in the street.

Tate and Klaus Kuhlemann live in London, in a Camden Town mews house converted from an early-Victorian stable. They have designed the interior themselves and have created a place of order and tranquillity which serves Tate as a refuge. Entering their home is rather like walking into a Vermeer painting. The house is tiny but uncluttered, and kept to the essentials. Each object, including the flower arrangements, seems to occupy its rightful place, and contributes to the beauty. Their most prized treasure is a collection of early Meissen porcelain. "It's our mania—a dangerously expensive mania," Tate told me.

"Every piece is irreplaceable," Kuhlemann added. "Our cleaning lady is terrified."

Since his days in the Kentish household, cooking has been one of

Tate's favorite pastimes. He specializes in French cuisine, and appoints himself official chef for complicated dinner parties. Tate and Kuhlemann served me a "modest" lunch consisting of smoked-mackerel pâté, vegetable salad, taramosalata (a Greek salad made from cod roe), prosciutto, Stilton cheese, a baguette of French bread, and vintage champagne. Tate owns a Porsche; he cannot drive, but with Kuhlemann at the wheel he likes to speed around the countryside. They once drove from Aix-en-Provence to Salzburg in a single day, mostly on side roads. "Jeffrey has a wonderful trait," Kuhlemann says. "He enjoys everything—whatever it may be—at the time he does it."

"Jeffrey has had material success, and he's the first one to value that," Sir John Pritchard told me. "I've known of no one other than myself who's so much a bon vivant. But you must never forget what a really hard life a conductor has. It's the other side of the coin from the very pleasant material advantages. You can never, never go onstage and conduct without placing yourself before judgment one more time."

Tate's achievements have elicited a warm response from disabled people. He is now a board member of three organizations concerned with the handicapped, including the Association for Spina Bifida and Hydrocephalus, of which he is president. He feels rather guilty about not having more time to give to these institutions, but his musical work is, in itself, doing much to change the way handicapped people are perceived.

One day when Tate was in Italy, a man came up to him, said, "*Scusi, per favore,*" and touched him on the curvature of his back. "The gesture was meant to bring good luck or fertility," Tate told me. "Abnormal objects are supposed to ward off malignant influences. I tried to dissociate myself from what was going on, yet I couldn't help feeling uncomfortable. I knew that I was being used as some sort of totem. That's all well and fine, but when you're on the receiving end—totem or not—you're also *you*. Once when I was visiting Crete, a woman made the evil-eye sign when she saw me. I still suffer slightly when children turn around in the street to look at me. Inevitably, there is a sense of anger involved with disability. I'd be lying if I said it wasn't so. I feel that to repress such things would be very foolish of me, so I try to be aware of these elements in myself and to use them somehow creatively. I try not to direct the anger toward other people. There are, of course, exceptions. Once, at the Frankfurt airport, an attendant refused to help me carry my heavy case of orchestral scores. As bureaucracy would have it, I was planted in a wheelchair. I felt perfectly humiliated; my self-esteem was involved.

"Sometimes I wonder what it would be like to live inside a healthy body. My body being flawed and my mind being—thank God—relatively able, I can, in a rather Cartesian way, occasionally shift outside my body for a while. It belongs to me, and yet it doesn't belong to me. I can look at myself in the mirror and be somewhat depressed at what I see, yet I know at the same time that I have the ability to stand outside myself while I make that judgment. I'm rather ferociously aware of my own faults. It's part of what I suppose is an urge to see oneself as completely as possible—to see the negative as well as the positive side of my achievement. If you're aware of these polarizing and opposing elements within you, you gain a certain objectivity. You're not pushed into one corner, believing that there's only one truth."

Tate's mother, a devout Christian says, "I often think of Jeffrey's disability and ask, If there is a God, why has He allowed this? A local vicar once told me, 'You know, if your faith were strong enough Jeffrey would be made whole.' I never forgot that; I didn't go back to that church for years. I wish I knew the answer. But, then, Thy will be done; I'm sure it will all be revealed one day. Nowadays they can test for spina bifida in the first part of pregnancy. Would I accept the risk of having a deformed, or even a mentally retarded, child? I'm thankful that I wasn't called upon to make that decision. The important thing is that Jeffrey has made so much of his life, and he's not sorry for himself—not in any way."

Tate himself says, "I can conceive of the possibility that forces exist in the universe which dictate in some broad way how things behave. However, I don't believe in a deity which, in accordance with Judeo-Christian tradition, is God the Father, with all those human attributes, and which thinks in human terms. I understand and admire many people who do believe this, and I'm grateful for the marvellous works of art that have come into being as a result. But I cannot see that my disability was dictated by God, any more than my gifts were dictated by God. It was caused by a gene mutation, which could have happened to anyone. Every person is different, just as every tree is different. Some people who claim a religious calling have told me that I've been given a good mind because I have this disability—as though God distributed his gifts like Santa Claus. The fact is that you are as you are. I can't think of a time when I haven't been fascinated by all that's around me, and whether I would have been that way without the disability I can't really tell. I would say, however, that *if* you have been given a fairly keen sensibility the disability can sharpen that—if you want to use it that way. With it, I've tended to see the world in a more quirky way, with more open eyes. The disability can act on one's mind as a kind of refiner's fire."

In the fall of 1991, Tate will become the music director of the Rotterdam Philharmonic Orchestra. He chose this position over a more lucrative one, offered by another major European orchestra, because of his respect for the Rotterdam players and because of the favorable artistic conditions in which he'll be able to work—five rehearsals for every concert. "I have many plans for the future," Tate says. "I want to divide my time about equally between opera and symphony concerts—I hope without a lot of frenetic travel. When I'm conducting opera, I want to work with people who can define the dramatic content. I'm not interested in revolution for revolution's sake, but I do want to wipe off the false layers of varnish that have accumulated on certain masterworks. I'll confess a secret ambition: I've long nursed a desire to direct a film—a film noir like Clouzot's 'Les Diaboliques.' My greatest dream, which doesn't need to have a time put on it, is to conduct 'The Ring' and 'Parsifal' at Bayreuth."

Tate still reads avidly. He can hardly enter a bookstore without carrying away a dozen books. He enjoys biographies (early-twentieth-century, Bloomsbury), history (Roman, Byzantine, and medieval), and, on performance days, thrillers. But the book that has continued to haunt his imagination since adolescence is that strange, captivating, almost mythological tale "Le Grand Meaulnes."

"On the surface, Alain-Fournier's work is fragile and elusive, but it has powerful undercurrents," Tate says. Faced with the harsh and unpromising reality that surrounds them, the crippled boy François and his friend Meaulnes follow an irresistible inner calling to pursue their mysterious quest. As François grows into manhood, he begins to participate actively in the unfolding of his destiny. Two-thirds of the way through the story, he manages—by perseverance helped along by chance—to discover the whereabouts of the lost domain he and his friend have so long sought.

> And I knew that, with Meaulnes far away, and all hope abandoned, it was I who had before me, like some familiar well-trodden pathway, the road which led to the domain for which we had no name.
>
> I who had always been a dreamy, reserved, unhappy sort of boy turned overnight into what was known among us as a "decided character" when I saw that the opening of a new chapter in this important adventure depended on me.
>
> And it is from that evening, I believe, that my knee stopped hurting me for good.

This interview, conducted in London, England, first appeared in *The New Yorker*, 30 April 1990.

CHAPTER THREE

A Gold Coin

One day toward the end of May, 1927, Josef Gingold, seventeen years old, accompanied by his mother, appeared with violin in hand at the door of 48 Avenue Brugmann, in Brussels. Mother and son had come from America in the hope that Eugène Ysaÿe would accept Josef as a student. They were ushered inside and taken upstairs to the study. There, seated in an armchair, was the legendary violinist—a huge presence, wearing a velvet jacket and practicing his instrument with intense concentration. A student of Wieniawski and Vieuxtemps, Ysaÿe had by 1895 become the most widely admired violinist in the world, and he had held that position unchallenged until shortly before the First World War. César Franck had dedicated his Violin Sonata to Ysaÿe, Debussy his Quartet, Chausson his "Poème." Ysaÿe's constitution, mighty as it was, had given way to diabetes in his later years. Now, at sixty-eight, he had largely retired from the concert stage.

Josef had brought with him a letter of recommendation from one of Ysaÿe's American friends, but he never showed it. He took out his violin and was about to begin the Brahms Concerto when Ysaÿe asked him to play a three-octave scale in G major, a deceptively simple assignment. Ysaÿe listened closely for smooth bow changes, for flawless intonation. He then asked that the scale be played with different bowing patterns: the Viotti, the Paganini. Only after what seemed an eternity to Josef did Ysaÿe let him play the concerto. Afterward, Josef's mother asked, *"Maître*, will you accept him?" *"Mais naturellement,"* Ysaÿe replied. *"Il est un violoniste né."*

Born to the instrument—and all the more aware of his obligation to

Josef Gingold. Photograph by David Blum, Bloomington, Indiana, June, 1993.

work at it. Ysaÿe's lessons often lasted three hours. Every piece had to be memorized. "Ysaÿe never yelled or threatened; he treated me like an adult," Josef Gingold told me as we talked together sixty-three years later, in his home in Bloomington, Indiana. "He worked with me on my bow arm. The bow is your artist in tone production—in color, power, delicacy, and articulation. Every once in a while, he'd pick up his fiddle and speak through the medium of his glorious Guarneri del Gesù. His music-making was full of fantasy; it was poetry. He spoke like a poet—he even wrote poetry. We have masterly fiddlers today, who are products of our age. Ysaÿe was a product of an age when Sarah Bernhardt could recite the alphabet and make it seem a work of art. Ysaÿe could play a scale and it was the most heavenly thing you had ever heard. The first piece I studied with him was Vieuxtemps's Fifth Concerto. In one passage he made plaintive downward slides between certain notes in the way a singer might do. 'Every time I change positions here, there is a tear in my playing,' Ysaÿe told me. 'I'm not playing, I'm crying.' He taught that the most important thing in music-making is to bring out the character of a piece. By doing that, one goes right to the heart of an audience. When I played Beethoven's 'Kreutzer' Sonata, I began the variation in minor key rather quickly. Ysaÿe stopped me. *'Non, non, mon petit!'* he said, and he played it for me, taking his time as he did so. I had never been so deeply moved by anything—the accents were so grief-stricken and dramatic. It was as if the composer were listening in. When Ysaÿe finished, it was all I could do to continue the lesson. Whenever I play that variation, I still try to reach for the unreachable."

Once, Josef arrived early for a lesson and strummed some chords on the piano, an ornate Pleyel. Ysaÿe appeared at the doorway and said, "Treat the instrument gently. Debussy composed 'Pelléas et Mélisande' on it."

"The walls of Ysaÿe's studio were lined with finely bound classics," Gingold recalls. "He had read every one of them. A picture of Tolstoy hung on the wall. Ysaÿe was interested in my obtaining a broad culture; he even corrected my French grammar. Violin playing wasn't enough in itself. It had to be a part of life."

In 1974, Andrés Cárdenes, a sixteen-year-old violinist, entered the Denver Young Artists' Competition. Andrés realized that he had over-reached himself, and was soon eliminated. He was therefore amazed when he was approached by a member of the jury—Josef

Gingold, renowned for his career as soloist, chamber-music player, concertmaster of the Cleveland Orchestra, and Distinguished Professor Emeritus of Music at Indiana University. "Keep working," Gingold told Andrés. "Keep your head up, because you've got something special. I advise you not to look at this as a deterrent." Cárdenes, who is now concertmaster of the Pittsburgh Symphony, recently said to me, "Why did he bother to speak to me? After all, I was one of the losers. Yet it wasn't in his nature to separate the vanquished from the victors. He knew that music is an art form—that it's older than all of us combined." Gingold invited Cárdenes to study with him, and a year or so later the young man entered Studio No. 154 in the Indiana University music building, the room that students sometimes call the Gingold Museum. The shelves there are crammed with books on music. More than a hundred autograph letters and etchings and photographs of famous violinists of the past two centuries fill every inch of wall space. Pride of place belongs to a photograph that carries the inscription *"A son cher disciple, avec profonde affection et la certitude d'une brillante carrière—Eugène Ysaïe, 1929."*

"I was a very confused eighteen-year-old with a highly competitive attitude," Cárdenes recalls. "Mr. Gingold taught me that the beauty in playing the instrument is not to be better than the next person but to stay true to oneself, to set one's own standards and keep to them, not just in violin playing but in life itself. He instills in his students the idea that there is no such thing as a trite phrase, that every minute you have the fiddle under your chin you're striving to find depth and meaning. One day, I brought Richard Strauss's Violin Sonata to a lesson. I had practiced the slow movement with special care. As I played it, I thought, All right, Andrés, it's great—you're doing your best, and it's coming off splendidly. When I finished, Mr. Gingold said quietly, 'That was lovely, but it just needs a little more patience.' Then he played the opening for me. After two bars, I felt that I didn't know the piece at all—the beauty of his sound, the sensitivity of his intonation and of his slides! He took more time over the notes and between phrases—yet without making it slow. After he played, I just couldn't speak. Suddenly, I realized how little I knew about violin playing. It's not a question of preparing a piece for a week; it's a lifetime devotion."

It is rumored in violin circles that Josef Gingold knows everything there is to know about the violin and its history. Players from all over the world approach him for the most arcane points of information. He is a storyteller, always ready to delve into his storehouse of musical lore. Some students initially question the relevance of these tales to their immediate needs, but they soon realize that the stories impart more than knowledge: they illuminate questions of musical interpretation; they connect the present with the past and bring the young players into a family circle that is two hundred years old. "I don't want a student of mine to be a *Notenfresser*," Gingold says. "There's more to music than merely playing notes. If my students become teachers or play in symphony orchestras, they shouldn't be ignorant. They should respect their art."

The lore of the past lives on not only in Gingold's words but in his playing and his teaching. He restores artistic dignity to the vast nineteenth-century violin virtuoso literature, which many players value primarily for its technical brilliance. ("Wieniawski is the closest thing we violinists have to Chopin," he says.) He draws upon an encyclopedic knowledge of the repertoire and a detailed recollection of the playing of great violinists to offer his students solutions to virtually every musical problem. He'll show a student a fingering that gives access to a particular, subtle type of slide—say, of Heifetz or of Kreisler—and ask, "You buy it?"

Perhaps Gingold's most valuable service as a mentor is to heal the artistic division between technique and expression, between matter and spirit. He never teaches technique as an abstraction. A constant refrain of his students is "Every étude becomes a wonderful piece of music." He refers to technique as "the vocabulary—a know-how." It becomes a means to every expressive end.

Raymond Kobler, a past student of Gingold's who is now concertmaster of the San Francisco Symphony, says, "Gingold's humanity comes out in his playing as in no one else's that I know of. It's a unique, heartfelt expression. You can say it's representative of an era that's gone by, but for me it's as current as anything. I don't believe in this 'old-fashioned' thing. Either something is beautiful or it isn't."

"I happen to be in love with my muse—a beautiful expression that's rarely used nowadays," Gingold says. "Ysaÿe would say, 'I didn't play well—the muse wasn't with me tonight.' It was another time, before the mechanical influences began to creep into our art."

The eminent cellist János Starker, who is a colleague of Gingold's at Indiana University, told me, "I consider Josef Gingold the greatest violin teacher I have ever known. His background is almost unparalleled; he has done practically everything that a string player can do in music—even played in Broadway shows. He's the only teacher I know who is equally qualified to teach the instrument, solo repertoire, orchestral repertoire, and chamber music. He also happens to be one of the most genuine human beings I've ever met."

Pinchas Zukerman says, "I can honestly say he is the kind of man who comes once in a century."

In his comfortable but not lavish living room, in a neocolonial apartment house ten blocks from the Indiana University music building, Josef Gingold settled down into what he calls his Archie Bunker chair and urged me to call him Joe. He had recently celebrated his eightieth birthday. Forty-seven former students had come to Bloomington to pay him homage, and his colleague Paul Biss had organized a gala concert. Gingold expressed regret that he had thus far succeeded in answering only a hundred and fifty of four hundred cards he had received. He still teaches at least twenty-five students a week. But now, just after New Year's, he had a few days free to reminisce about his life.

Joe Gingold is nobly pear-shaped (he is a devotee of hamburger steak and chocolate cake), but the sense of roundness he conveys is more than physical. His manner is genial and jovial. He wears his long, silver hair swept back, and he sports a touch of mustache. As outgoing as he is, he has a natural dignity that keeps him from excess, sentimentality, or any coarsening of his private world. Everything about him seems rooted. He is pragmatic with his time—a philosopher not prone to philosophizing. A trace of Russian accent betrays his origins; he takes care to express himself clearly in English. His words have a resonance of feeling; sometimes he nearly sings them. His gestures have the expressivity of violin bowings. His voice, imitated by violinists the world over, is as gravelly as that of Louis Armstrong.

"The violin is my life," he said. "I have no hobbies. I don't play cards; I'm too old for sports. Four years ago, I walked all the way from school to my home; I sat down and couldn't move. The doctor called it nerve stress in the leg. It's terrible; it seems I'm a one-sided man. But I am what I am." We discussed the fact that many people of his age tend to reject their past. "Don't you think that they were unhappy with what they were doing?" he asked. "I have such a beautiful life to remember. Imagine—I can tell my students how Heifetz played when he was twenty! Even the unhappy things that have left a little hurt to this day have, in their own way, been helpful to me." I suggested that every experience from his past had been a creative building block. He took a puff on a forbidden cigar, and said, "But, you see, my dear—my past is my present."

Anna Leiserowitz was an unusual woman. The daughter of an Orthodox rabbi, she was born in 1874 in the Russian town of Brest Litovsk, on the Polish border. At fifteen, she entered into an arranged marriage, meeting her bridegroom for the first time under the canopy at the wedding ceremony. She detested her husband, but in those days, and in her society, divorce was considered a disgrace. However, after a year and a half, and the birth of a son, Israel, she took matters into her own hands and obtained a divorce; thereafter, she was looked upon as the black sheep not only of the family but of the community. Anna eventually married Meyer Gingold, who owned a shoe factory. Meyer, whose first wife had died in childbirth, already had two children, a boy and a girl.

Two girls were born to Meyer and Anna, and on October 28, 1909, their last child, Josef, came into the world. Meyer wasn't musical at all, but his son from his first marriage, Willy, who was seventeen years Josef's senior, was an enthusiastic violinist. From the day he was born, Josef heard the sound of a fiddle. "One day when I was three, my father came home with a small violin for me," Gingold told me. "It was only about seventy-seven years ago—why shouldn't I remember? I was thrilled, and asked, 'What makes it play?' He explained that a little man lived in the violin who began to dance when you put the bow on the string. I wanted to have a look inside, and so I smashed the violin. My mother came to my rescue: 'Why do you tell the boy such fairy stories?' " While waiting for his next violin, Josef would get hold of Willy's fiddle and, with one or two fingers, try to play by ear the "Kreutzer" études his brother was studying. "Many years later, when I studied these same pieces with a real teacher, I found myself making all the mistakes I had heard my brother make," Gingold said. As Josef neared five, his progress on the violin was so considerable that arrangements were made to take him to Warsaw to play for a teacher at the conservatory. Before that plan could be carried out, the European balance of power collapsed, and Germany declared war on Russia.

Brest Litovsk was an arsenal town, and the civilian population was given twenty-four hours to evacuate the city. "Pandemonium broke loose," Gingold said. "All trains were reserved for the military. My family joined a group of about two hundred people from town who took refuge in the fields between the Russian and the German lines. We wandered about, without any definite plan. When we walked at night, we held hands, so that we could stay together. We slept in the open. Food was scarce. My mother picked apples from orchards and cooked them, so that it would seem we were having a hot meal. She held the family together; she was wise, and had a wonderful head. One bright, chilly day, I was chasing about with a playmate. My mother's nerves were frayed, and to separate me from my friend she took our family for a walk. A shell suddenly fell and killed almost everyone who had stayed behind. The carnage was horrendous. My mother used to say that it was I who had saved our family."

After several weeks, the refugees came to the Russian town of Pruzhany, but found, to their dismay, that it had been occupied by the Germans. The refugees were rounded up and, "for hygienic reasons," put in a big armory, where everyone slept on the floor. Meyer and Willy did forced labor, but the small ration they received barely sufficed for the family. "We were fortunate that these German soldiers—unlike those in the Second World War—weren't indoctrinated to hate Jews," Gingold said. "One day, I heard a fiddle out in the yard. A German soldier was trying to play a tune for his colleagues. I motioned that I, too, played the violin. I must have been a pest, because the sentry let me through the barbed wire. I picked up that enormous fiddle and somehow managed to play the tune. That night, two soldiers carrying guns with bayonets suddenly appeared in the armory and demanded to know which boy played the violin. My mother was desperately afraid, but she woke me from my sleep, and the soldiers took me to a party they were throwing. Oberleutnant Krock announced that a little Russian boy was going to play a song on the violin. I managed to find some notes, and then—I don't know how—played a mazurka by Wieniawski. The audience broke into applause, but I was terrified, not knowing what it meant. The Oberleutnant collected money for me in a hat, but I just pointed to my open mouth and rubbed my belly. I can still see this man as if he were right in front of me now. His eyes filled with tears, and he ordered four soldiers to accompany me back to the armory, carrying bags of food. That was the first fee I ever got for playing. My mother, fine woman that she was, woke up the entire barracks, so that we could share the bread, chicory, and cans of meat. What made the greatest impression on me was the sardines. They were the tastiest things I'd ever eaten in my life. A half century later, when I was teaching during the summer at the Meadowmount School, in upstate New York, I created a near-scandal by eating everybody's sardines at lunch.

"I was made a big fuss over that night, but it was exceptional. My family never thought that I was God's gift to music, never spoiled me, never believed that I didn't get what I deserved in life—ridiculous. What a wonderful way to bring up a child! Today, you have to send your child to a psychiatrist to find out why he doesn't like sardines. That comes to fifteen thousand dollars, and when the treatment ends he still doesn't like sardines. The upshot of my little concert was that when Oberleutnant Krock went on leave to Berlin he brought me back a small violin of my own."

After six months, the refugees were permitted to leave the armory, and the Gingolds found lodgings in Pruzhany, which was still under German occupation. One of Willy's buddies, a violinist named Yablonovich, whose studies at the Warsaw Conservatory had been interrupted by the war, took an interest in Josef; he taught him how to read music and how to use four fingers when he played. Gingold can still play from memory the book of studies he used at that time.

One night, the Germans ordered Willy to play at a party. Because there was no pianist available, he took Josef along to provide accompaniment on the violin. Gingold recalls, "I did as well as I could, but I would fall asleep between numbers. Suddenly, as we were playing, a soldier came rushing in and shouted, 'All officers on duty! The Russians are counterattacking!' My brother strapped our violin cases around him with a rope, and, carrying me piggyback, made a run for it. Shells were exploding all around us. There was no pavement— nothing but mud. When we finally managed to get home, we found our parents in hysterics."

At the conclusion of the war, the Gingolds returned to Brest Litovsk. Gingold remembers his father's taking him at the age of eight to the station to see Trotsky arriving to negotiate the peace treaty that was signed on March 3, 1918. Meyer expressed amazement that Trotsky, a Jew, could have risen to such prominence in Russia. Brest Litovsk was now in Polish hands, and Meyer risked being conscripted into the Polish Army, where anti-Semitism was rampant. Gingold recalls, "One day, I was looking out of the window and saw an elderly Jewish man being taunted by a group of Polish soldiers. They began to pull at his beard, and finally ripped it completely off his face. My mother hurriedly closed the shutters. We knew that we had no choice but to leave."

In 1919, Meyer and Anna set out on an odyssey across Europe with their three daughters and Josef to find a ship that would grant passage for six to America. (Josef's two half brothers had already emigrated—Israel to Buenos Aires and Willy to New York.) After obtaining visas in Warsaw, they travelled to Danzig, Hamburg, and Antwerp—but to no avail. As a last resort, they went to Paris, and there Meyer renewed an old acquaintance. His friend, now a furrier, gave a party for Meyer's three marriageable daughters. Fanya, the eldest, met a young man who soon proposed marriage; she decided to stay in Paris. (Fanya's story is worth remembering. During the German Occupation in the Second World War, her husband was murdered by Klaus Barbie. She was given refuge in the basement of a Christian family's house, and didn't see the light of day for four years. After the war, she met one of her husband's employees and married him, although he was seventeen years her junior. They lived happily together for thirty-seven years, until her death, at the age of eighty-seven.)

Finally, in September of 1920, the Gingold family of five managed to get passage on the tanker Niagara, which made the voyage from Le Havre to New York in three weeks. They arrived on Yom Kippur. A new life began for the Gingolds, on the Lower East Side. They lived on Madison Street for two and a half years and then moved to East Second Street. "Conditions were not the easiest," Gingold recalls. "We had to walk up five flights. There was only one toilet for four families. We didn't have a bath—only cold water. But we found it marvellous. We were no longer afraid that someone would kill us for being Jewish. We were free, and life was beautiful."

Meyer had always been his own boss, and considered menial work to be beneath him. He now became an insurance salesman, but with only moderate success. Josef's sisters went to work in a sweatshop. Willy worked in a factory by day and played the violin for silent movies at night. One evening, he asked Josef to substitute for him. "I didn't know how to play the movie music, so I played Vieuxtemps's Second Concerto," Gingold told me. "Hearing the applause, the manager became curious, and, to my consternation, ordered me out of the theatre. I learned later that he was afraid of being caught breaking the child-labor law."

The more intellectual members of the family came from Anna's side. One of her brothers was the editor of a newspaper in Warsaw, and another was an Orthodox rabbi living in New York. A third, Yacov, who also lived in New York, wrote the lyrics for "Di Greeneh Kusineh" ("The Greenhorn Cousin"), a song that describes the struggles of an immigrant girl. (It was stolen and published, and became an enormous hit. Yacov, who had not taken out a copyright, never saw a penny from it.) Yacov appreciated classical music and sensed an unusual quality in Josef's playing. He took him to Charles D. Isaacson, the music critic of the New York *Globe*, and Isaacson arranged for Josef to perform in a "prodigy concert." "I played reasonably well in tune, and didn't scratch or scrape," Gingold recalls. "A six-year-old boy named Morton Gould played a piano piece of his own called 'Just Six.' After the concert, I was introduced to Joseph Fuchs, who was then twenty and was already a fine violinist. My bow had cost two dollars—one turn and the hair would just pop up tightly. I didn't know the difference; it was a bow to play with. Fuchs took one look at it, and said, 'Oh, my God!' He invited me to come the next day to meet his family, including his sister Lillian, the violist—she is now the grandmother of one of my students. He then gave me a gift I'll never forget: my first decent bow."

On Isaacson's recommendation, Josef took up violin studies at the Music School Settlement (which is now called the Society of the Third Street Music School Settlement). "The school was set up to get the kids off the street," Gingold says. "It made no pretense of being a conservatory, but for several months it provided me with free lessons. I later taught at the Cleveland Music School Settlement for thirteen years. I remembered what had been done for me as a kid." At Public School 62, Gingold had his first experience playing in an orchestra. "It consisted of seventy-nine violinists—almost all Italian and Jewish—and one pianist," he recalls. "I showed the kids how to improve their fingering. We played an arrangement of Schubert's 'Unfinished' Symphony, and I thought it the most beautiful piece of music I had ever heard.

"During all this time, my mother held the family together in a natural way, and she kept track of our finances—right up until the time I married. She had a special place in her heart for me, and believed in my promise as a violinist. When I practiced a concerto, she'd be in the kitchen singing the piano part. She truly knew how to listen, and, as I later discovered, had perfect pitch. She had a lively curiosity. For instance, she would ask me to explain what made a Stradivarius so very special. Her questions were simple but relevant. She taught me not to speak badly of people, to be helpful to those who had less than we did, never to feel that money is everything. She lived by these principles—and I live by them, too, I assure you. My mother encouraged me to read. My favorite books were on American history. My heroes were Lincoln and Jefferson. Did you know that Jefferson played the violin and had music of Corelli and Vivaldi in his library at Monticello? I was proud to be an American, and ashamed of my parents for not making an effort to learn English.

"I went to the first day of my seventh-grade American-history class at P.S. 62 with great expectation. The teacher asked the students to rise when she read their names. She pronounced mine 'Jingold,' and I said, 'Please, my name is pronounced "Gingold." ' She said, 'Young man, take a failing mark for the rest of the year.' I turned in a perfect paper for the first test—dates have always fascinated me—but she said, 'I told you that you would fail,' and tore it up. She was far from the worst of my teachers, if you can believe it. One day, I played the violin for the school assembly. The applause went on for so long that the principal became annoyed and ordered that it be stopped. Two days later, I had an art class with Miss Eberhardt—a tall, statuesque blonde with her hair tightly wound in a bun. She asked me, 'Are you the young man who played the violin the other day?' I thought, My God—can you imagine it? A teacher values what I'm able to do! She continued, 'Show me the hand that makes such beautiful music.' She was carrying a long wooden pointer, and suddenly cracked it over the palm of my left hand with all her force. It was so painful that I screamed. I left the class and, although it was winter, ran without a coat the twelve blocks to our apartment. My hand had swollen badly. After treating it with cold compresses, my mother put on her hat and coat. Our neighbors heard her shouting. They begged her, 'Anna, don't make trouble for the teacher, or they'll send you back to the Old Country.' Finally, they calmed her down and talked her out of going, and it's probably good that they did; she was ready to kill that woman. I never went back to the class. So I flunked art as well as American history." (While performing the cycle of Beethoven violin sonatas at Indiana University in 1961, Gingold felt an unusual pain in his left hand. He told me, "I went to see a specialist, and he found a ridgelike spur running along the inner palm, which had caused an inflammation of a nerve. He said that, as I was a violinist, an operation would be too risky, and that I should consider myself lucky not to have been bothered by it more frequently. He asked me if in earlier years I had fallen on my hand or had had a severe blow to it. Then it came back to me: Miss Eberhardt and her pointer! I told him the story. He said, 'Miss Eberhardt could have ruined your career forever.' ")

Josef found another sort of educator in Melzar Chaffee, the director of the Music School Settlement. A man of exceptional kindness, Chaffee took a warm interest in Josef. He felt that the boy, who was now twelve, needed a first-rate violin teacher, and recommended him to Vladimir Graffman, who was the assistant to the famed Leopold Auer. Aside from his few months with his brother's friend Yablonovich,

Josef had never had a formal teacher, yet a photograph taken of him playing the violin a few days after his arrival in America shows an ideal left-hand position. When I asked Gingold how he had acquired this position, and if any teacher had ever thought it should be corrected, he said, "No one corrected it then, and no one has corrected it since." Graffman put Josef on a stiff regime of études and taught him to pay meticulous attention to his intonation. "It felt just great," Gingold told me. "I was making up for all the years I had missed." Graffman charged three dollars a lesson, but after a while he refused to allow Josef to pay. When Josef was seventeen, he played at Graffman's wedding. (Graffman's son is the pianist Gary Graffman, who is now the director of the Curtis Institute of Music, in Philadelphia.)

When Josef was thirteen, he took on his first violin student, charging him twenty-five cents a lesson. When Anna heard about it, she insisted that he return the money. "You don't know enough yet to teach anyone else," she said. "He'll get another teacher. Don't feel so important."

On New Year's Day, 1922, Josef heard the twenty-year-old Heifetz in Carnegie Hall. "Heifetz's playing was a model for any violinist," Gingold told me. "He stood like a statue, and never moved a muscle in his face. What came out was the most marvellous fiddling. He brought the violin to a state of virtuosity that we're still trying to emulate. He had an ideal vibrato—a little on the fast side and very narrow. When he shifted positions, his thumb led the way, moving as fast as the hand of a prestidigitator doing a card trick. But his playing was more than just fingers. It was moving. He was the greatest violin talent of the century." Vladimir Graffman knew Heifetz—they had both come from Vilna—and a year later he took Josef to play for him. Gingold says of the meeting, "I overheard Heifetz say in Russian that I had a lot of talent and was worth watching. Then Heifetz called me over and demanded, 'Why do you play so fast?' He, of all people, to say that!"

Josef seized every opportunity to hear the finest performers of his day: "Casals, who showed how elegantly a cello can be played—at a time when most cellists scraped and moaned on their instruments. Josef Hofmann, who made the piano sound so majestic." Among the singers were Titta Ruffo and Galli-Curci. The theatre, too, made an indelible impression—particularly Walter Hampden playing "Hamlet."

In 1923, Josef heard Fritz Kreisler for the first time. "I couldn't afford to buy a ticket," Gingold told me. "So I waited outside Carnegie Hall, and, when the concert was over, ran in to hear the encores. Some time later, I heard Kreisler play a whole recital. His rubato was incomparable. 'Rubato' is the Italian word for 'robbed'—what is taken has to be restored. No matter what freedom he took, he'd come out together with the beat at the end of the bar. In the age of virtuosity, when every musician was playing faster than the next, he never raced; he always gave time for a phrase to expand. And I heard Mischa Elman, with whom I later played chamber music. A remarkable violinist. Today, he's almost forgotten. He had the most heavenly, golden tone. One of the most important goals of my teaching is beauty of tone. If you listen to the recording Elman made with Caruso, you don't know who is the greater Italian singer. I'll tell you a story about Mischa. He once attended a master class given by the famous teacher Carl Flesch at the Berlin Hochschule für Musik. Flesch could be merciless in his criticism of other violinists, but he himself didn't have the most wonderful tone. One boy got up and played in a terribly dry way. Flesch announced, 'Ladies and gentlemen, there is someone here who knows more about tone than anyone in the world. Mischa Elman, would you define a beautiful tone for the student?' Elman told the boy, 'Exactly what your teacher doesn't have.'

"It was fascinating to hear Heifetz, Elman, Kreisler, Szigeti, Hubermann, Thibaud—each player had his own unmistakable style. I could call them—without belittling them—string-playing crooners; they had a special quality of communication. Some students make exciting débuts, but only time evaluates a career. There are many violinists who can play ninety-five per cent. That remaining five per cent is a precious and indefinable quality."

One day, a truant officer came to the Gingolds' door. Josef overheard him tell Anna, "Your son has missed four Fridays in a row. He's a no-good kid. He's probably out playing pool with the bums."

"As a matter of fact, he's in the other room practicing," Anna replied, and she picked up a rolling pin. "He goes to the New York Philharmonic on Friday afternoons. Do me a favor and leave this house. Next time I see your face, you're going to get it over the head."

At junior-high commencement, the principal announced to the

graduating class that one day the name Gingold would appear on the marquee of Carnegie Hall. He put his arm around Josef and awarded him a special gold medal. "I had never been so proud of anything in my life," Gingold told me. "I raced home to show the beautiful medal to my parents but discovered, to my horror, that I had lost it while running. I felt terribly humiliated. My mother suggested that I go back to school and explain what had happened. I found the principal alone in his office. After hearing my explanation, he turned on me savagely and said, 'It serves you right for being so careless. There's the door—get out of here. You'll get no other gold medal.' I went out, detesting what school stood for, and began to think over what was going on. I promised myself that if, one day, I should ever become a teacher I'd treat my students differently. I've kept my word."

When Josef was not quite sixteen, Graffman took him to play for Leopold Auer. "As we entered Auer's studio, he was teaching a girl named Anita, who was playing like an automaton," Gingold recalls. "Auer, who was then eighty, shouted, 'Anita! A violinist without any temperament is no violinist!' He snatched up his violin, and his bow scratched at the strings, but that didn't matter: he showed her what temperament is. He became so red in the face that I was afraid he was going to die. I thought, My God, this old man plays like a twenty-year-old. He couldn't help himself. He gave of his best as a teacher."

Then it was Josef's turn to play. Auer listened with mounting approval. After eight bars, he asked Graffman, "A Russian boy?" After another eight bars: "Is he Jewish?" And by the next page: "He doesn't pay for lessons, does he?" Then Auer walked slowly over to Josef.

"He was short and myopic," Gingold told me. "We virtually touched noses. He looked me right in the face and said, with a sinister solemnity, 'Why don't you have staccato?' " Staccato bowing, a hallmark of virtuoso playing, is a series of short, rapid strokes executed while the bow is drawn in one direction. " 'Put your bow on the string,' Auer said. 'Make the upper arm tight—TIGHT,' he roared. Then he shouted 'Play!' And I found myself doing a staccato bowing; he scared it out of me."

At about that time, the family moved to Hewitt Place, in the Bronx.

"That was a step upward," Gingold says. "At least, we had a bath." Josef would walk everywhere to save a nickel's carfare. On one occasion, to while away the time before attending a concert, he went into the New York Public Library on Forty-second Street and asked for the music division. "The atmosphere was like electricity to me," he remembers. "The librarian brought me a book called 'Violin Mastery,' by Frederick H. Martens, which consisted of interviews with well-known violinists. I couldn't put the book down—read it from cover to cover. I missed the concert that night. Above all, I was fascinated by one violinist, whose picture mesmerized me: Eugène Ysaÿe."

A plan was eventually developed, with Graffman's encouragement, for Josef to go to Belgium to study with Ysaÿe. A family friend, Joseph Milner, set about raising the necessary funds, to which Josef added the receipts from a recital he had given in Brooklyn. Something of a family crisis occurred. Anna felt that, at the age of seventeen, Josef was too young to be left on his own in Europe. She insisted on going with him. Meyer didn't want the family broken up, but she prevailed, and in May, 1927, she and Josef sailed on the Berengaria. In Paris, they witnessed the acclamation given Charles Lindbergh after his solo flight across the Atlantic. A few days later, they were in Brussels, ringing the bell at 48 Avenue Brugmann.

Belgium had been hard hit economically after the First World War, and Anna was able to find an apartment of five rooms for eighteen dollars a month. Gingold reminisces: "My mother was a marvellous companion. She gave me all the freedom I wanted. I played the violin ten hours a day. I had gone to Europe to get an education, not to be a star. I never had dreams of playing in Carnegie Hall. I had dreams that my next lesson might be good. I wouldn't have let Ysaÿe down for anything." Ysaÿe, as a measure of his esteem, entrusted Josef, at eighteen, with the first public performance of his Third Sonata for Solo Violin, "Ballade": Josef included it in a recital he gave at the Brussels Conservatory on February 23, 1928. "I did nothing at all but practice," Gingold told me. "I've never played a concert better in my life."

Anna, because she was still awaiting her naturalization papers, had to return to America before a year was out. Josef, on his own for the first time, moved into a pension, and played a series of concerts in

Belgium, Holland, and France, always including the "Ballade." "I regret that more performers today aren't composers themselves, as Ysaÿe, Kreisler, and Enesco were," Gingold says. "Whether their music will live or not is beside the point. Their understanding of the art of composition helped them as performing artists—they were at one with the composer."

By late 1929, Ysaÿe was often bedridden, and he could not go on teaching. In saying goodbye to Josef, he presented him with his photograph, which he slowly and painfully signed. Gingold arrived in New York a week after the stock-market crash. His sisters were now married, and he felt that it was his responsibility to support his parents. He was not at his best in a New York recital, and it proved less successful than he had hoped. A brilliant solo appearance with the Minneapolis Symphony did not lead to further engagements. Conditions were such that it would be impossible for Gingold to contemplate a solo career: concerts would be so few and far between that he would not be able to provide for his family. "It's hard for anybody who didn't live in that period to realize what hardships were endured during the Depression," Gingold told me. "I joined a walking fiddle corporation—some of them superb players—who were seeking any kind of job." He played at the Ritz-Carlton Hotel and in the Manhattan Symphony Orchestra, and eventually joined the A. & P. Gypsies for an appearance at the Chicago World's Fair.

In October, 1931, he finally found steady employment, as assistant concertmaster for the Broadway production of Jerome Kern's "The Cat and the Fiddle." "I earned eighty dollars a week for fifty-six weeks, and felt like a millionaire," Gingold said. "I was able to pay off our debts, and we could move into a nicer apartment. I eventually played three other shows, as concertmaster—two by Jerome Kern, one by Cole Porter. Playing in 'The Cat and the Fiddle' taught me two things that stood me in good stead throughout my performing career. First, never take your eyes off the baton for a split second; no two performances are alike. Second, what may be the hundredth performance for you is the first performance for the audience. Never become a *routinier*. One night years later, I was playing one of several performances of Tchaikovsky's Fourth Symphony, on tour with the Cleveland Orchestra. After the first movement, George Szell whispered to me, 'Joe, take it easy. What are you giving so much for?' That was the first time Szell had ever told an orchestra musician to give less. I said, 'George, I love this piece.' 'I love it, too,' he whispered back, 'but not every night.' "

Gingold maintained his connection with classical music by studying chamber music with Adolfo Betti, of the Flonzaley Quartet, and music theory with Harold Morris. But there were less serious moments. There is a tale of a boisterous party of musicians on West End Avenue and, in the early hours of the morning, an upright piano being thrown out of the apartment window.

Gladys Anderson was born in 1908, to Norwegian-immigrant parents, in Culbertson, Montana, where her father was a superintendent of the Great Northern Railroad. She met Josef Gingold, from Brest Litovsk, in the Times Square subway station. "It was the winter of 1932," Gingold told me. "Gladys was with my colleague Benno Rabinof. As he had to catch a midnight train, he asked me to see her home. When I struck up a conversation with her, I noticed that she had the loveliest brown eyes. I invited her to attend the Wednesday matinée of 'The Cat and the Fiddle.' I told her I could get all the tickets I wanted. Of course, I had to buy a ticket, and, luckily, one was available. After the show, she came backstage to say hello, and we went out to an Italian restaurant. Gladys was a fine violinist—she played in the Dorian Quartet, which was unusual at that time because it consisted of three women and one man—and she was also an accomplished pianist. We saw each other for two years, and I gradually realized that I couldn't live without her.

"I had had lots of girlfriends, including some chorus girls from the theatre. After my mother met each of them, she'd say, 'No good.' She'd also make an issue of a girl's not being Jewish. When I first brought Gladys home to dinner, I had to leave early to play the show, and Gladys stayed on to talk with my mother. When I got home, about midnight, my mother, who always waited up for me, asked me my intentions. 'Don't talk to me about Gladys,' I said. 'After all, she isn't Jewish.' But my mother said, 'I think you've finally met a girl who can understand you and who can be your partner. It's not a question of religion. She'll make you a proper wife.' And Gladys had been told by her father that Jewish men make good husbands. How he learned that out in Montana, building the railroad, I have no idea.

"When I proposed to Gladys, we had, between us, twenty-four dollars—exactly what Manhattan Island was bought for. In my family, it would have been unthinkable for us to be married by anyone but my uncle the Orthodox rabbi. That meant a ceremony of conversion, to which Gladys agreed. We were married on October 14, 1934. Heifetz was scheduled to play over the radio that day. My uncle was slow in completing the ceremony. The instant it was over, there was a mad rush to the radio, leaving Gladys and me standing like two dummies, with no one to congratulate us."

The Gingolds' marriage lasted until Gladys's death, forty-three years later. "I know that even happily married people often fight and shout at each other, but when it relates to me I don't get it," Gingold told me. "Gladys and I never had such quarrels. We always talked over our differences. She was the most honest person I've ever known. Sometimes, in a situation where I might risk hurting someone, in my own mind I'm not sinning if I tell a little fib. Gladys called a spade a spade. She would tell me that I was too trusting. That's the way I am—I can't help it. But she was more discriminating. Thanks to her, I resumed practicing seriously. She was afraid I was getting too satisfied with my way of life just because I was doing well commercially. She was confident that I would eventually find my rightful place, and she wanted me to be in the best instrumental shape at all times. Her musical criticism was right on the nose. The two people to whom I owe most in my life are my mother and my wife."

In 1936, Anna Gingold became seriously ill with diabetes. Shortly before her death, she made a silk violin sack, and told Josef that she hoped someday he would have a Stradivarius to put in it. "I'm only sorry that she didn't live to see that day, and to see her grandson," Gingold said. "And what joy it would have brought her to know that I've been granted the chance to give knowledge to others. My mother valued education more than anything else. When my students at Indiana complain about all the extramusical subjects they have to take, they're wrong. They don't see it with my age and with my eyes. I have travelled a lot and read a lot, and have been with highly educated people. Yet I regret that I didn't have a college education. I'm left feeling a little incomplete."

Gingold eventually fulfilled his mother's dream and obtained a Strad. "My instrument was made in 1683," he told me. "That was two years before the birth of Bach and Handel. It's beautiful to realize that this violin has lived all these years alongside their music. Ysaÿe referred to his violin as '*elle.*' And mine is a jealous mistress. When I don't practice for a week, she looks back at me: You're scratching, you're hurting, you're playing out of tune! I have to take care, because she has gorgeous overtones. When I'm in good shape and I hit those notes on the head, she begins to sing. I needn't vibrate much—just touch her. In my younger days, such fine Italian instruments, though not cheap, were obtainable. It breaks my heart when I see some big talents today who can't buy those violins, many of which are owned by collectors and aren't being played."

One day in early 1937, Gladys saw an announcement that NBC was forming an orchestra for Toscanini. Gingold recalls, "I told Gladys that Toscanini was supposed to be a holy terror in rehearsals and I didn't want my life ruined. She said, 'First take the audition, then worry about Toscanini. You might not even be able to make it.' That didn't sit too well with me." Gingold took the audition and was accepted in the first-violin section. He remained in the NBC Symphony for seven years.

"I'll never forget Toscanini's first rehearsal," Gingold told me. "The old man entered—a small, sober figure—and the whole orchestra rose. He muttered, '*Grazie. Allora,* Brahms,' and immediately began the First Symphony. His beat had an incredible intensity; it conveyed a tremendous sense of power. He began singing along, in his croaking voice. I was actually shaking—not from nervousness but from the effect this man and the music had on me. In these few minutes he changed my outlook on music. Toscanini's most impressive musicmaking was during the rehearsals. He never spared himself. He always stood, and was completely drenched in perspiration. You couldn't help being a partner in this sweat. I used to play my heart out for him, and I wasn't the only one. The outer part of Toscanini was sometimes difficult to take, because of his abusive nature, but we had a terrific love for the inner man.

"Once, I found myself in the elevator with him; he was studying the score of Beethoven's 'Eroica,' which we were to rehearse that day. '*Caro*, I've studied fifty-five years this symphony,' he told me. 'But is always possible, eh, that I could forget about one sforzando.' When we started to play, I found myself more conscious than ever of the implications of Beethoven's markings—the many sforzandi at various dynamic levels, a crescendo over two bars that should be paced differently from a crescendo over four bars—and I realized that on the first page I had already made several mistakes. Toscanini not only read the lines but knew how to read between the lines. They say that he played only what was written. Other people also play only what is written. But with Toscanini something happened."

In addition to playing with Toscanini, Gingold had other responsibilities at NBC. One was performing with the Primrose Quartet, named after its renowned violist, William Primrose. Oscar Shumsky played first violin; Gingold, second violin; and Harvey Shapiro, cello. I quoted to Gingold from Primrose's autobiography: "I am quite convinced—and I am conceited enough to say so—that no quartet ever played that had the instrumental ability of my quartet." Gingold smiled, and said, "I loved playing in that quartet! All four of us respected each other. And I never minded playing second violin. I never had that kind of false pride. Music is greater than Mr. Gingold. Bill Primrose and I used to devote hours to rehearsing just the two inner voices."

Subsequently, Gingold played first violin in the NBC Quartet. "Sunday was my busiest day," Gingold told me. "From 8 to 8:30 A.M., I'd be on the air with a trio I'd formed with Harvey Shapiro and Earl Wild. Then Harvey and I would run into the next studio to rehearse with the Primrose Quartet before its broadcast, from 10 to 10:30 A.M. I'd then go to the NBC Concert Orchestra and rehearse light or semi-popular music until our broadcast, from 12:30 to 1 P.M. Then I'd go home and rest up for the five-o'clock concert with Toscanini. One day, after I played a solo with the Concert Orchestra, a colleague was noticeably depressed by the considerable success I'd had. I told him, 'Cheer up, Spielberg, it wasn't that good.' "

In August, 1939, the Gingold's only child, George, was born. George was talented musically, but he eventually chose to follow a career in law. His name has appeared back to back with his father's in *Who's Who.* "My parents gave me an extraordinary amount of affection and saw to it that I received the best possible education," George told me. "They cared deeply about me, but they had a limited understanding of the real world, outside the realm of music. In many ways, the normal roles were reversed, and from an early age it was I who was taking care of them." At nine, George urged his parents to open their first savings account; at thirteen, he prepared their income-tax return. "I more or less grew up on my own," he went on. "Dad and his music were inevitably the focal point of the household. It wasn't until I was in my thirties that I really felt I was no longer living in the shadow of being Josef Gingold's son. Now I regard my father with a mixture of admiration and amusement." Gingold likes to say of his son, "Thank goodness, he inherited my sense of humor and his mother's common sense, and not the other way around."

In 1944, Gingold made the difficult decision to leave the NBC Symphony and become the concertmaster of the Detroit Symphony. "After a concert, Toscanini called me to his dressing room," Gingold recalls. " '*Caro*,' Toscanini began, 'you don't like Maestro?' I said that I adored him. 'Then, why you leave? Is a good orchestra here, a good Maestro.' I explained that I had always wanted to be a concertmaster and that such opportunities were hard to come by. He seemed to understand, and invited me to visit him with my family at his home in Riverdale. We spent a memorable afternoon with him. He told me of how highly he esteemed Ysaÿe, who had played with him in 1897. I'll never forget Toscanini's searching, piercing eyes. Today, whenever I do something stupid when I'm teaching or playing, I see those charcoal-black eyes looking at me, and saying, '*Vergogna!*'—'Shame on you!' "

Gingold spent three seasons in Detroit. While there, he taught the twelve-year-old Joseph Silverstein, who recalls the lessons as opening a world of color for him in violin playing. Gingold found it rewarding to work with the Detroit Symphony, a highly professional orchestra conducted by Karl Krueger, but his years of true fulfillment as a concertmaster were yet to come.

Enter George Szell. Hungarian by birth, Szell had studied in Vienna, and while he was still a very young man his talent as a conductor caught the attention of Richard Strauss. In 1939, after establishing a major European career, notably in Berlin and Prague, he came to America. Szell's knowledge of music was unsurpassed. It was said that any musical score could be brought to him with all the notes covered up except those in a single bar, and he would invariably identify the piece. Szell was a musical idealist. He took over the Cleveland Orchestra in 1946 and was determined to engage the finest instrumentalists America could provide. Above all, he sought a concertmaster who shared his ideals.

As guest conductor of the NBC Symphony, Szell had noticed Gingold's playing as outstanding, even in a fiddle section where no player succumbed to routine. Subsequently, when Szell was guest conductor of the Detroit Symphony, he was so impressed by the combination of musical and personal attributes Gingold brought to his work as concertmaster that he knew he had found his man, and offered him the position in Cleveland for the following season. Gingold hesitated: he knew Szell to be an exceptional musician, but he felt a sense of loyalty to the Detroit Symphony. Not to be deterred, Szell arranged a second meeting. After describing his plans to develop the Cleveland Orchestra, Szell delivered an ultimatum: Gingold would have twenty minutes to make up his mind. He decided to accept. A reporter in Cleveland got wind of the decision, and printed the story a week before Gingold submitted his resignation. Karl Krueger, surprised and incensed, accused Szell of piracy.

Gingold went to Cleveland in 1947, and he stayed there for thirteen years. He entered into a remarkable relationship with Szell—a friendship of opposites—and helped him build the Cleveland Orchestra from a good ensemble into one of the great orchestras of the world.

George Szell lived in an age of autocratic conductors. Even so, it was not every conductor who earned the distinction of being referred to by his musicians as Dr. Cyclops. Szell had no children of his own; the members of the orchestra were his progeny. From his office window, he would watch them as they arrived for rehearsals, and note those who had taken their music home to practice. Severance Hall was his domain. He told the musicians how to play, the trustees how to plan, and the cleaning women how to hold their brooms. A member of the orchestra told me, "Among the players, fear joined with a sense of privilege. It was a feudal kingdom, with the conductor as the king, the first-desk players as dukes, and everybody else as serfs." Szell demanded the utmost of himself and gave it twenty-four hours a day, and he expected his players to do the same. He was obsessed with perfection. He said, "In Cleveland, we begin to rehearse where most orchestras leave off." Typically, he once warned a woodwind player before a difficult passage, "Look out—the last time you played it, it was perfect!" No one escaped his caustic tongue. When a famous violin soloist who was admittedly beyond his prime asked during a rehearsal to begin again from scratch, Szell replied, "You never said a truer word in your life." Szell set Olympian standards, and there was no denying the artistic result.

Abraham Shernick, who was the solo violist of the Cleveland Orchestra for twenty-seven years, told me, "Szell taught us how to listen. He didn't stand up there and say, 'Follow my stick.' He'd say, 'I'm conducting the oboe; you go with him.' We became aware of the relative importance of each part. We were a hundred players playing like a string quartet. Players and audience alike found themselves listening to the whole score." Szell's perfectionism could also be damaging: his performances were sometimes stiff and unyielding. At their best, they had a clarity and a vitality that speak undiminished in his recordings to this day.

Given a conductor who dared, in his own way, to reach for the unreachable, and the presence of a superlative ensemble, Gingold could now fully realize his gifts as a concertmaster. Arnold Steinhardt, who played as assistant concertmaster to Gingold before joining the Guarneri Quartet, says, "Musically, Joe made up for Szell's limitations. Szell thought he knew everything and would impose his own bowings. But Joe truly knows everything there is to know about bowings. When the orchestra's string sound became tight and lacking in sheen, he'd suggest using more bow to get more suppleness. When Szell had lapses in his conducting technique—especially in twentieth-century music—Joe would discreetly lead the ensemble. Joe practiced the orchestral parts as thoroughly as solo pieces." In his position, Gingold couldn't be outspoken, but behind the scenes he did whatever he could to protect the interests of the players. He was held in affection not only by the orchestra but by the musical public. It is said that when he came onstage and acknowledged the applause, with his beatific smile, it was as though he were entering a large room filled with friends. His solos in orchestral works are still remembered for their extraordinary personality—not least in Strauss's "Ein Heldenleben," where the violin depicts the composer's wife in all her unpredictable moods.

Gingold tells his students, "In an orchestra, there's only one boss, and that's the conductor. By cooperating with the conductor, the concertmaster becomes a model for all the other players." In Cleveland, Gingold often went beyond the call of duty and became a lightning rod for the orchestra. Steinhardt recalls, "Joe has always loved practical jokes. His specialty is an amazing doubletalk of his own invention, in which nine words out of ten have no meaning at all. During rehearsals, when Szell was driving the orchestra to the breaking point, Joe would raise his bow and say with great flourish, 'Dr. Szell, as far as the bowings are concerned'—and launch into this doubletalk, interspersed with a few strategically placed string-playing terms. The orchestra would hold its breath. Szell would study his score for some time and say, 'Well, in *this* case, I'll leave the bowing up to you.' He never caught on—or never wanted to admit that he didn't understand. It was *heroic* of Joe."

Behind Szell's façade of tyrannical grimness, another personality lurked. Off the podium, Szell could be a delightful friend: he was a linguist, a wit, and a superb chef. (True to form, on arriving at the Gingold's for dinner he would go into the kitchen, taste the food, and say, "More salt.") He often came to the aid of players with serious personal or health problems, but at such times he chose to remain anonymous. When one of his good deeds was revealed, he told some orchestra members, "Ever since you found out that I'm somewhat human, you've tried to take advantage of me."

Szell's relationship with Gingold was no less complex. Gingold recalls, "Once, after a performance of a Haydn symphony, Szell told me, 'Joe, your leadership and playing were an inspiration. I take no responsibility for this performance; it's yours.' I didn't know what he was talking about. My leadership and playing were at the same level as for every other concert." Each year, Gingold played a concerto with the orchestra. Szell told him, "Joe, I take my hat off to you. Despite all the work you do here, you always play with the impeccable technique of a seasoned soloist." But when Gingold didn't play a particular eighth note in the "Moldau" short enough for Szell, the conductor roared at him as he came offstage, "Joe, you ruined my concert!" The closer Szell got to someone, the freer he felt to subject that person to abuse. Gingold recalls, "On another occasion, when I was playing the solo violin in the slow movement of Brahms' First Symphony, Szell suddenly—for no apparent reason—had a violent fit while conducting and gave me a look as though I had committed murder. For once, I really lost my temper. After the performance, I burst into Szell's dressing room without knocking. At first, he denied that anything had displeased him, but he finally said, 'You took a little too much time between the F-sharp and the C-sharp.' I walked out, slammed the door, and didn't talk to him for two months."

The one soloist Szell didn't dare criticize was Jascha Heifetz. Gingold felt honored to have both Heifetz and Szell over to dinner after a concert. At the table, the conversation turned to violinists of the past, and Gingold politely corrected Heifetz's statement that Sarasate had died in 1910. "I say 1910—and 1910 it is!" Heifetz insisted. Gingold didn't press the point, but Szell, remembering a hundred-dollar bet he had recently lost to Gingold about an obscure point of musical history, said, "If Joe says 1908—1908 it is!" Szell jumped up, verified 1908 in Grove's Dictionary, and thrust the page under Heifetz's nose. Heifetz virtually threw the book in Gingold's face.

The same three musicians played a more dramatic scene in Severance Hall during a midwinter rehearsal of the Tchaikovsky Violin Concerto. A rumbling was heard as violent winds unsettled snowdrifts from the roof. Debris began to fall from the ceiling, and a spike plummeted to the stage, missing Heifetz's violin by inches. Szell ran off the stage as quickly as he could. Gingold leaped from his seat, put his arm protectively around Heifetz, and led him to the sanctuary of the greenroom.

Gingold summarized his relations with Szell: "In his private life, he could be the most lovable person. He did some wonderful things for me. And I overlooked some other things—I don't know who else would have stood for them. When I weigh the evidence, I have to say that musically he was a giant. If I've amounted to anything as a teacher, it's largely due to him."

For Christmas in 1955, Szell sent Gingold a coin, minted in 1915, bearing a portrait of the Emperor Francis Joseph. Szell wrote:

My Dear Joe,

A gift more symbolic than useful calls for a commentary. . . . I give you a little souvenir which, akin to the second half of your name which you so well deserve, should be a token of what I feel for you. Gold, since time immemorial, has been considered the safest standard of true worth and value. Let me say that it symbolizes *you* for me, the true and trusted friend and outstanding collaborator whose worth and value is unchanging, or, rather, ever increasing. In this tenth of my years with the C.O., when we can look back on very considerable progress, I am convinced that this type of unfolding of a variety of virtues of an orchestra would have been unthinkable without you. This broad statement is meant to cover both your superb artistry and your moral influence on the consciences of all of us. So I am asking you to accept this piece of gold which has yet another hidden meaning. It is the last (or one of the last) 100-kronen piece struck in the old Austro-Hungarian monarchy during the First World War, shortly before its collapse and disintegration—in that Empire whence I come and on the territory of which most of the immortal masterpieces were written which are inspiring us in our daily work and to which our lives are devoted. In deep affection—from your

GEORGE

Fate sometimes has a way of replacing an object lost in one's youth, particularly if it is gold.

During Gingold's Cleveland years, his teaching expanded considerably. In 1954, he was invited by the distinguished violin teacher Ivan Galamian to head the chamber-music program at Meadowmount. Gingold taught there regularly for thirty years, and influenced a generation of string players. He introduced the thirteen-year-old Itzhak Perlman to chamber music and the fourteen-year-old

Pinchas Zukerman to the viola. In 1947, Gingold had begun teaching at the Cleveland Music School Settlement, and among his students was Jaime Laredo, who started studying with Gingold at age of twelve. Gingold remembers him as "remarkable, very musical, in every sense a most promising child." Laredo says, "One thinks of scales as real drudgery. Joe made them so interesting and exciting for me as a kid that I was never bored for an instant. After I worked with him for nearly a year, he felt that I needed the atmosphere of a music school, with its student body, and recommended me to Galamian at Curtis. I didn't want to leave him. He instilled in me an incredible love of the violin."

Was it not inevitable that the gift for instilling such love should become a vocation? Circumstances pointed the way. In the fifties, the Cleveland Orchestra's pension plan didn't offer the degree of security it does today, and Gingold, remembering his childhood, wanted to assure his family's future. He also had no wish to slip back into the ranks of an orchestra as he grew older. While Gingold was in Cleveland, he was offered the position of concertmaster in Chicago, Los Angeles, and Philadelphia. He told Szell that as long as he played in an orchestra he would not leave Cleveland, but that someday he might consider joining the faculty of a university if he should be asked. Szell assured him that if that day ever came he would not only let him go but help him secure the post. In the spring of 1959, Gingold received a telephone call from Wilfred Bain, the dean of the School of Music at Indiana University. Like George Szell, Bain was a man with a mission. He was intent on creating at Bloomington one of the finest music schools in America.

"There was only one way to go, and that was first class," Bain told me. "I wanted to have real professionals on the faculty. I wanted to create an atmosphere in which colleagues felt comfortable with one another, where the students would be part of a musical family. I had heard reports about Josef Gingold's teaching. The Cleveland Orchestra was an incomparable ensemble. I wanted someone who could impart the musical discipline that Szell imparted."

Gingold had just signed a new three-year contract with the Cleveland Orchestra. However, he paid a visit to the Indiana campus and was impressed by what he found. He wrote to Szell asking to be released. Szell and Bain thrashed out a compromise: the university would hold the position vacant for a year, during which time Gingold would help Szell find another concert-master. Auditions were held in secret. When the news of Gingold's departure was announced, Herbert Elwell, the music critic of the Cleveland *Plain Dealer*, described the resignation as "a blow not only to the orchestra, but to the entire musical community."

In the safe in his teaching studio at Indiana University, where Gingold keeps his most precious possessions, the gold coin came to rest. "When I began to teach here, I felt at home right away," Gingold told me. "I had more freedom artistically than ever before in my life." I asked him if he had had a sense of relief at escaping from the imposing domain of George Szell. "I prefer to say that this appointment was the next wonderful thing that happened to me," he said. But during his early days at Indiana he had told a friend, "For the first time in fourteen years, I sleep well every night."

In addition to teaching at Indiana, Gingold has given master classes at more than thirty music schools, from the Paris Conservatory to Tokyo's Toho Music College, and seminars in orchestral playing from Denmark to Colorado. He has received seven honorary doctorates, and has served on the juries of most of the leading international violin competitions, including the Indianapolis competition, of which he was a founder. Three of his students—Miriam Fried, Jaime Laredo, and Nai Yuan Hu—have won first prize in the Queen Elisabeth of Belgium competition. Among his many other gifted students—several of them prize-winners—have been Joshua Bell, Ulf Hoelscher, Dylana Jenson, Leonidas Kavakos, William Preucil, and concertmasters of eight major orchestras.

Gingold's students admire him no less as a performer than as a teacher. Carol Sindell, who studied with both Gingold and Heifetz, says, "In certain profound ways, they were very much the same— their sense of commitment, their integrity, their passion for music. They were both poetic players. Heifetz was more aggressive. Gingold brought intimacy to his poetry."

When Gingold takes up his Strad, the instrument becomes one with the expressive bulk of his form. Gingold and his violin would have made an admirable subject for Rodin. It's not by chance that the tone he draws forth is as centered and vibrant as a bell, so sure is the contact between bow and string. His sound has a radiant sweetness that seems to flow directly from his personality. In Gingold's recordings, dating from 1942 to 1976—Fauré, Walton, Kodály, Roy Harris, Wieniawski, Kreisler—the poetry is tangible. He transforms "passage work" into the kind of playful arabesques one hears on recordings of Galli-Curci. He brings vitality to every rhythmic element. (While teaching, he once stamped a polonaise rhythm with such force that he injured his foot and limped about for three weeks.) Technically, he is fearless. He promised George Szell that he would give him fifty dollars if, during all his years in Cleveland, he ever missed the treacherous high E-flat in the violin solo in Strauss's "Till Eulenspiegel." He never had to pay. If now, with age, Gingold's playing has lost some of its power, it has lost nothing in the way of élan.

True to Ysaÿe's dictum that the most important thing in music-making is to bring out the character of a piece, the quality that most typifies Gingold's students is an ability to enter into communion with whatever music they are playing. Otherwise, one would be hard pressed to know that they all came from the same studio. Unlike many string teachers, Gingold does not impose a preconceived sequence of études and concertos on his students, nor does he ask for uniform fingerings and bowings; he allows a wide latitude in artistic conception. He says, "I encourage my students to develop their individuality, because without individuality music is nothing."

Although he could easily teach at only the most advanced level, Gingold enjoys working with students at every level, especially if he senses latent talent. "Sometimes students come to me with bad habits that have to be eradicated," he says. "Some aren't sufficiently conscious of their intonation, or lack variety in tone color. Physical tension can be a problem. Not every student of mine is a very strong player. But one must have patience. A teacher who has no patience is no teacher." There have been occasions when the chemistry between teacher and student didn't work. A colleague says, "Joe has been known to throw students out of his class, but, of the hundreds who have passed through his studio, they have been few and far between." Once, when somebody asked Gingold to name his favorite student, he said, "The one I'm teaching at the moment." His colleague

Paul Biss comments, "He knows how to reach every student. Real psychology is involved. There are lessons when you are going through agony and unhappiness about your playing, and he says very little. He knows you don't need a teacher to tell you that it's terrible. But when he really needs to put the screws on, he will." Herbert Greenberg, the concert-master of the Baltimore Symphony, remembers that once when he wasn't playing well at a lesson Gingold asked, "Herby, what's on your mind—the World Series?" Gingold took him out to get some doughnuts, and they watched the World Series together. Later that week, they had a real lesson.

Gingold has always exceeded his official university teaching load of eighteen students, in some years taking as many as forty, and he still teaches weekly master classes. "They're like forums," he says. "The students learn from each other." He has sometimes begun teaching at eight-thirty in the morning and continued with lessons and student recitals until late into the night. And his relationship with his students does not end when they leave his studio. He follows their careers closely, and is always available if they need his advice. He says, "I see a human being who is trying to express himself or herself through the medium of a violin. To use the beautiful Hebrew word, it's a *mitzvah*— a blessed service—to be a teacher." When friends caution him not to overwork, he says that he is having the time of his life. He put it somewhat differently when, in an offhand moment, he told a colleague, "In Cleveland, I used to have one problem. Now I have forty."

One of Gingold's strengths as a teacher is that he prepares his students to cope with being on their own once they have left his studio. The first step is autonomy. If Gingold feels that a student hasn't bothered to think out a musical problem, he may be less forthcoming than usual in offering specific advice. He will demonstrate less for those who tend to copy what he does, and more for those who really need inspiration. He teaches his students how to practice—how to take a passage apart and work on it like a study while retaining its musical value. Corey Cerovsek, who, at eighteen, is already a promising concert artist, told me, "Mr. Gingold began by putting fingerings into my music, but eventually I had to do all the preparation myself. Now he won't even tell me what repertoire to play, and insists that I choose my own recital programs."

The second step is to match one's expectations with reality. Herbert Greenberg recalls, "At my first lesson, Mr. Gingold asked me, in a fatherly way, 'Herby, what do you want to do when you leave school?' I told him that I'd like to be a concertmaster. 'That's great!' he exclaimed. 'But don't forget that you have to be a first-class instrumentalist, because some of the concertmaster's solos are as difficult as any concerto you'll ever find.' Right from the beginning, he devoted lesson time to all the aspects of orchestra playing. You won't find too many teachers who will hit you with that question at the very beginning and then actually go about making a plan to teach you the things that are necessary to accomplish the goal you have in life." Gingold said, "Some of my students plan to become teachers. I tell them that if they want to help their future students become soloists, quartet players, orchestral players, section leaders, it's important that they themselves have practical experience. I sometimes advise them to wait before taking a teaching position—to join a good orchestra first, and continue their education by playing. It will all add up to a gold mine of experience."

The third step is to know how to deal with the demands of a musical career. "Take stage deportment," Gingold said. "I'm very strict about that. One shouldn't come onstage too quickly, or bow too abruptly—just accept the applause simply, taking plenty of time, and then tune discreetly. A girl asked me, 'Why all this fuss?' I said, 'Listen, darling, the audience looks first; then it starts listening. Every woman is scrutinizing you: Is she fat? Is she thin? The hairdo, the blouse, the shoes. If when you tune with the piano you bend your derrière to the audience, that's insulting.' Enesco used to come onstage wearing a dress suit that looked as though it hadn't been cleaned or pressed for five years. He must have kept it rolled up. Of course, there was something there beyond a rumpled suit. My God, what an artist! But I know some young players who have seriously harmed their careers by being careless in this way. Nerves can be another problem. Sometimes they stem from inadequate preparation. If you've prepared at a hundred and fifty per cent, you can be sure that you'll perform at eighty per cent—and that's a high number. The art is to know how to prepare. Things aren't always milk and honey on the concert stage. You rely on an instrument that you hope will be in good order, on the acoustics of the hall, on the receptivity of the audience, on your health. You may have personal problems, or suffer a memory lapse, or have a feeling of routine about a work to which you've already given your best in preparation. You'll be lucky if all the conditions are favorable in two concerts out of fifty. You must play the others so immaculately that, even though you're not at your best, something comes out. For this you pay a price: you have to work."

Gingold makes a point of not interfering in his students' private lives. "They're in college; they can take care of themselves," he says. Yet, inevitably, many of them regard him as a second father. (And, evidently, as a matchmaker: several of his students have formed bonds of matrimony, one couple held their wedding ceremony in his studio, and four couples have given their first male child the middle name Josef.) Gingold remains the least possessive of fathers. He has never hesitated to recommend that his students continue their studies with other teachers. His attitude is felt through the whole string department and has helped create an atmosphere in which any student can feel free to attend any teacher's master classes. One colleague expressed the reservation that, given Gingold's propensity for avoiding conflict, certain problems may at times remain insufficiently addressed. But everyone acknowledges Gingold's contribution to the exceptional degree of harmony that prevails among the faculty. Charles Webb, who in 1973 succeeded Wilfred Bain as dean of the School of Music, told me, "I can show you artists of the highest calibre who are so insecure in themselves that they can't say one kind word about anybody else. Joe Gingold lives what I call an unfettered life. He carries around very little excess baggage."

Fullness of personality can be an eloquent teacher. Miriam Fried told me that once, while on tour, she and the pianist Garrick Ohlsson had played through their recital program for Gingold: "He made a few suggestions here and there, but it wasn't really a lesson. That night, we gave the best concert of the entire tour. Nothing about the occasion or the atmosphere would have made us play so well. We both felt that the only reason for it was that we had spent the morning with Mr. Gingold."

In January, 1978, Gladys died of cancer. "I still haven't got over it," Gingold told me. "To see this perfectly gorgeous woman shrivel up to nothing in front of your eyes—sometimes you wonder if God always rewards those whom he loves." In her memory Indiana University set up the Gladys Gingold Memorial Scholarship Fund, for gifted violin students. All Gingold's private teaching fees go to it. Herbert Greenberg says, "Joe and Gladys lived in an epoch when he would take the subway and go to the other end of town to court her. Time was set aside for human relationships. There was a flavor, an elegance, to their way of life. You felt this whenever you were with them."

Gingold now lives alone, but his activities are monitored around the clock by friends and students. He gets up at five-thirty, has some cereal and coffee, takes out his violin, and goes for what he calls an hour's promenade on the fingerboard. "Every day, when I pick the violin up it's like the first time," he told me. "She looks at me and says, 'I dare you.' When I retire—if my hands are still in order—I'm going to start practicing more than ever, and really work from the very beginning. Maybe my colleagues will think enough of me to invite me to play chamber music. But if my standard drops I'll play for myself, in the privacy of my own room. After all, it's not easy to give up the violin. I remember meeting Joseph Szigeti after he retired from the concert stage. I had played for him in 1924, and now, in 1971, we were serving together on the jury of the Paganini competition, in Genoa. I saw that he had a violin case with him, and asked if he was playing again. He explained that he couldn't touch the strings without his fingers being cut in grooves to the nerves. 'But,' he said, 'since I was six years old I've been travelling with the violin. It feels so nice to hold it.' " Gingold is no less attached to the violin. In 1979, in Victoria, British Columbia, while holding his Strad in its case with his left hand, he opened what he thought was an exit door and fell down eighteen concrete steps to a cellar floor. As he fell, his first thought was for the violin; he clutched it so tightly that he neglected to protect himself, and broke his left wrist. He couldn't play for months. The Strad was neither scratched nor out of tune.

Gingold has a way of transmuting the afflictions of life into a positive force, or else of simply ignoring them. One Christmas, he visited his son and daughter-in-law, George and Anne, at their home, in West Hartford, Connecticut. Anne noticed that one of his eyelids was drooping, and asked why he hadn't told them. "I don't like to say things like that over the phone" was the unconcerned reply. He had come for three days but stayed for five weeks, and had emergency surgery for glaucoma performed on both eyes. "You see what happens when you go near doctors," he complained. In 1982, he had several blackouts. He told me, "I went to a neurosurgeon in Indiana, who said that the carotid artery was blocked, and that it would be too dangerous to operate. The doctor told George, 'Let your father die in peace.' George said, 'Not until I've explored every avenue.' I don't know if I'm going to die in peace; I know that I'm going to rest in peace. Anyway, they operated on me in Boston, and I'm still here."

"Keeping track of Dad's health is like white-water rafting," George says. "One doesn't know what's coming around the next bend. Amazingly, he pulls through each episode."

Anne adds, "He defies all the laws of nature. He's got the secret: he's happy. And we're going to die first from worrying about him."

"Death is a mystery, and I refuse to spend time thinking about it," Gingold told me. "I'm just too busy. I don't know if there is life after death. But if there should be I'd like to meet Paganini and say, 'I want to know if what they wrote about your playing is true'—but I'll put it nicely. And I'd like to meet Beethoven. In the slow movement of his Violin Concerto he ascends to heaven and looks over the rest of us. I had a student who played a Beethoven sonata—all the notes, but with little understanding. I told her, 'Beethoven's music is my credo. Someday, maybe, after life, I'll get on my knees and thank him with all my heart for what he's given us.' I was almost in tears at my own words. I told her that, as she was a good girl, she'd certainly be going to heaven, and asked whom she would like to meet there. She said, 'John Wayne.' "

I am spending the afternoon with Joe Gingold in his teaching studio. Paganini, Joachim, Wieniawski, Sarasate, and Heifetz are looking down at us. Rieko Suzuki, who has taken a year's leave of absence as associate concertmaster of the New Japan Philharmonic to study with Gingold, is playing a series of études. Gingold sits in his chair and, in the tradition of Ysaÿe, invents quiet violin accompaniments that produce an expressive musical counterpoint. Rieko responds with playing of enhanced sensitivity. Gingold shows her how he practices études creatively, by varying their rhythms, phrasings, and bowings.

The lesson becomes an exploration. A study by Jacob Dont is dramatically transformed into a preparation for the finale of the Sibelius Concerto. "Darling, let your fingers travel without clutching tightly," Gingold suggests. "It will make the fingerboard seem half as long." His own fingers, at eighty, are as fleet as any student's.

Chin Kim, a young concert violinist, has flown in from New York for a lesson. He begins to play Paganini's D-Major Concerto. At the lyrical second theme, Gingold says, "This is *musica italiana bel canto*. I want to hear a soprano, and then a tenor singing in response—imagine a song with words to it. And here there's a little bit of a sigh: don't be afraid to slide—it gives the violin a wonderful chance to sing." Later in the movement, when the melody is repeated in a lower register, Gingold says, "This time, the soprano has a new boyfriend, a baritone; let's widen the vibrato and get deeper into the string. This is an opera by Rossini on the violin."

The Sibelius Concerto follows. Gingold stops Chin shortly after the beginning and describes Sibelius's home, set in a bleak Finnish landscape dotted with stark white birches. He suggests that something of this pensive atmosphere may be conveyed in the concerto's opening five-bar phrase, and recommends that it be played less sweetly, without vibrato; then the subsequent phrase—where the melodic line mounts—can burst forth like an anguished cry. "We need more than one kind of vibrato to find these colors," Gingold says. He picks up his Strad and demonstrates. The young man listens intently. The veil of generalized expression is lifted. The unique features of this passage are revealed; the music has *character*. In his gravelly voice Gingold asks, "You buy it?"

This interview, conducted in Bloomington, Indiana, first appeared in *The New Yorker*, 4 February 1991.

CHAPTER FOUR

Going to the Core

R ichard Goode had been at the piano for most of the day. It was a Tuesday evening in January; he was in the midst of a ten-day-long tour that had brought him to San Francisco, and he was scheduled to give a recital there at the Herbst Theatre on the following day and one in Berkeley on Friday, with the programs built around three of the most musically demanding works in the repertoire—the last piano sonatas of Schubert. As we walked together along San Francisco's Opera Plaza, enjoying the mild early evening, he wore an overcoat more suitable for January in New York City, where he lives. His shirt collar was open, as usual, and he wore a gray woollen cap from Verona, of the sort worn by Italian fishermen.

Goode suggested that we visit a nearby bookstore. His love of music is nearly matched by his love of books, and when we got to the shop he moved from shelf to shelf for more than an hour, quietly absorbed, a benign expression on his face as he collected an armful of books and literary periodicals. Goode has accumulated more than five thousand books in the three-room East Side apartment he occupies with his wife, Marcia. When the Goodes go on tour, some of the books go with them in a satchel, which increases in weight as they progress from city to city.

We left the bookstore already late for dinner, and picked up Marcia at the Inn at the Opera, where the Goodes were staying. Marcia is a violinist, and two days earlier, while Richard was giving a master class in Houston, she had played in a performance of Beethoven's Missa Solemnis, in Carnegie Hall. Now she was singing the melody of the Benedictus, which kept going through her head. Much of the Goodes'

Richard Goode. Photograph copyright © Dorothea von Haeften. Reproduced with permission of the photographer.

conversation, I've learned, consists of their singing music to each other.

At the Zuni Café—a favorite of theirs, built on peculiar triangular lines and decorated in a Mediterranean style—Goode was relaxed and jovial, feeling a sense of release after his day's work. We discussed the latest book acquisitions, which included additions to his collection of Irish literature. "Sometimes when Richard's on tour he'll feel the need to have a certain book with him even if he already has it at home," Marcia said. "He has five copies of 'Moby Dick.' "

"I did have five copies, but I gave most of them away," Goode protested. "However, I recently got a new edition—one that I've always wanted, with beautiful woodcuts. So I think I've come to terms with 'Moby Dick' for a while. It's nice to have an extra copy around of a book you really love." He asked me if I knew Schubert's last letter, in which the composer asked his friend Schober to send him books by James Fenimore Cooper. "Think of it!" Goode exclaimed. "He hadn't eaten for eleven days. He had typhoid fever as well as syphilis. Did he know he was going to die? And, if so, why Fenimore Cooper?"

In a radio interview taped the previous evening, Goode had spoken at length about Schubert's last sonatas. Contact with the media is a rather new phenomenon for him and still makes him uncomfortable. Although he felt the interview had gone well, he expressed the hope that it would be broadcast too early the next morning for anyone to hear it.

"Schubert is the composer I'd most like to have met," he went on. "I have a feeling of at-homeness with him on a personal level, more so than with Beethoven—I'm still too overwhelmed by Beethoven. I love Schubert's modesty. But, you know, once when he had been drinking he was approached by two musicians from the Vienna Opera who wanted to commission a composition from him, and he rudely refused them. They protested that they were artists, and he shouted, 'Artists! Artists? Musical hacks are what you are! Crawling, gnawing worms that ought to be crushed under my foot—the foot of a man who is reaching to the stars!' "

Goode read from the menu, "Wild mushrooms roasted in the brick oven, with garlic, parsley, and hazelnuts." He growled voraciously. With the mushrooms he ordered a roasted chicken and a bottle of Pilsner Urquell. "Some people feel that there's a premonition of death in those last sonatas," he said. "Yes, there's darkness and fatalism, but you find those qualities in Schubert from way back, not only in his last year. One of the things that move you in Schubert is the coexistence of marvellous beauty, sweetness, and grace with a kind of terror waiting to be disclosed. More than Beethoven, he evokes the uncanny. You feel how vulnerable that beauty is."

In conversation, Goode often holds his broad hands together, the fingers interlaced. When he wants to make a point, he'll lean forward and free a hand to gesticulate at keyboard level. His appearance resists precise description. He is stocky, broad-chested, and seems earthbound, almost peasantlike. Yet there is something gentle and unworldly about him. He is forty-nine years old, and over the years his face has become at once craggy and soft, monumental and tender. As if to complete a Rembrandt self-portrait from the sixteen-fifties, the nose is ample and pronounced. The neck is thick, the lips sensuous, the eyebrows bushy, the hair silvery, nearly shoulder-length, and often scraggly. In his eyes, which are greenish-gray, one can see his thoughts evolving. His voice is a sympathetic, light tenor that tends to trail off to pianissimo as he gets toward the end of a thought, at which time he'll sometimes append, as though musing to himself, some paradoxical comment. These asides reveal unexpected corners of his mind and will often be followed by an outburst of guttural baritone laughter.

Until a very few years ago, Richard Goode was little known as a solo pianist. "A career has a dark and a light side," he said now. "Take playing with an orchestra. It means that you have to fight for rehearsal time. The concerto is usually shunted aside, as if its orchestral part didn't need much attention. It also means that you play with a lot of conductors, and until you find those with whom you see eye to eye it's not much fun."

"Especially when the conductor is a shallow jerk," Marcia said.

"Marcia's more outspoken than I am," Richard commented. "She speaks my id for me. I once studied conducting myself, but I was uncomfortable with it. I need the actual contact with the sound at the piano to feel that I'm really participating in the music."

The conversation turned to the hut in which Grieg composed, at the edge of a fjord; to ghost towns in the American Southwest; to the marvel of a two-thousand-year-old cypress near Oaxaca. Goode takes a lively interest in almost any subject. "Richard can so easily get involved," Marcia says. "He reflects on virtually everything he observes. If the purpose of life is getting from A to B as fast as possible, he's failed in that."

When we returned to the Inn at the Opera, a tape of a Chopin nocturne was being played in the elevator. I suggested to Goode that the Inn should use one of his recordings. "If they did, I wouldn't stay here," he said. He quickly became absorbed in the music, and when we arrived at our floor he held the elevator door open, so that he could go on listening. "Just for a second," he said. "I hope nobody wants to use the elevator." He listened all the way to the end.

The next morning, I joined the Goodes in the hotel's dining room. On the wall behind Richard hung a large watercolor depicting members of a nineteenth-century music public lunging dramatically toward a violinist. That morning's San Francisco *Chronicle* had a sizable article about Goode. He opened the paper no more than a crack and spied on it.

The two Bay Area concerts were to be given in relatively small halls, each seating fewer than a thousand, which was as Goode liked it; the more intimate the setting, the more at ease he tends to be. We talked about a concert he had recently given at Camphill Village, a home for the mentally handicapped, in Copake, New York. Goode's connection to Camphill is through a friend, Anne Ratner, who presents an annual concert series in support of Camphill at her apartment in New York and, at eighty-seven, remains unflagging in her devotion and enthusiasm. He had included in his Camphill program the Schubert A-Major Sonata—a forty-minute work, with which he would conclude his San Francisco concert. It is a challenge to any audience, but the Camphill community had no difficulty responding to it. "It was wonderful to see how enormously concentrated they were," Mrs. Ratner had remarked to me afterward. "Their emotional openness was beautiful."

Schubert wrote his last three piano sonatas in less than a month, following directly upon the completion of the C-Major Quintet. They weren't published until a decade after his death, and then they remained largely neglected. As late as 1928, the centenary of Schubert's death, even so complete a musician as Sergei Rachmaninoff did not know of their existence. Musicologists generally stigmatized them as rambling and overlong, especially compared with Beethoven's sonatas.

"Analysis is one thing; reality is another—the reality of experience that can't be entirely explained," Goode said. "What makes Schubert so compelling? Beethoven is an architect, and Schubert is a weaver. His sonatas are more singerly, more transparent than Beethoven's, and they include more kinds of fantasy. When you begin one, you feel that you're setting out on a long journey through Schubert country— a country unlike any other. There are strange happenings—harmonic marvels—everywhere. But there's always a thread to follow. In his last years, he deepens the content while developing the form. He manages to have his dreams and make the whole thing cohere at the same time."

Goode generally gives scant attention to external demarcations of time. But this was a concert day. He rose before finishing his coffee, and picked up a canvas sack containing several volumes of sonatas and a book or two. The piano would be available at ten o'clock; we set off for the Herbst Theatre, which was diagonally across the street, at ten minutes to ten. Goode, who is not prone to exercise, sniffed the morning air and exclaimed with the brio of an aerobics instructor, "Taking this walk twice today will do me a world of good!"

At the hall, Goode and the stagehands tried out various placements for the piano, in order to get the best acoustics, and tested the lighting. Lighting is important to Goode; his eyes are weak, and he can't tolerate bright lights onstage. At home, he often begins practicing toward dusk and continues in complete darkness. When everything was as he wished, he began to play the Schubert. Until that moment, he had been affable and gregarious. Now, in an instant, the world around him dropped away.

Anyone who has seen Goode enter, however informally, into his musical element will have noticed the immediacy of his transformation, and the totality of its effect upon him. He doesn't practice in the normal sense of the word; he re-creates, striving for continuity of expression just as intensely as he does when he is giving a concert. "Richard's practicing always comes from how he feels the work as a whole," Marcia says. "He never attacks it in pieces and then puts it together. When he goes into his music, he shuts the world out completely." She and I both knew we were in the way; she embraced him, and we left.

That evening at six-thirty, after a two-hour nap, Goode returned to the theatre. Without hesitation, he chose the most cramped of three dressing rooms, because its lighting was harsher than that of the others and would better prepare him for the light onstage. He was noticeably less talkative than he had been in the morning.

Since childhood, he has suffered from stagefright. "Cold hands, physical stiffness," he had told me. "But, above all, mental anguish: worry about memory, a refusal to believe that I've done this thing successfully before. I've often felt like a runner who has devoted his best effort to preparing and then has a hundred-pound load put on his back.

I went to some workshops on stagefright, to no avail— and I went to a psychiatrist for a while. That led in interesting directions, but it yielded nothing I could pass on to anyone else. I haven't yet found the all-purpose pre-concert calming ritual. I'll sit quietly and try to empty my mind, or even read until the last minute, but no elaborate yoga techniques. A certain amount of obsessive hand washing goes on—that is, when I'm lucky enough to have hot water available backstage."

The tuner was late finishing his work and was still onstage. Goode hid himself away in a corner of the wings and read his book of the moment, John Millington Synge's "The Aran Islands." When the piano was finally ready, he began to play Mozart's Sonata K. 570 in flowing lyrical lines that spanned long phrases, coaxing the instrument, caressing it. I remembered that he had once told me, "I often imagine the sound of a piano without the hammers." He went on practicing until it was time to let the audience in to the hall.

When, at a few minutes past eight, Goode came back onstage, his demeanor betrayed nothing of the inner battle he had waged, or of the musical forces now to be unleashed. Quiet and self-contained, he disappeared to the extent that the bulk of his frame would allow, and walked directly and quickly to the piano—more like a librarian going to a shelf for a favorite book than like a celebrated musician about to begin a concert. He bowed simply and rather formally before settling himself at the keyboard and didn't take much time before beginning to play—no excessive fiddling with the piano bench. His continuity of mental preparation was not to be broken. Everything nonessential had been pared away.

Onstage, Goode is not a "personality" who enthralls by his presence but a medium, insignificant in itself, through which matters of import will pass. He seems to be playing as if in his own living room, yet his communication with audiences is powerful and bonding. The entirety of his being engages itself in his music-making. A pliable weight is transmitted from his shoulders into the instrument. The hands do more than play the music: they mold it. At times, his back curves toward the keyboard like a sea pine in a storm; at other times, he'll distance himself from the keys, his head swaying in the dream of a lyrical phrase. His lips nibble goldfishlike, silent coworkers in the formation of musical patterns.

What one remembers most from Goode's playing is not its beauty—exceptional as it is—but his way of coming to grips with the composer's central thought, so that a work tends to make sense beyond one's previous perception of it. This concert was no exception. There was a palpable immediacy of experience throughout—in the Italianate lyricism of the Mozart, the dynamic energy of Beethoven's Opus 10, No. 3, and the evocation of color in four Debussy preludes. Then came Schubert's A-Major Sonata.

Goode doesn't adopt a retrospective view of the Schubert journey: he travels along with the composer. Taking hold of the first movement's diverse strands, he gave life to particularities while retaining the proportions of the whole. There was inevitability in the way heroic passages gathered cumulative energy, in the way the lyric second subject was set forth in quiet repose.

The melody of the slow movement, which Goode describes as "a nocturnal song of intense stillness," is interrupted by one of the most remarkable passages in all music: harmonically audacious, rhythmically tumultuous—an unbridled expression of despair. The immediacy of experience now became positively dangerous; the torrent of notes seemed improvisatory, cataclysmic. ("There's nothing more wrenching," Goode has said. "From a relatively quiet passage, the music suddenly flares up in a terrifying way into near-chaos. I've always accepted these outbursts in Schubert as making enormous sense. Irrational things do make sense. We all have them. These passages come out of the substratum of the soul, and people respond to them in a very deep way.") A lyrical transition leads back to the movement's opening theme, but this transition is punctuated by fortissimo chords—horrifying aftershocks. Goode snatched these chords from the keys with unmitigated fury, once bringing up his hand with such violence as to shake his fist.

When the first theme returns, it is accompanied by haunting new rhythmic figures: "night sounds—incipient Bartók," Goode calls them. "In performance, you wonder how you can get out of the darkness," he has said. "But light dawns with the Scherzo. The theme of the finale is related to the song 'Im Frühling.' It's the most wonderful thing to give people this melody; it's totally openhearted and, in a way, a resolution of all the dissonances of the past movements." As

Goode guided us through the finale's extended rondo form, along by-ways into distant regions, he captured the implication of mood in each modulation, and we never felt lost. Schumann once spoke of Schubert's "heavenly lengths," and we cherished them. Every time the melody returned, it seemed more eloquent than before. And when it appeared for the last time, fragmented by rests and touching on new harmonic spheres, each moment of silence was imbued with a poignant expectancy. The spontaneous formulating process of the creator was tangible in the concert hall.

How Schubert might have reacted to Goode's playing can only be conjectured, but the distinguished living composer George Perle told me, "I'm privileged to have Richard as an interpreter of my works. I once felt that I had miscalculated the way I had written a certain passage in my 'Ballade for Piano,' and told Richard that I wanted to add octaves to the bass. But Richard said, 'I think I can find a way to realize the effect you want without your making any changes.' Usually, it's up to the composer to urge the interpreter to fulfill the musical intention; with Richard, it was the opposite—he was being my conscience. Richard reconnects to where the music came from. He makes a piece his own, yet he's true to the piece. He's a revelatory pianist, like Artur Schnabel."

Goode himself fights shy of any comparison with the great Austrian pianist who brought home to our century the full spiritual legacy of the keyboard music of Beethoven and Schubert. But, increasingly, others are making the point. Schnabel's son, Karl Ulrich Schnabel, now eighty-two and a remarkable pianist and teacher in his own right, put it this way to me: "Richard's playing has many of the qualities of my father's: his sense of continuity of tempo, so that any flexibility of rhythm never disturbs the whole, and, above all, his deep respect for the text. Fidelity to the text was the crux of my father's playing. He and Toscanini both fought an uphill battle to establish that the composer is more important than the performer. Richard makes the most of the intention of the composer: he goes to the core."

When the applause had ended, Marcia and I found Richard alone in his dressing room. He sat in a chair, drained and white, and somewhat dazed, as if felled by a heavy weight. He declined a drink, but suddenly seized a bottle of orange juice and gulped down the contents. Dress shirts and undershirts were strewn about, thoroughly drenched. With a decisive effort, he drew himself up and changed his clothes once again. In his pre-Marcia days, his soggy after-concert embrace was proverbial; she now provides him with three sets of shirts. Donning a blue sports jacket over his black striped trousers, he went out to greet a throng of well-wishers, and was soon immersed in conversation, speaking with each person at length and heedless of the line of people waiting patiently to talk to him. He is always engaged with the other—to the extent that he finds it difficult to say no, even when he risks being taken advantage of. One of his friends told me, "Richard never changes his relationship to people according to who they are. He doesn't care if you're the chairman of the board or the janitor. Some people find this disconcerting."

It was quite late when we left the hall for dinner at Stars, a lively restaurant whose walls are adorned with gaudy Pop art. "A quiet painting, that," Goode commented, pointing to one of the gaudiest. He ordered a hamburger and three Pilsner Urquells—one for Marcia and two for himself. "Eating after a concert is wonderful—almost makes the playing worthwhile," he declared. "If a concert has gone poorly, I console myself with a big meal. If it's gone well, I reward myself with a big meal."

We began talking about programming. "I'd like to play programs with fewer composers," he said. "To stay longer in one area, and get deeper into it. Sometimes the changeover can be quite disturbing." A few minutes later, he said, almost as a matter of course, "I love the idea of putting Debussy in the middle of a program, of doing something completely different—clearing the palate, like having sherbet in the middle of a meal."

Goode's thought processes seem naturally to embrace opposites. Discuss with him his decades-long struggle against bourgeois attitudes, and he'll defend the bourgeoisie as having produced the greatest artists. Mention the dramatic conflicts raging within Beethoven, and he'll praise Beethoven's pastoral side, where the battle is stilled. Refer to the manner in which he merges piano technique and musical expression, and he'll uphold the virtues of scale practice. Goode's predilection for seeing more than one side of an issue is born less from a spirit of contentiousness than from one of completeness. The paradox scans the fullness of life—though, as Goode has learned in the course of his career, it can sometimes hold back the flow of life.

By the time we started back to the Inn at the Opera, it was one o'clock in the morning. The Schubert journey, one-third undertaken, would be completed Friday evening in Hertz Hall, at the University of California. A brisk wind had come up, and it had turned cold, but Goode's collar was unbuttoned, as usual. And, as usual, the heavy sack of music and books was slung over his shoulder. I had stopped offering to carry it for him a while ago, when I realized that he feels better having it near him.

Two things strike one about Richard Goode the pianist: the depth of his achievement as an artist, and the time it has taken for him to receive due recognition. Goode gave his first New York recital in February of 1962, when he was eighteen, in an improvised concert hall in an Armenian restaurant in Greenwich Village. Over the next couple of decades, he became a consummate chamber-music player and a New York cult figure, with a reputation as a musician's musician. He was forty-seven years old by the time he gave his first concert in Carnegie Hall. Of that evening Donal Henahan wrote in the *Times*:

> It is difficult to understand why it took 29 years for Richard Goode to make his Carnegie Hall debut, but the event was worth waiting for. . . . In a perfect world all debutants would be so well prepared, musically and technically. . . . He commands, in fact, a wider spectrum of tone color than any pianist of his generation whose name comes quickly to mind. . . . Those who remember him as one of the founding members of the Chamber Music Society of Lincoln Center two decades ago can be assured that the quicksilver temperament and total immersion in the score that distinguished his playing then continue in force. . . . His aptly moody and mercurial performance of the Schumann Davidsbündlertänze won this listener's vote as the high point of a recital that lived throughout on an extremely lofty plateau.

Was the twenty-nine years' delay a misfortune or a blessing? The answer depends on your point of view. (When it comes to Richard Goode, you feel free to have several points of view running concurrently.) A longtime chamber-music colleague, the clarinettist Richard Stoltzman, says, "Can you imagine Richard if he had become a well-known soloist at twenty-five? He would have missed the depth and breadth of intensive meditation on music which only an enormous amount of time has made possible. His concentration is what separates him from most musicians." The pianist Denise Kahn, who has known Goode since 1970, says, "Every little bit of progress he made in his career was an incredible struggle, as opposed to those people who just trot out there like racehorses. There was no stopping his talent—it simply had to express itself. But, God knows, he did everything he could to sabotage his career." In the espousal of these two viewpoints Goode's friends fall into two roughly equal camps. He once summarized for me his own ambivalence in the matter of his career by reciting the lyrics of an old Jimmy Durante song: "Did you ever have the feeling that you wanted to go—still have the feeling that you wanted to stay?"

There was no ambivalence in Goode's primary musical impulse, which, he says, "was always vocal." His mother, Helen Kaiser Goode, told me that when he was three he began to sing along with Bing Crosby records, and that when he was taken to see the film "The Jolson Story," starring Larry Parks as Al Jolson, he came home overflowing with song. "The pathos really got to me," he recalls.

Richard's father, Samuel, was a piano tuner and had once played the violin, but neither parent had ever been a professional musician. The family lived in a three-bedroom second-floor apartment on Arnow Avenue, in the East Bronx. (The original family name was Guzman; it was Anglicized when Richard's grandfather, who emigrated from the Ukraine in 1912, became a citizen.) "The avenues had big apartment houses, mainly Jewish," Richard recalls. "The cross streets had little houses, mainly Italian. The ladies would sit out on their doorsteps; whenever you came home, you had to run this gauntlet of elderly well-wishers. I still think that's how neighborhoods should be."

Richard, who was born on June 1, 1943, shared a bedroom with his elder brother, Robert, now a professor of biology at City College of New York. The boys' maternal grandmother, Anna, had a bedroom to herself. Her presence was powerfully felt in the small household. "As much as possible, my grandmother wanted to re-create in the Bronx the conditions of the old country," Richard told me. "She lived in her private world, as if removed from us in time, and devoted herself to reading—mostly prayer books in Hebrew, but also Tolstoy, whom she venerated. Her religiosity seemed a grim and dour thing to me. There was no joy in it. But I was impressed by her devoutness."

Samuel Goode hoped that Richard would take up the violin, and, by way of preparation for this, had him begin piano lessons at the age of six. After an unrewarding start with a neighborhood piano teacher, Richard was brought to Elvira Szigeti, whose nephew was the violinist Joseph Szigeti. This was a stroke of fortune: she proved to be the ideal person to nurture his talent. "Mrs. Szigeti's home had an Old World aura—lots of dark wood and heavy furniture," Goode recalls. "She was a majestic woman—stern and indulgent in the right mixture. She had arthritis, so she never demonstrated. But this may have liberated me. I was a fairly timid kid, and if I had heard impressive piano playing I might have felt inhibited. Music was an intense, emotional experience for her. She constantly used the word 'feeling,' and wouldn't let me rattle through scales and exercises unmusically. I was rather slow at learning—I'd get my fingers mixed up. But certain music had a magical effect on me, especially Bach."

In fact, Richard progressed rapidly and soon found himself deeply responsive to the piano. When a neighbor of the Goodes, the beatific Rabbi Ginzburg, asked Richard's father why it was that the boy played the same thing over and over, Samuel replied, "Rabbi, haven't you been saying the same prayers over and over since you were a child?" Thereafter, the rabbi could often be seen walking slowly around the block, his hands behind his back, humming Richard's piano music to himself.

"My brother practiced then as he practices now, singing and swaying, his whole body becoming part of his music-making," Robert Goode recalls. "The atmosphere of our home was rather confining, and the piano became for him a kind of emotional release."

Release had also come in the form of the written word, even before Richard's hands touched the keyboard: when he was only four years old he obtained a library card from the Wakefield Public Library. "My favorite books had animal protagonists," he recalls. "In fact, I was obsessed with animals throughout my childhood. I fantasized about having an exotic pet, like a marmoset—an adorable Amazon monkey, the smallest known—or a fennec, which is a desert fox with big ears. I did manage to get a cat, but it proved too mischievous for us to keep. I'd spend hours in the zoo, sketching the antelopes. In 'Song of Myself' Walt Whitman wrote, 'I think I could turn and live with animals. . . . Not one is respectable or unhappy over the whole earth.' "

Something of a Victorian spirit prevailed in the Bronx in those days. Piano playing was thought to be an accomplishment fit for girls, and Richard was the only boy among Mrs. Szigeti's students when, at the age of eight, he made his first public appearance, playing Mozart's D-Minor Fantasy. "I was blissfully unaware of the fact that it was to be my last concert without stagefright," he says. His schoolmates identified him with Liberace, the reigning pianist of the culture; his schoolteachers lionized him, and a great fuss was made over his playing. Richard responded by dutifully fulfilling everyone's expectations while managing to remain unpretentious—immune then, as now, to self-aggrandizement. But the adulation cast a shadow. As Marcia Goode put it to me, "Richard somehow felt that he was being primarily valued for his musical talent rather than for himself. The focus on his playing was a driving force, yet a damaging force. He didn't have a chance to sort out what feelings were truly his own."

When Richard was nine, Mrs. Szigeti retired from teaching, and he was sent to the noted pedagogue Isabelle Vengerova. "Her studio was *really* dark," he told me. "But, unlike Mrs. Szigeti, she seemed as remote and austere as possible. She turned me over to her assistant, Olga Stroumillo, a Russian lady with a big, Brillo head of hair, who assigned me just one exercise: I was to raise the wrist at right angles to the keyboard and let it fall suddenly, so that a note would resound with terrific force. Five seconds later, I would attack another note. I had been used to playing wonderful music, and now I was reduced to a starvation diet. Mme. Stroumillo wasn't sadistic—she was just the concentration-camp guard. Mme. Vengerova apparently had good results with some people, but I never got to see her again, because when I was returning on the subway from one of the lessons I threw a tantrum and told my father that I'd never go back."

At this critical moment, a friend of Mrs. Szigeti's brought Richard to the attention of Rosalie Leventritt, the well-known patron of the arts. Mrs. Leventritt is remembered both for the foundation she created to help young musicians and for her personal devotion to their cause. Although not trained as a musician, she had fine musical intuition, and she sensed an unusual potential in the ten-year-old. She asked the advice of Rudolf Serkin, the pianist she most respected. Goode denies having been a child prodigy, but his playing was sufficiently compelling to move Serkin to say, "This boy is so gifted and quick that he'll be easy to teach. He needs only to be given the right piece at the right time." Learning of the Goode family's modest circumstances, Mrs. Leventritt made an extraordinary offer: she would sponsor the whole of Richard's musical and academic education. "It took me some years to feel completely at ease with this remarkable woman who seemed to have taken charge of my life," Goode recalls. "Mrs. Leventritt had a Southern graciousness and warmth, an air of distinction, a wonderful bearing, and a strong will."

On Serkin's recommendation, Richard began studying with Claude Frank, then twenty-seven and already a leading interpreter of the Central European repertoire. "Richard's musical intelligence was such that he could easily comprehend a five-voice fugue by Bach," Frank told me recently. "Whatever musical faults he had were typical of a boy of his years. He liked to make huge ritards and crescendos at the end of every piece. He needed to learn to love the right things. When he wasn't studying music, he was reading. I asked his father if Richard was getting enough rest, and he replied, 'Richard doesn't sleep at all. He thinks it's a waste of time.' "

"Claude was the first truly outstanding pianist I had heard from close up," Goode says. "He played in a really grand style and opened a new world of expression for me. It was overwhelming—and hard work. I was a sensitive plant and prone to burst into tears when any criticism became too severe."

When Richard was twelve, Mrs. Leventritt felt that he needed the stimulation of a conservatory atmosphere, and she arranged for him to work with Nadia Reisenberg, at the Mannes College of Music. Reisenberg, who was Russian by birth, had studied with Josef Hofmann and during the 1939–40 season had given the first complete series of Mozart piano concertos in the United States. She was a player of uncommon facility, and could routinely demonstrate difficult right-hand passages with her left hand. She put Richard through an exacting regimen of "kitchen work" in the form of études, her emphasis being on fluidity of line and beauty of tone. Colleagues of Goode recognize to this day the benefits of her teaching. "Nadia was terribly nice to me," Goode says. "And, incidentally, she introduced me to Schubert's sonatas. I recognized her distinction as a pianist—a sort of limpid perfection. Yet I never had a true temperamental compatibility with her playing. At that point in my adolescence, the emphasis on elegance seemed to thwart my feelings—to focus on what wasn't essential."

When Rudolf Serkin played Brahms' First Piano Concerto in Carnegie Hall in March of 1957, the thirteen-year-old Goode heard what he felt *was* essential. "The playing was titanic," he recalls. "The performance seemed a matter of life and death. The sweep, the drama, the sense of immediacy astonished me." Serkin had kept abreast of Goode's progress, and the following summer he invited him to take part in the Marlboro Music Festival, in Vermont. Along with Serkin's son, Peter, with whom he formed a lasting friendship, Goode was one of the youngest musicians ever to participate. After an initial period of bewilderment, he settled into Marlboro life, and he returned for the next six summers. Goode refers to his experience at Marlboro—in company with such musicians as Pablo Casals, Marcel Moyse, Felix Galimir, and Serkin himself—as "perhaps the most important part of my musical education." A film produced there for German television gives glimpses of Goode, at fourteen, playing a Beethoven trio with an organic connection to the keyboard indicative of his present approach, and singing a melody of Mozart to a young colleague with the concern for musical shape that he manifests today.

Goode appears in the Marlboro film as a neatly groomed, well-adjusted youngster; there is no hint of conflict under the surface. But during his early teens he was "profoundly dissatisfied" with life. As a sort of talisman, he kept in his pocket a volume of Flaubert's letters. "I felt alienated from the world around me," he says. "This was a secret I kept largely to myself. Flaubert basically asserted that life is raw material for art—that art is the only way to redeem and justify this messy existence of ours. There was something beautiful but grim in his outlook. He was enmeshed in his surroundings, and had a great deal of hate and spleen. These letters were a consolation to me—an outlet for my dissatisfaction as well as for the deep feelings I had about art."

Goode's relationship to the everyday world was not enhanced by the McBurney School, a private boys' school in midtown Manhattan that Mrs. Leventritt had selected for his high-school education. "I didn't let anyone know how deeply unhappy I was at McBurney," Goode told me. "There was a lot of sham. The emphasis was on athletics. Nude swimming was required once a week—and each week the prospect filled me with trepidation. The classes were mostly without interest, and I sleepwalked through them."

Around this time, Goode encountered "Moby Dick." He had already been fascinated by the seventy-six-foot model of a blue whale hanging in the American Museum of Natural History. "The book utterly entranced me," he recalls. "Not so much because of the Ahab story as because it tied in with my sense of awe at the power of nature. During that period, too, visual art began to mean a great deal to me: the great splashes of the Abstract Expressionists in the Whitney Museum; Paul Klee's paintings, with their mystery and their vivid sense of presence. I read French poetry, and I was taken with Rimbaud's wild imagery: he created a world as far away as possible from the world he lived in. A friend who was in college introduced me to 'Finnegans Wake'—this huge book written in a special language, with the punctuation missing and the end going back to the beginning. These extraordinary man-made things evoked in me something of the sense of wonder I had felt about animals and natural history."

The impact of Rudolf Serkin's playing stayed with Goode. After his second summer at Marlboro, he asked Serkin if he might study with him at the Curtis Institute of Music, in Philadelphia, and he was accepted. "I had assumed that Nadia Reisenberg had somehow read my mind and knew that I wanted to go to Serkin," Goode said. "However, she was completely unprepared for this idea. I must have presented it rather badly. It was not a happy moment."

After graduating from McBurney, Goode took a year off and devoted himself to reading and to visiting Serkin's home in Philadelphia every so often to work with him privately. Lessons would begin in midafternoon and often continue after dinner. On walks, Serkin would reminisce about his studies with Arnold Schoenberg in Vienna after the First World War. In the fall of 1961, Goode moved to Philadelphia, rented a tiny studio apartment overlooking a fire escape, and entered Curtis as a full-time student.

None of Rudolf Serkin's students will ever forget the quality of Serkin's listening. Huddled in a corner with his eyes closed and his face buried in one hand, he would concentrate intently on whatever piece was being played. His main concern was interpretation; he said little about technique. He was uncompromising in his demand for textual fidelity. He rarely demonstrated, and he discouraged his students from taking notes. "You'll remember what I say if it's important to you," he would tell them. Lesson material had to be prepared to concert level. Any lack of commitment was blasphemy.

"On occasions when I did disappoint Serkin, as when I played Chopin's Barcarolle too vehemently, a grave and sad look would come over his face, as if to say that I had transgressed—that perhaps something had even been killed but maybe there was a chance of bringing it back to life," Goode told me. "In Serkin's teaching, the unspoken was what was most remembered. We learned most from the feeling with which everything was charged—from the totality of his dedication. Serkin never allowed himself the luxury of self-satisfaction—even the nourishing kind, à la Rubinstein. And if he couldn't be satisfied with himself how could he be satisfied with you? Much of the incredible tension Serkin communicated as an interpreter was related to the anguish—the inner resistance—he experienced in performing. There are, of course, artists who bring different qualities to the concert stage—a greater relaxation, an untroubled ease in communicating. But such musicians may have other shortcomings—perhaps a certain glibness in their facility, or a lack of idealism. It's difficult to separate the virtues and defects in an artistic personality. Either they come together into a convincing whole or they don't. In Serkin's case, they came together in a uniquely expressive way, and the suffering he endured was part of it."

Goode had to contend with his own sense of dissatisfaction. "Since my first student recital, a drastic change had come over me," he said. "During my Curtis years, I began to play a lot in public, and I suffered from such extreme stagefright that I didn't know how I could possibly continue performing. After a concert I gave in Wyoming, I wrote to Serkin about this—partly as a catharsis, partly pleading for his advice. He told me that my letter had touched him but that, regretfully, he didn't know what advice he could offer. I was disappointed, but I wasn't terribly surprised. I began to wonder, What's a lifetime of this going to be like? I definitely wanted to be a musician, but being a musician and being a performer are two different things."

The dichotomy was not restricted to Goode's waking hours. He still remembers a nightmare he had at the time: "I was playing the piano in the Allerton Avenue subway station, in the Bronx. Judges, who were seated in the shadows, announced that every time I played a wrong note I'd lose a finger." But there were other sorts of dreams: "Sometimes, wonderful music that I'd never heard before would come to me. I couldn't wait to write it down, but when I awoke it would be forgotten."

One day while Goode was at Curtis, he visited the Philadelphia public library and listened to Arthur Schnabel's recording of Beethoven's "Hammerklavier" Sonata. "A light bulb went on in my head," Goode told me. "I said to myself, 'He plays the music as if he had written it!' He had a way of discovering meanings that might have eluded us—a delight in the articulation of the unexpected. It was a new vocabulary—a kind of sculpturing, such as you find in certain great paintings. Mantegna's Roman soldiers seem to be so real that you could almost grasp them. Schnabel did that when he played Beethoven: he made the contours of the music seem tangible."

I asked Goode what role his fascination with visual art plays in his approach to music.

"I don't think of colors—yellow, green, and so on," he said. "But I do think of spaces, textures, and moods. The more you pour into the hopper of the imagination, the better. Certain works do call up images, although these are, of course, entirely subjective. For example, at the beginning of Schumann's C-Major Fantasy I hear an enormous bell. The whole opening section seems enveloped in its reverberations. In the middle of the movement, after the trills die away, the spirit of the music seems to recede into the historical past: a shrouded forest image. In much music I feel shifts in time between the present and the past, especially in Schumann and Chopin—the Ballades, for instance. Or shifts in space, the music moving nearer or farther away—as in Beethoven's Diabelli Variations. Some painters achieved marvelous effects in their use of space—Piero della Francesca, for instance, in 'The Flagellation.' In Rembrandt you have all kinds of effects of depth, darkness, recession, uncertainty, mystery—qualities that exist also in music. And that's the challenge. The piano is the great instrument of illusion, of transformation. In the recordings of Rachmaninoff or Cortot, the piano becomes a voice, singing and speaking; it becomes an orchestra; it becomes nature. It doesn't remain itself."

Seven years after leaving Curtis, Goode returned there to give a recital. The day after the concert, Serkin took him into his office and, announcing solemnly, "Our ways have diverged," proceeded to chide Goode for the amount of rhythmic freedom in his playing. "Serkin's rigor sometimes made people react against it," Goode recalled. "For me, it was a question of working through his profound influence, fighting it at certain points, and later finding my way toward a synthesis. I've learned that too much liberty can disturb the unity of the large design. In the performance of any work, there's a constant dialogue between freedom and regularity. The first thing one thinks about is flow. If the freedom is right, it will help the piece generate itself; if the freedom is excessive, it will detract from the flow. The piece must always seem to unfold naturally."

Divergence notwithstanding, Goode's relationship with Serkin continued until Serkin's death, in 1991. A letter Serkin wrote to Goode in 1979 evidences the bond that existed between them on more than one level: "I wish we could see each other more often and talk about the really important things in life. . . . With fear and horror I am becoming aware that in two weeks I shall be playing in Lisbon." And he noted in conclusion, "Be happy, reasonably happy."

Goode graduated from Curtis in 1964, when he was twenty-one. It was at that point in his life—a crossroads for a young musician—that his inner dualism met conventional expectations head on. It was taken for granted that he would actively pursue a major solo career and begin to enter competitions—the traditional and most effective ladder toward success. As the pressure to succeed increased, so did his resistance. "I had a revulsion against the idea of ambition," Goode told me. "Sometimes I've felt that I was carrying out some-body else's wish. This, combined with my doubts about myself, re-sulted in a lack of confidence as a player. Serkin tried to get me to do more solo playing, but I needed other processes to take place before I was able to make that step. I've often felt that simply being on the stage is so difficult for me that my natural love of music forsakes me when I'm there. I always fantasized that I would quit one day. At the same time, I didn't want to give it up. The fact that I was involved in a career was something I almost kept secret from myself. My way of ignoring it—until quite recently—was just to let it happen, and not admit consciously that it was shaping my life in any significant way."

A young musician in America today is confronted by a society that feeds on success—particularly, rapid success. But Richard Goode, by his very nature, was a misfit in the world of high-pressure competi-tions and managerial promotion. "I was anything but a salesman's dream," Goode says. "I wasn't a great virtuoso; I was a rather serious, intense, sweaty young musician. I played repertoire that many con-cert sponsors didn't love. And I was at odds with myself." In 1970, when he had been with a New York concert management for four years, the sales representatives called him in to a meeting. Their chair-man said, "Richard, your image is still unclear to us. It's hard for us to market you. Are you a scholar with a touch of the poet? Are you a classical pianist with a romantic side? Who *are* you?"

Goode would have had few performing opportunities when he left Curtis had it not been for Charles and Susan Wadsworth. In 1961, Susan had founded Young Concert Artists, a non-profit organization designed to promote the careers of gifted but little-known musicians. Her criterion was artistic merit rather than salability, and she took no commission on her artists' performance fees. While Goode was still at Curtis, she presented him in her first New York series, and continued to find concert engagements for him until he was taken on by com-mercial management. In 1964, Charles invited him to play at the Spo-leto Festival, and five years later he engaged Goode as a founding member of the Chamber Music Society of Lincoln Center.

By this time, Goode had made a decisive turn toward chamber music. "It's a shared experience—a friendly thing to do, because of the company onstage," he says. "I still did occasional solo playing, but I was acutely uncomfortable with it." In 1967, with Serkin's encouragement, Goode had made his London début in Wigmore Hall, with a Beethoven, Schubert, and Schumann program. The London Times headed its review "UNUSUALLY SUCCESSFUL RECITAL BY YOUNG PIANIST," and commented, "One predicts for Mr. Richard Goode an exceptional career." Goode was furious. He was deeply disturbed that anyone should have words of praise for the travesty he thought he had committed.

"It was helpful to learn the chamber-music and vocal repertoire so early," Goode told me. "I wasn't boxed in, in a pianistic sense. Thinking in terms of other instruments can immeasureably change the way you play. Take the beginning of Mozart's D-Major Sonata K. 576—a dialogue between horns and flutes. Or the last song of Schumann's 'Frauenliebe und Leben,' a blow of fate—three trombones."

In the Wadsworths' New York apartment, Charles played me a tape, from the 1966 Spoleto Festival, of Schumann's Fantasy Pieces for cello and piano, in which Goode was joined by Jacqueline du Pré. The two had met in Spoleto and formed a close friendship. Their music-making there generated a white heat of excitement. Du Pré afterward called Goode "a life force."

Charles, for his part, was impressed with Goode's way of incessantly exploring the possibilities of interpretation. "A page of music is a living thing to Richard," he told me. "It was typical of him, just before going onstage, to turn to page fourteen and whisper to his colleagues, 'You know, we really make too much crescendo here. We should save it for the next bar—and why don't we take a little more time at the top of the phrase?' "

When I mentioned this to Goode, he said, "I know I can be annoying—very annoying. I once pestered a member of the Boston Symphony Chamber Players about so many details that he told me, 'Richie, this is chamber music. You play your way, I'll play my way."

A year or so after graduating from Curtis, Goode returned to Mannes, in order to continue to deepen his understanding of music. He studied conducting with Carl Bamberger and theory with Carl Schachter, with whom he had also worked during the Reisenberg years. "Schachter showed me how each piece is permeated by certain characteristic musical ideas and generated by its own specific kinds of laws," Goode recalled. "For instance, in the 'Pastoral Symphony' there are places when the harmony doesn't change for many bars at a time—Beethoven's intimation of the long, slow cycle of nature. When you view a work from a variety of perspectives and ask 'What is it that makes this piece unique?' you begin to see connections that you wouldn't have thought of before. I had often felt awash in a sea of feelings that music aroused in me. This fuller realization of music as an intellectual object freed me, in a way. It didn't dissolve the mystery of the beauty—it intensified it."

At Mannes, Goode came into contact with Karl Ulrich Schnabel, and, in master classes and private lessons with him, he was drawn into a historical continuum: Mr. Schnabel has preserved the heritage of his father's musicianship without sacrificing his own musical individuality. "He combines an Old World geniality with a scholar's passion for detail," Goode told me. "Like a good Talmudist, he showed me how to understand the text, and how to communicate it. His attitude was that, despite his greater experience, we were both students. One felt that the music had limitless possibilities." Schnabel, too, recalls those lessons. "All great music contains two ingredients—expression and form," he said. "Richard and I worked on combining the two. It's not that he destroyed form—he was just not yet building it. Over the years, his playing has become more substantial and authoritative. Form has become one of his greatest strengths."

In a historic BBC interview in 1935, the composer Ethel Smyth, then in her late seventies, gave this firsthand account of Brahms' piano playing: "Overwhelming in power, it was never noisy, nor what today is called percussive. And when presently, with what he called his tenor thumb, he lifted some warm, tender passage out of the tangle of sound, the look on his face was a thing one never forgot. Best of all, I like to think of his playing Bach's mighty organ fugues, sometimes accompanying himself with a sort of muffled roar, as of Titans moved to sympathy in the bowels of the earth." Goode's playing shares much with this description, and sometimes the roar has gone unmuffled. "Had I not been a pianist, I'd have liked to be a singer," he told me. Anyone who takes Goode's statement as merely figurative should hear him practice. The singing in question would do no credit to Pavarotti; it is an ecstatic humming, a moaning, a keening, a crooning. Little wonder that while Goode was practicing backstage shortly before he was to perform a Beethoven concerto in Naples in 1984, he remained unaware of an earthquake that caused near-panic among the public and the orchestra.

"Singing along was always something of a problem for my father, and it has been for me as well," Mr. Schnabel told me. "One sings along for two possible reasons. First, you still imagine something that is better than you can realize at the keyboard. Second, you don't like what you hear from the orchestra. In Richard's early days, if anything was wrong it was the appearance, not the substance."

The primal freedom of Goode's approach to practicing was carried over in large measure to the more formal precincts of the concert stage. "He is . . . in constant motion, rolling, pouncing, shaking his head, rocking," Harold C. Schonberg wrote in the *Times* in February of 1966; and the London *Times* commented in September of 1973, "A pianist more agreeably heard than seen, so ardently does he exteriorize his feelings—but audibly too."

"Richard's gestures and vocalism were a huge problem," a friend says. "They were distracting to many members of the public and injurious to his career. He was very annoyed when people mentioned this to him. It almost drove him further into it. He felt that people were focussing on the wrong thing."

Other friends take the point of view articulated by the pianist-composer Franklin Latner: "Creativity sometimes demands a rough edge. If Richard had suppressed that jaggedness, his playing might not be what it is today. I'd be respectful of this part of his personality. There's a truthfulness behind it that's frequently lacking in a world that rewards uninhibited music-making."

Bruno Walter tells of the gradual evolution of Mahler's gestures as a conductor from the "astounding mobility" of his early years in Vienna to the "almost uncanny calm" of his late years "with no loss in intensity of effect." Today, Goode's approach to the keyboard has become simpler. The roar, though manifestly yet within him, is generally muted. The change can be credited in part to the demands of recording—which have forced him to control his singing and the piano bench's squeaking—and in part to an economy, a fullness in concision, that comes with maturity.

"I agree that my manner at the piano may have held back my career," Goode said when I raised the point with him. "I think the supreme accomplishment is stillness—not frozen stillness but quiet stillness that's supple and can move in any direction—although I doubt if I could achieve that ideal in *this* life. And it's more gratifying to see somebody doing something with ease than with effort. Stage-fright may have played a role: with those gestures, I've tried to throw off a sense of oppression. Sometimes I've felt that it's difficult enough to perform at all—to do it in the approved manner is intolerable."

"**B**reak with the outside world, live like a bear," Flaubert wrote. During the sixties and seventies, Goode appeared to have something of the sort in mind. His friends still speak with incredulity of the state of the small West Side apartment he was living in then: the bed in swirls; clothing, music, records, and magazines on art, theatre, and poetry strewn everywhere; and, of course, books, a number of them years overdue at the library. "A tempest of life," says Harry Jensen, who studied with Goode for fifteen years. "The order in Richard is in the intensity of his experience. When he was involved in music, I didn't exist, he didn't exist, time didn't exist. Once, when we had been working on a few measures of Bach for over two hours, we heard a loud crash. A cabinet had fallen off the kitchen wall, and all the crockery lay broken on the floor. Richard continued teaching as if nothing had happened. When I went for my next lesson, two weeks later, the mess was still there, untouched."

"I was intransigent by neglect rather than by design," Goode says. "People looking at me might have thought I was engaged in a certain form of revolt, but I didn't think of myself that way. It's just that I'm horribly disorderly. A lot of what I do is surrounded by chaos."

One casualty—or, depending on one's point of view, distinction—of Goode's bohemianism was the state of his dress. He is remembered from his bachelor days as "an inspired tatterdemalion" and as being "in the great tradition of clothes crumplers." Appearances on the concert stage with shirttails hanging below his evening jacket or with a safety pin affixed to his music-reading glasses did nothing to dispel such impressions. On one occasion, he had to be sewn into his trousers, which, just before a concert, had split open at the fly. The Chamber Music Society of Lincoln Center received letters from subscribers wondering why Goode had to sit on the Manhattan telephone directory while he was playing, or wear anklets with his dress suit. "As a performer, one has to appear in reasonably decent attire on certain evenings," Goode says. "That was not impossible for me, but it was a bit of a burden." Some of Goode's efforts to achieve sartorial splendor have passed into legend, such as the time he ran the bath (without pulling the plug) to steam the wrinkles out of his tailcoat and was notified an hour later that the ceiling of the apartment below had collapsed. Or the time he washed his white bow tie, put it in the toaster oven to dry, and then covered the singed places with talcum powder.

Goode's attitude toward money has also been a cause of concern to his friends. Harry Jensen recalls, "I'd pay for my lessons with a check, and he'd ask me to put it in a drawer. The drawer was filled with checks that had never been cashed, some from years back. I tried to pay him with groceries, but he never ate what I left." Children visiting the apartment found money lying about on the floor, and decided that Goode must surely be a very rich man.

Goode's career as a pianist almost came to an end in 1970, when he and a girlfriend were in an automobile accident in Mexico. The car they were in turned over twice and landed upside down in a riverbed. Miraculously, both escaped serious permanent injury. Goode's injuries included two fractured vertebrae, which required him to wear a back brace for several months, and a severed extensor tendon in his left hand; the glass had just missed cutting two other tendons. "My fourth finger is still a bit of a bother to me," Goode says. "It doesn't always clear the keys in a satisfactory way. With the combination of the hand and the back injuries, I had to train myself to become more economical in my movements when I was playing. Imagine what I was like before 1970!"

A few years earlier—telling almost no one—he had entered his first international competition: the Busoni, in Bolzano, Italy. "I played with cold hands," he told me. "I felt miserable—always the same story, ever since I was ten. But being in the competition was not as painful as I'd expected, because every concert I'd given had required so much psychic energy as to seem virtually like a competition. In the end, I was awarded the second prize. Garrick Ohlsson won the first prize. Having got that far, I was deeply disappointed not to win, but I didn't admit that to myself for several months."

In 1973, at the urging of the eminent pianist Mieczyslaw Horszowski, Goode relented one more time, and entered the Clara Haskil Competition, in Vevey, Switzerland. At thirty, he had almost reached the competition's age limit. ("He had to be dragged there in chains," a friend says.) He played the Mozart D-Minor Concerto in the finals, and this time he won the first prize; Mitsuko Uchida was the runner-up. Thereafter Goode was awarded a number of European engagements, but by that time the odds were against his achieving a major career: he had been before the public for over a decade and was no longer a bright new face. Relatively few knew of the soloist living within the chamber-music player—a situation that his friends tried to remedy.

In 1977, the pianist Shirley Rhoads asked Leonard Bernstein to hear Goode. She told me of the meeting: "After Richard performed Beethoven's Sonata Opus 110 and Brahms' Fantasies Opus 116, Lenny said that Richard's playing was the 'classiest' he had heard in years, and asked him why he wasn't performing Brahms concertos all over the world. Richard was nonplussed. Lenny undoubtedly sensed that Richard himself hadn't yet decided that he wanted a solo career."

"It was a curious interview," Goode told me, even now somewhat abashed at the recollection. "Bernstein's reaction to my playing was encouraging, but I was taken by surprise when he seemed to throw the responsibility back to me. I was very shy about getting into a discussion of psychological problems, which I felt were probably at the root of the whole thing. So we didn't have much of a conversation."

The previous summer, Goode had spent ten days at the Grand Teton Music Festival, in Wyoming. "I felt a sense of freedom, being up in the mountains," he recalls. "I realized that life, hemmed in by the next concert, had become too narrow. I couldn't face it anymore—I had to get off the treadmill." Now he acted on this awareness, and for ten months in 1978 he played no concerts at all. "For much of the time, I was lying fallow," he told me. "I read a lot, went to auctions and art exhibitions, found a new apartment, and practiced without being under constant pressure." While lying fallow, Goode made what was for him a painful decision. He withdrew from the Chamber Music Society of Lincoln Center, despite the intense loyalty he felt toward the colleagues with whom he had worked for a decade. "I realized that chamber music had become a refuge from pursuing something that would be more difficult for me," he said. "It had been the path of least resistance." Bernstein's challenge was beginning to strike home.

In fact, Goode's withdrawal from the Society was only partial—his participation continued, with a reduced commitment, for another decade—but he now began to direct time and energy toward a new goal. Significantly, in 1980 he was awarded the Avery Fisher Prize, which carried with it a solo appearance with the New York Philharmonic. "The prize is given in the nicest possible way," Goode told me. "You don't have to *do* anything to get it—you're just nominated."

Early in 1983, Goode and Jay K. Hoffman, who had recently become his personal representative, were returning from Westchester County after looking at a concert hall that Goode had been asked to inaugurate. As they drove along the Saw Mill River Parkway, Hoffman asked Goode which works he would choose if he were given the opportunity to record absolutely anything he wanted. Goode laughed, and said, "Oh, all the Beethoven sonatas." Hoffman said, "Why don't I give it a try?" He approached Book-of-the-Month Records with the proposal, and, to Goode's astonishment, it was accepted.

Goode made the first of the Beethoven recordings in the fall of 1983. Because of his critical standards and his unwillingness to regard any performance as definitive, the project wasn't completed until this year, by which time it had been taken over by Elektra Nonesuch Records. "I stretched everyone's endurance to the limit, including my own," Goode says.

During the early stages of the recordings, Goode made a decision that was to have a vital effect on his career: he committed himself to playing all thirty-two Beethoven sonatas in public in a single season. He postponed the project once, but achieved his goal during the 1987–88 season, in a series of seven concerts, which he gave both in Kansas City and at New York's 92nd Street Y.

Learning and performing all the Beethoven sonatas was a watershed in Goode's development. From the first concert, there was a sense among his dedicated New York public that something momentous was taking place. The *Times* described the series as "among the season's most important and memorable events." Hoffman, who had followed Goode's career for many years before they formed their professional relationship, told me, "The fact that Richard had to learn and play all the Beethoven sonatas in a time frame—to make the necessary psychic decision to compress time—forced out certain extraneous things, and gave him, if you will, more power. I contend that with this power came a moment that transformed his career, and that moment was the Sunday afternoon of his first Beethoven recital in New York. The review came out, and suddenly, as if people understood that something important had happened, his management started to get calls from all over the country."

I asked Goode what effect the year's dedication to Beethoven had had on him.

"When you're immersed in Beethoven, you feel that he's right in the center, and everything else is radiating out from him," he said. "There's an enormous sense of room in him. He gives strength to people, because of the hugeness of his heart and his will, his refusal to give way. There's a redemptive force in his music. Its strong shaping power focussed my energies in a way that I hadn't known before. If a composer is great enough, he forces the interpreter in a certain direction. Beethoven forces you in a direction where the parts can't take over the whole. He was fanatically occupied with coherence of design. Like a Roman architect, he made the structures profoundly right; his works are less destructible than those of other composers. If you build a Roman wall, the individual bricks, strong as they are, might not be so important in themselves. Beethoven avoids details that can be diverting—the kind of fantastic, purple detail that one finds so often in Schubert. The spirit is so monumental, the structures are so austere, that I sometimes felt a bit of a sensuous deprivation, and wished there were a little flower growing nearby."

During the series, Goode performed many of the sonatas for the first time, including the "Waldstein" and the "Appassionata." "A benefit of playing so much chamber music was that certain staples of the solo repertoire remained fresh to me," he said. "I had to learn many of the early sonatas. In each of them, Beethoven explored new territory. There's a daring unpredictability in the inspiration. Beethoven's dynamics are often confrontational. He rarely allows his lyric quality, compelling as it is, to go unchallenged for long. He'll often interrupt with a brusque statement, as if to place the surrounding serenity in greater relief. One shouldn't soften those corners. The boldness of these works is most apparent in halls small enough for the powerful passages to sound loud, and not recede into a framework. The *essence* of this music is the bursting out of a framework."

I recalled his May, 1989, Beethoven recital in London's Wigmore Hall, which seats only five hundred and forty. The hall had rocked with the energy of the music, and the response of the audience was a roar, an explosion. "I gather that it was pretty powerful for Wigmore Hall," Goode said, smiling sheepishly. "It may not altogether have been to the English taste."

Sibelius once said that "every note must be experienced." The words are simple; the application—whether by composer or performer—is difficult. In master classes that Goode gave at the University of British Columbia in Vancouver in January of 1991, he was constantly asking questions: "Why do you think Beethoven has marked a sforzando here?" "Where is this chord going to lead?" "What sort of mood do these notes imply?" A student began Beethoven's Sonata Opus 22 with physical bravura, but the music itself lacked character. Goode said, "You have energy in your playing, but not enough comic spirit. It's a question of rhythm—the sort of thing that can't be written down." He then played the passage himself, gathering together the six notes of the opening motif into a more concise group and creating a sense of expectancy during the short rest that precedes the next group. The change was almost imperceptible, but a new rhythmic poise was present. One suddenly understood the idea behind the notes and, hence, behind the movement. Mantegna's Roman soldiers came into focus: they were standing by their wall and were in high spirits.

Goode's way of evoking the mood of each piece, of speaking softly—almost hypnotically, and often forgetful of his auditors—and of finding simple, creative analogies helped free the musculature and the imagination of the young players, even during the short period of time available for the lessons. "Don't think of the fingers at all, but of the movement of the hand and forearm as they take you over two measures," he suggested while teaching one of Schumann's Davids-bündler Dances. "It's a spring song—something gossamer, softly textured, not precisely focussed. Feel the sound as relaxed and serene from within. Imagine the legato line as if it's on a long violin bow, and translate that into whatever gesture will make for the greatest smoothness of flow. The piano will dictate to you unless you tame it. In other words, you create the motion first—a motion that mirrors the musical idea. Then the notes follow."

"Finger playing per se is anathema to me," Goode explained to me later, as we trudged through the snow blanketing the campus. "Some pianists' fingers seem almost to be separated from their bodies. The gestural quality gives me the sense of proportion in shaping a phrase, and provides an expressive basis for the whole technique. For me, the actual playing has to come from a somewhat larger gesture than is strictly necessary, because when you aim precisely at the mark you get something smaller and more inflexible than you want."

"He possesses all different touches imaginable," Mme. Auguste Boissier wrote of Liszt, in 1832. "His hands are so limber and pliable that they maintain no definite fixed position. They contact the keys in all manners and forms." Goode follows in a worthy tradition. In the Allegro finale of Beethoven's Sonata Opus 26, his hands will glide almost weightlessly over the keys; in the D-minor Largo of Beethoven's Sonata Opus 10, No. 3, they will seem weighted down, as if, he says, "subject to the gravity of Jupiter." In the fugue of the "Hammerklavier," they stab the keys, dragger-like, from above. As Goode explores the immense range of Beethoven's creativity, no two walls are similar, no brick remains unexperienced.

After a concert in Houston in 1987, a member of the audience came up to him and exclaimed, "Mr. Goode, you *are* Beethoven!"

Goode leaned forward, cupped his hand to his ear, and asked, "What did you say?"

San Francisco was hazy in the winter sunlight as the Goodes and I were driven across the Bay Bridge by the conductor Robert Cole, who is the director of Berkeley's Cal Performances series. It was 11

A.M. on Thursday. Schubert's heavenly lengths had extended beyond the A-Major Sonata's conclusion the previous night: Cole was talking about the melody of the finale, and for Marcia it had replaced the Benedictus from Beethoven's Missa Solemnis. Richard, however, said that he was already thinking in C minor and B-flat major, the keys of the Schubert sonatas for his Berkeley concert.

We arrived at the campus at eleven-thirty and went directly to Hertz Hall, because it would be free that day only until noon, and Goode wanted to choose between two pianos that were available for the concert. One was distinctly brighter in tone; he chose the other, which he called "warmer and gentler." Cole took us on to Zellerbach Hall, where, two flights down, in a storage room at the farthest extremity of the basement, in which many pianos were crammed together, Goode could practice in peace for the next five or six hours. He appeared content to be so safely sequestered.

"When I met Richard, I didn't know much about careers," Marcia told me later, over lunch. "I assumed he was doing just what he wanted to do. It was only gradually that I became aware of his desire to do more and yet his fear of it. His ambivalence was like a seesaw. I jumped on one end of the seesaw, and became an advocate for the part of his personality that wanted him to express himself fully. I thought, He can always reject a solo career if he wants to, but why not see what it's like to have the opportunity?"

Marcia's appearance is striking. She is slender and somewhat shorter than Richard, with long, straight dark-brown hair, an almond-shaped face, and a classical Roman nose. If Goode is something of a Rembrandt self-portrait, she is a Duccio Madonna—but a Madonna with a sense of humor. Born Marcia Weinfeld, she was raised in Buffalo, went to Smith College, and, in 1973, took a master's degree at Yale in music performance. She and Richard became acquainted in February of 1983, in Ottawa, when, as a violinist in the National Arts Centre Orchestra, she participated in a chamber-music concert in which he also performed. "At the first rehearsal, Richard came into the hall and greeted us," she told me. "There was something about his voice and his presence—this sounds corny, but I just fell in love with him, even before he began to play. I didn't know how to flirt with him. I saw that he had come with a plastic bag full of books, so the next day I brought with me something I'd been reading by Elias Canetti. After the rehearsals, we would go with the other musicians for a bite to eat. As the week went on, the number of people going out together dwindled, until Richard and I found ourselves alone. He flew up to visit me several times during the next few months. In August, I sold everything and put myself on a plane for New York. I had never met anybody connected with Richard, nor had I ever seen where he lived. I loved him—what more did I need to know? He tells me that he made a huge effort to clean up his apartment for me but that my face fell when I saw the kitchen. That was immaterial. Richard was there, and all this richness surrounding him. I still haven't explored all the books and records. I still don't know quite what's going on there."

The consensus among Goode's friends had been that he would probably never get married. His relationships with women usually ran in seven-year cycles. (No matter how dishevelled Goode became, he was always successful in attracting women.) And Goode—who was not known for being decisive, or for allowing himself to be imprisoned by the traditional forms of things—remained irresolute. One of his previous girlfriends had given him an ultimatum, with the result that he backed out of the relationship. "I found that instructive," Marcia said. "I wasn't going to make the same mistake. It was already a huge commitment for him when we decided to live together. He had never before invited anyone to share his apartment. I wasn't worried about marriage; I was sure that things would work out." (Later, when I raised the subject with Goode, he said, "Even though I knew I had met the right person in Marcia, marriage was very hard for me to accept. But resistance has its own law: you can hold on just so long. Among other things, marriage was a great relief to me—the relief of throwing off the burden of resisting it.") "Richard didn't want a big wedding," Marcia said. "The production aspect of it would have been almost as frightening as the marriage itself." On April 10, 1987, they embarked on two adventures: a first-time ferry ride to Staten Island, and marriage in its pleasant borough hall.

After lunch, I took a stroll and happened to look into the University Press bookstore. There was Goode, in his overcoat and woollen cap, quietly absorbed, as he always is while he scans bookshelves. I was surprised to see him, yet his presence seemed inevitable. He looked at me rather guiltily and said that he had only come out for a cup of coffee but hadn't been able to resist the bookstore when he passed it on his way. Armed with *The Yale Review,* a book for Marcia about the Missa Solemnis, and a double espresso, he returned to his practicing.

That evening, a friend of the Goodes joined us for dinner at the Chez Panisse Café. Richard ordered a bottle of Lamborn Zinfandel, and sampled something from each of our plates. Presently, he began talking about one of the more arcane of his wide-ranging interests. "Swamps fascinate me," he said, and a glint came into his eyes. "I guess the personal parallel isn't hard to find. For some reason, whenever I propose a tour of the swamps of New Jersey, Marcia always has something else to do. But don't laugh. Swamps happen to have the highest concentration of life—plant, animal, amphibian—of any environment on the planet."

I asked if he had ever visited a swamp.

"No—actually, I haven't," Goode said. "I just think about them. After all, I married a woman named Marcia. There must be something in that."

He changed the subject to Schubert and the voice: "If we come down to it, people love to play Schubert because they love to sing. One associates Schubert with the lied, and Chopin with Italian bel canto. It's terribly important to imagine ideal vocal shape, and not to fall into the habit of equalizing things that aren't meant to be equal. When I was ten, I was tremendously taken with recordings of Cantor Rosenblatt. In fact, at Curtis they said that when I sang solfège exercises I sounded like a cantor."

"So that's why you sing when you play," his friend said.

Goode seemed less than pleased at this and fell speechless for a long moment.

"At least you play when you sing," I ventured, and he exploded with laughter.

On Friday morning, during breakfast, Goode received a call from his agent in London, who was pressing him to agree to perform all the Beethoven sonatas there and in several other European cities. Goode would not commit himself. "A legacy of my chamber-music career is that I haven't yet caught up with the solo repertoire," he told me. "There are still so many works I'd like to play; I need time to learn them."

At the hall, later that morning, Goode checked the lighting and the positioning of the piano. The concert was sold out, and stage seats were being set up. Marcia asked that they be arranged so that nobody would be in Richard's line of vision. The day would be consecrated to Schubert: the Sonata in C Minor, which Goode had characterized as "intensely dramatic," and the one in B-flat, "a lyrical transformation."

On July 3, 1822, the twenty-five-year-old Schubert had a dream so impressive that he took the unusual step of writing down his recollection of it. It is a unique document:

> I was deeply and lovingly devoted to [my family]. Once my father took us to a feast . . . and bade me enjoy the delicious dishes. But I could not, whereupon he became angry, and banished me from his sight. . . . I wandered into far-off regions, my heart filled with infinite love. . . . The news of my mother's death reached me. . . . We followed her body in sorrow. . . . Then my father once more took me to his favorite garden. . . . Did the garden please me? I denied it, trembling. At that, my father struck me, and I fled. . . . I again wandered far away. For many years I sang songs. Whenever I attempted to sing of love, it turned to pain. And again, when I tried to sing of pain, it turned to love.
>
> Thus were love and pain divided in me.
>
> And one day I had news of a gentle maiden who had just died. And a circle formed around her grave in which many youths and old men moved as though in everlasting bliss. . . . Heavenly thoughts seemed forever to be showered on the youths from the maiden's gravestone, like fine sparks, producing a gentle rustling. . . . I went to the gravestone with slow steps and lowered gaze, filled with devotion and firm belief, and before I was aware of it, I found myself in the circle, which uttered a wondrously lovely sound; and I felt as though eternal bliss were gathered together into a single moment. My father too I saw, reconciled and loving.

I have quoted the essential narrative of the dream not to suggest that any Schubert composition adheres to it programmatically, or to set forth any psychological hypothesis, but because, more than any source I know, it expresses in words the kind of journey on which Schubert takes us in his last sonatas.

That evening, as I walked in the darkness with Goode across the university campus toward Hertz Hall, he stumbled and almost fell. Obviously disconcerted, a moment later he dropped his bag of music and books on the ground. "When I'm on tour, I'm forced to hold myself together in a certain delicate equilibrium," he had said to me that morning. "It's when the tour ends and I return to normal life that I realize how enormous the tension has been." We arrived at the hall without further incident, and I left him to carry out his pre-concert rituals.

The C-Minor Sonata begins with a forceful, Beethoven-like gesture—Goode seized on it impetuously—but then the music sets out in directions quite unlike Beethoven: slithery pianissimo chromatic scales, which Goode has likened to "a fast ride in a sled on a chilly wintry night, with some sort of fearful pursuit"; an agitated, unsettlingly fragmented Menuetto; a finale in the relentless rhythm of the tarantella, sister movement to the finale of the "Death and the Maiden" Quartet. Sinister forces invade even the requiem-like slow movement. Goode's performance plumbed a dark disquietude that often rose to a pitch of harrowing confrontation.

After the intermission and Debussy's preludes came Schubert's last sonata, the one in B-flat major. Goode had told me of Karl Ulrich Schnabel's description of its opening theme: "There are some melodies that float, and some that are on the earth. This one is perfectly poised between the two." The liedlike melody, which Goode set forth as though it had no bar lines, is interrupted by long pianissimo trills deep in the bass, which are followed by enigmatic rests. These trills are not mere ornaments; they are more like the murmurs of lurking furies. Goode led us unerringly through this strange dialogue of light, shadow, and silence. Because the movement is unusually long, pianists rarely make the optional repeat of its opening section. But Goode did, and it was a choice determined less by musicology than by high drama. There is an extraordinary transition passage—it remains unplayed if the repeat is not observed—in which, for the only time in the movement, the trill is declaimed fortissimo. Goode brought this transition to an abrupt, alarming climax and then let loose the furies in all their terrible grandeur. The silence that followed seemed a colossus astride an infinity. When the lied melody returned, it seemed even more consoling than before, and the whispered trills more ominous. With the repeat, the spatial dimensions became almost those of a Bruckner symphony, but we had become wanderers with Schubert and gladly travelled the terrain again. Goode held the architecture together by means of a subtle rhythmic flexibility that flowed with the dramatic gradients. The sense of organic growth reminded me not so much of any other pianist as of the conductor Wilhelm Furtwängler.

The slow movement was a rite of passage, sublime and mysterious. The Scherzo was angelic and childlike; the finale, hovering between minor and major, juxtaposed menace and radiant song. When the journey had come to an end, Goode received a standing ovation. But, more than ever, he was not there. The audience, knowingly or not, was applauding not the unassuming, bearlike pianist but the bespectacled man of five feet two inches who on November 19, 1828, in his thirty-second year, seven weeks after completing this last instrumental essay on the division of love and pain, turned to the wall and said, "Here, here is my end."

In its days of grandeur, the building in which the Goodes live was the home of Mary Pickford. Much of the ornate molding from 1910 still exists, but the floors have long since been divided into apartments; the Goodes live in two rooms and an eat-in kitchen. It takes a certain determination for two musicians to function successfully in such a relatively small space. "I practice in the bedroom, and often we practice simultaneously," Marcia told me recently, when I visited them there.

"This took some getting used to," Goode said, and he added, "What we really need is a two-bedroom apartment over a fantastic restaurant where the owner knows us, loves us, and feeds us for the price of a recital or two a year."

Goode gave me a tour of his books. Most (aside from seven trunkloads in the building's basement) are not only shelved but categorized. "Since my marriage, the book collecting has become both more virulent and more ordered," he said. An L-shaped entrance hallway is lined with bookcases devoted to fiction (double shelved), essays, biography, theatre, cinema, travel, science, and history. Moving into the living room—or what could more aptly be called the piano room—one finds poetry, music, and art. In the bedroom there's a shelf for literary criticism, and most of the kitchen cabinets are filled with musical scores. Every horizontal surface, including the piano, is covered with a miscellany of music, books, and art works. "Richard is often attracted to some object but doesn't bother to think about where it might go," Marcia said. "He has wonderful taste in individual things but no concept of the total." Goode's favorite among his eclectic art collection is a nineteenth-century Japanese ceramic piece, which he bought twelve years ago. It's a brooding monk about seven inches high, cradling one knee, with a somewhat simian aspect and fashioned with precision and delicacy. "Nobody else seems to like him," Goode said. "He's half human, half animal. Perhaps he's a mythological figure. He's eloquent, in a way; he has a look of remorse—of sorrow for what might have been."

These days, Goode plays recitals in the major halls of the world, but he still prefers a church in Litchfield, Connecticut, to Carnegie Hall any time. In reference to his forthcoming tours, his first thought is not of concert halls but of bookstores: Powell's, in Portland; the Tattered Cover, in Denver; Blackwell's, in Oxford. "Do you want to know what the high point of my career was?" he asked, the glint appearing. "It was in 1981, when I went to Rio de Janeiro for the first time. I was soloist with the Orpheus Chamber Orchestra. As soon as we got there, I came down with a fever and had to go to bed. When I awoke, it was evening. I felt groggy, but I thought I'd go out for a walk. I went through a dark alleyway and suddenly came upon a large, illuminated square. Magical lights were twinkling everywhere. It was a book fair. I thought I had died and gone to Heaven."

Although Goode seldom finds time for chamber music now, he takes special pleasure in giving recitals with the soprano Dawn Upshaw when their schedules permit. "The song texts—for instance, in Schubert and Wolf—give a whole world of imagery that's reflected in the piano parts," he told me. "The challenge is to create the largest range of feelings in three or four minutes. I've always been attracted to concision, to density, to having every note charged with feeling. That's also the way I read lyric poetry. The most fulfilling thing you can do is to create these different worlds of expression. After all, we pianists need all the help we can get, the piano being a miraculously limited instrument—limited in such fundamental ways that it stimulates the imagination no end."

I asked Goode what advice he would give a young musician. He thought for a moment or two, and replied, "I don't know how helpful it may be, but I'll give the only answer I can: Pay attention to your deepest response to music, get as close to it as possible. I don't think there is an external path to something like that. Your strength as a performer comes from where your need is—from saying the things in music you really have to say. Audiences will respond to that—they hear the accent of honest feeling."

Goode is an aficionado of old recordings, and they are amassed in his piano room. If he still venerates the masters of the past, he has come to realize over the years that he has something to say in his own right.

"I've felt it best to get back to my basic instincts about music-making, about how to get the piano to sing like a human voice," he told me. "This really started happening about ten years ago. I've found that I can go out onstage and speak through the instrument in a very direct and simple way. When that happens, giving concerts is wonderful, and I feel that this is really what I should be doing. But at other times—even now, when, as they say, my career has been taking off—the stagefright comes to me as strongly as ever. Often, it's a horizon of darkness, tension, and anxiety. But you have to try to let the music express itself even when you don't feel up to it. As Serkin said, 'It's no trick to play well when you're not nervous.'

"A few years ago, I dreamed that I was standing before a large bookcase. From a vast collection of books on music, I chose biographies of three composers—Berlioz, Mahler, and Sibelius. Actually, I love Sibelius, but I have very mixed feelings about Berlioz and Mahler. However, it's striking that all three of these composers have one thing in common: they never wrote anything significant for the piano. I've always fantasized that one day I'd quit playing in public. Every three weeks or so, I tell Marcia that there must be a better way to live. After all, why should we always be under the shadow of this experience? We could go to a small town and open a bookstore. But then I'd have to part with the books. I don't know if I could do that."

This interview, conducted in San Francisco, California, first appeared in *The New Yorker*, 29 June 1992.

CHAPTER FIVE

The Farm Girl and the Stones

On a fine morning in late June, a few days after the Midsummer celebrations, Birgit Nilsson, one of the greatest singers of the century, now in her seventy-fifth year, brought me to the church of her native parish of West Karup in Skåne, Sweden's southernmost province. Two hours earlier, we had set out by car from her home in Kristianstad, in northeastern Skåne near the Baltic, where I had spent several days with Nilsson and her husband. Now, on the final day of my visit, we had come to the Bjäre peninsula on the Atlantic coast where she was born and raised.

Since the twelfth century there has been a church on this site, set among peaceful fields, not far from the sea. Part of the original walls are still standing. The present building, dating largely from the eighteenth century and painted white, closely resembles a New England village church, except that it is built of stone and lacks a spire over its bell tower. As we entered the churchyard, Nilsson told me that many of her ancestors had been laid to rest here, beginning with her great-grandfather born in 1805. "I want to put some water on my parents' grave," she said. She fetched the watering-can that hung together with gardening tools near the gate, filled it, and freshened the flowers on the gravesite of Nils and Justina Svensson. Above her father's name the word *Lantbrukare* (land-cultivator) is inscribed. "He was the sixth generation of farmers," Nilsson told me. "I felt I should leave more than just the name. Otherwise, after thirty or forty years no one will remember what a person did." Lines from an old hymn are engraved on the stone; she translated them to me: "One generation follows another; the pilgrims' song is never silenced in heaven."

Birgit Nilsson and David Blum. Photograph by Sarah Blum, West Karup, Sweden, June 1995.

She sang the opening phrase softly, almost to herself, cherishing the simple melodic line.

We entered the church. The interior, like many in rural Scandinavia, is both sober and elegant. The original eighteenth-century colors have been restored: a serene white and grayish blue. In keeping with the proximity of the ocean, a finely crafted model of a three-masted schooner is suspended from the ceiling. "I joined the choir here when I was fifteen," Nilsson said. "In the country it was the only thing one could do with one's voice. I sang a solo at our pastor's wedding; I remember how nervous I was." Two artisans, who were retouching the gilding above the altar, called down to Nilsson from their scaffolding and assured her that their work would be finished in time for the concert due to take place some days later. Nilsson has presented concerts in the church since 1955 to insure the upkeep of the local Heritage Society Museum. Since her retirement nine years ago, she has invited gifted young singers to perform in her stead. She had told me that she now never sings in public. "It's true—I don't sing," she reaffirmed, when I gently pressed her on the point. "But last year, when Gösta Winbergh—a fine tenor—had finished his recital here, he began the duet from 'Tosca.' Well, I was standing there with nothing to do—so I *had* to sing."

Birgit Nilsson's life began in Skåne, and it will end there. In a sense, it never left there. Many who heard her sing at the Metropolitan Opera, La Scala, Bayreuth, the Vienna State Opera, Covent Garden—to mention only a few of her homes away from home—might be surprised to learn that the daughter of Nils Svensson worked on the farm until she was twenty-three and first set foot on the opera stage when she was twenty-eight. Such beginnings might seem inauspicious, if not defeating. Yet Nilsson's origins are as inseparable from her art as stones are from the north Skåne landscape.

Throughout the morning's trip, stones had been very much in evidence: in the fences built of rocks that the farmers have gathered up from the earth; in the windward walls of old farmhouses. Other stones—huge ones, and less malleable—are strewn over the fields as if rained down by a giant. Some are haphazardly patterned—orphans of the ice age, lying where they were abandoned by melting glaciers; others were painstakingly patterned into circles or outlines of ships by men of the bronze or iron age who wished to consecrate places of burial or of judgment.

We left the church and returned to the car. Our next destination was the farm on which Nilsson had lived until she was twenty-three; she and her husband presently use it as a second home. As we drove off again, the fields shown green. They were planted with wheat, corn, potatoes, rye, or sugar beet. (Skåne is the granary of Sweden.) "We grow two kinds of beets here," Nilsson explained. "Both are yellow: one is for sugar, the other for the cows to eat. I harvested the beets for the cows, and I picked potatoes. It wasn't easy; we did everything by hand. My father worked by the sun, not the clock. He was never a slave to time. Nowadays, we are looking at our watch, running and rushing—he couldn't care less."

Soon another color washed across the fields: the golden-hue of mustard flower. The sea became visible in the distance. There was still shopping to do for our lunch, and, at the crest of a hill, we stopped at a farmhouse that has been transformed into a market. It was painted in *falüröd*, a deep red made from iron oxide mined in central Sweden. (Whole villages are painted in this striking color.) Nilsson made a careful selection from an array of fresh produce and deliberated at length with the fish vendor. We came away with mackerel that had been caught that morning, ingredients for a salad, and a spiral-like cake more than two-feet high called *spettkaka*, a confection of eggs and sugar baked around a long thimble.

As we left, Nilsson said, "In this very place, the son of a rich farmer once proposed to me. His main accomplishment was that he could ride a bull." Further down the road, she pointed from the car window to a large expanse of field where Holstein cows were grazing. "Here was that fantastic farm. My father hoped I would marry into the family, but I had another boyfriend: the church organist—he was my mother's choice. When I went out on a date I had to make my mother believe that I was seeing the organist and my father that I was seeing the farmer's son. I thought for a while that I might marry the organist, but it would never have worked out. He was very serious—quite the opposite of me. I am more or less outgoing." She added wistfully, "He never married."

Nilsson talked about things that happened more than a half century ago as if they had occurred yesterday. In all the time I had been with her, the reality of her age had failed to impinge itself upon me. Her vitality could, in fact, be daunting. When I had first met her in New York seven months before (she had come there for a gala concert given in her honor by the Manhattan School of Music), I was initially struck by her innate Swedish sense of propriety, her old-world courtesy, a reticence bordering on shyness. But another side of her personality was soon forthcoming: an immediacy in the expression of her feelings; a bracing candor verging on the slightly outrageous; an irrepressible wit, handled with rapier-like dexterity. That other side seemed Latin in temperament, and I now told her as much.

"Who knows?" she conjectured, as she looked out at the passing farmlands. "There may be some Latin blood in my family. Our peninsula was often visited by sailors. In this part of Sweden many people have dark hair—my whole family is dark. And people here have a very stately posture as they do in southern Europe where you'll often see women carrying pitchers of water on their heads." Her own bearing is as regal in everyday life as it was on the stage.

She was dressed in white slacks, a multi-colored print shirt, and open-toed red sandals; she wore a gold-link bracelet and a necklace from which hung a diamond-studded "B". Her face is wide and astonishingly unlined (it is virtually untouched by cosmetics). When she smiles, which is often, her eyes narrow considerably. Nilsson is the first to admit that her profile bears a striking resemblance to that of Richard Wagner. "Piercing eyes . . . sharply curved nose, a remarkably broad forehead, a projecting chin"—so reads a contemporary description of the composer. She claims that, as a Taurus, she has "the benefit of being built with a large chest and almost no neck—not bad for singing." She is barely five-foot six, but her personality is of a sort that fills big spaces.

Nilsson's accent in English has the flavor of Greta Garbo's. Her voice rings pure and clear and is produced from those regions of the head where her singing resonates. This was the voice that, when producing the high Cs in Puccini's "Turandot," carried so powerfully beyond the arena of Verona that passers-by thought the fire alarm had sounded. I told Nilsson that even the vibrations of her speaking voice are so penetrating that they can, over time, fatigue the ear. She laughed and said that once, when she was giving a concert in Skåne, her voice had cracked a church window, and, when she was singing in Teheran, it had split a turquoise earring. "I can tell you—it also caused problems for a lot of microphones," she went on. "I've had all the troubles in the world when recording. The producers would say, 'For a high note take three steps backward.' To tell the truth, I don't think any of my recordings capture my high notes as they were."

We now passed by the church of Hov. "The name means high or holy place," Nilsson commented. "The church was built where pagan rites were once held. There are several stone circles here where offerings were made to Odin. This is where I made my debut—when I was seven, in the school hall at a Christmas party. The workers had taught me a song about young lovers forced to meet in secret. My father adored it, because he recognized himself in it. When he courted my mother, he was so poor that her father opposed the marriage. A suitor from America had offered her a little sack of gold and had thrown it on the table—like in 'The Flying Dutchman'—but she refused him.

"My parents were quite different from each other. My mother was more the Latin one. She was lively and cheerful; she could get very angry, but the next minute forget why. Once my father got something into his head you could never convince him otherwise. Oh, was he stubborn! He had tremendous will-power, but he also had a sense of humor; it was his way of coping with life. My husband says that I inherited the characters of both of my parents—but they never unite."

Nilsson drew my attention to a simple white house on a nearby hill; it was the place where she had been born. "My father wanted a son so badly that he promised the midwife an extra fifty krone if I were a boy," she said. "In Sweden children are sometimes given their father's first name as their last name, and then '*son*' is added to it—not '*dotter*,' even if you are a daughter. So I became Nilsson. That was all the more convenient for my father. All his life he lamented that he didn't have a son who could take over the farm."

A moment later we were in an almost non-existent village called Svenstad, and drove into a large yard with a well in the middle. "Okay, here we are in one piece," she said.

Of the original eighteenth-century enclosed farmstead, three sides remain: a modest, two-story house that still serves as the living quarters, a harvest-shed that has been converted into a garage, and a cow-shed now used for storage. (The farm's fifty acres are rented out to be worked.) "When I was four or five, I began milking the cows," Nilsson told me. "It took me a while to figure out what side to sit on. I was often sent out here to fetch water. Sometimes I'd drop the bucket in the well, and there was hell to pay." She showed me several large hollowed-out stones that were set near the front gate. "These were prehistoric hand-mills," she said. "My father put them here. He was fascinated with things of the past."

Nilsson's husband Bertil Niklasson and their long-time house-keeper Karin had driven over from Kristianstad earlier in the morning to open up the house. They now came out to greet us. When I had first met Bertil four days earlier, his directness and simplicity of manner had immediately put me at ease. He is a large-framed man with a rough-hewn voice and a broad and open face. A sense of humor is evident in the kindly pale blue eyes behind his glasses. Although born into a Skåne farming family, he had hoped to become a doctor. Given the poor professional prospects in the early nineteen-forties, he opted for veterinarian work, and later became a prosperous businessman. Nilsson had told me of how they had first met, in 1945 on a train. Bertil had seen that she was studying music, and asked if it was difficult. "That depends," Nilsson replied. "If you can read music, it's not difficult." He was studying a textbook on veterinarian surgery and inquired if he might call her when he had finished reading it. Nilsson thought, Why not? and wrote her telephone number on the last page. She assumed that either he had forgotten her or he was a slow learner, because it took many months before he got around to making the call. They were married 10 September 1948 in the Swedish church in Copenhagen, with only the minister and a witness in attendance; Nilsson had wanted to avoid being fussed over by family and friends.

A close friend of the Niklassons calls the marriage "a genuine partnership of two strong personalities. They enjoy sparring with each other, but, behind it all, Bertil's quiet strength has always been a support for her. He's not the typical singer's husband; he doesn't constantly intervene in her career. Birgit hasn't much use for people she can't respect. She would never have asked him to stop his life and just follow her. He's too creative and energetic for that. Should she bring her diva-like qualities into the household, he knows when to draw the line. He treats her like an ordinary person, and she likes it."

Nilsson took me through the downstairs rooms of the farmhouse. Its interior has undergone only minor transformations since her childhood; the original low ceilings remain. The household decorations, homely and full of character, curiously intermingle life on the farmstead with that on the opera stage. Together with jars for distilled brandy from 1828, an antique clothes press, and the folk costume Nilsson wore on her sixteenth birthday, there is a bust of Verdi (a gift from the Teatro Regio in Parma), a painting of Nilsson as Agathe from "Der Freischütz" at the time of her Swedish debut, and a photo of her as Salome in 1972, holding a silver tray bearing the sculpted head of Rudolf Bing, then General Manager of the Metropolitan Opera.

The presence of Nils Svensson is strongly felt, whether in his collections—of porcelain, pewter, copper wear, oil lamps—or in his portrait that reveals a firmness of purpose worthy of the lineage of farmers who had, in the eighteen-twenties, bought their freedom from the nobility and established self-government in their parishes. An old embroidery, hanging in the kitchen, depicts a rustic domestic scene: a farmer plays the fiddle for his family gathered at the hearth. The inscription reads: *Hemma är bäst*. "My father was absolutely convinced that 'home is best,' " Nilsson said. "He visited Stockholm for the first time when he was over sixty. But then he loved it, and couldn't be kept away from the antique shops."

Nilsson excused herself: "I'm going to help Karin in the kitchen. I'm like my mother used to be. She would always say, 'Just wait; I can do it better myself.' "

Bertil poured me a drink of his own concoction, brewed from home-grown rhubarb and Elder flowers. I asked him if he had realized, when marrying Birgit, how far her career might take her.

"I don't know why, but, much earlier than others, I had the intuition that she would become a famous singer," he replied. "I was quite sure, and encouraged her to make an international career. Yet I was never tempted to become an impresario for her. Of course, we discussed things and I tried to help her from time to time—that's only normal. But Birgit is a woman who wants to protect herself; she is strong enough, and if you try to protect her too much she will not be happy. Later on, there was a danger when all those people were running around telling her how fantastic her singing was. Birgit was usually very self-critical, but once, for a short period, she didn't take the time to work properly with her voice. Normally, we don't talk much about that sort of thing, but I told her then that she must be careful—and she listened."

Nilsson, who had re-entered the room, said, "Bertil truly loves music. He gets deeply involved, to the point that he can hardly sit through a performance of 'Tosca'—it affects him so much. And he's learned a lot about the voice—perhaps too much. Some singers' husbands take away the bad critics and show them only the good ones. If my husband found the bad ones he'd be sure to give them to me."

Lunch consisted of two sorts of open sandwiches (Swedish caviar and paté with cucumbers); salad with vinaigrette; and the mackerel, poached, and accompanied by new potatoes garnished profusely with fresh dill. During my stay with the Niklassons, they had provided me with more hardy south-Swedish fare than any reasonable person could allow: *gravad lax*; lamb filet interlarded with garlic; yellow carrots; *äggakaka*—a Skåne speciality—a thick egg cake taken hot from the pan, sprinkled with sugar and chives and served with lingonberries and sausages.

The conversation turned to a favorite topic of the inhabitants of the region: the bureaucratic control exercised over their affairs by the central government in Stockholm. Many refer to their northern compatriots as "bloody 08s" (08 is the Stockholm area-code). The problems began in 1658 when Sweden wrested Skåne from Denmark. "We are still under occupation," Bertil said. "But we have kept our Danish character—a more open character." He began to sing a popular local folk song that translates roughly, "They speak much of our dung and muck, but think how useful our dirt has been." Birgit joined in, and then said, "We have our own dialect down here; our vowels are broader." She demonstrated the difference: the Stockholm dialect was quicker and more sing-song; she slightly parodied it, enjoying herself. "I can change when I'm in Stockholm," she said. "But Bertil can't."

"Birgit considers herself Swedish," Bertil rejoined. "She's been given the highest medal by the King. But in a hundred years Skåne will be Danish again."

"Unfortunately, you won't be around to see it."

"Everything here in Skåne is Danish—except Birgit Nilsson. But even she is imported. Her eyes are green-brown; not only the eyes but also the mind is imported."

Karin brought forth the *spettkaka*. Nilsson retired to the kitchen and emerged with a knife at least twenty inches long. I suddenly imagined her as I had last seen her on the opera stage, and told her that I thought Elektra had come into the room. She brandished the knife and sang with full voice Strauss's mighty invocation: A-GA-MEM-NON!

I remembered her singing that phrase one evening twenty years before at La Scala. The power she had unleashed came not only from the gleaming radiance of her voice, but from her unassailable presence: her will to fuse with the mighty spirit of the dead king. Nilsson had used her innate sense of irony with terrifying effect to lure Klytemnestra—her mother, the murderess of Agamemnon—off guard, before springing at her out of the darkness to deliver her curse. In the Recognition Scene—in which Elektra discovers a mysterious stranger to be her brother Orestes whom she had thought dead—her voice took on a warmer, more tender radiance. It soared over the orchestra as though its resources were limitless. "When you thought that a high note couldn't be sung better, she'd sing the next one equally gloriously," Sir Georg Solti had told me recently at his home in London. "Her singing had boundless energy—musicality, security. She was a marvel of vocal distinction. There will not be a better Elektra in the coming fifty years."

"I had waited a long time to sing Elektra," Nilsson said as she now cut into the cake. "When I finally got the chance, in 1965, I was worried that it would be a voice killer. I had heard an Elektra over the radio—she was shouting and screaming all the time. But when I opened the score, I found that there are so many places, especially after Klytemnestra leaves, where Elektra can sing softly and lyrically—that is, if the conductor doesn't overwhelm you with his hundred players."

One of the characteristics of Nilsson's vocal art—manifest in "Elektra"—was her way of attacking a high note with instantaneous tonal impact and absolute precision of pitch. I commented that many singers will reach for such a note from underneath. "One shouldn't reach for it, but stand over it," she said. Without any forewarning, while handing me my plate, she sang a high C that began as cleanly as though cut by a diamond. Even Bertil was startled. In the opera, Elektra has hidden away an axe. I told Nilsson that I suspected that she had one stashed away somewhere.

As it turned out, there were axes galore in the house, dating from even before Elektra's time. After lunch, the Niklassons took me upstairs and showed me a glass case in which nearly two hundred Stone-age artifacts had been carefully laid out. "One day my father discovered an ancient axe-head on the farm," Nilsson said. "From then on he became obsessed. If he heard that somebody had found a prehistoric relic, he'd go on his bicycle half a day to try to buy it." Bertil added, "He was most proud of having the Ring of Judgment on his land—a circle of stones from before the Vikings. It's on a hill overlooking the farm; we'll go up later to see it. It was the first thing he showed his visitors. Then he showed them his daughter. She was a little younger."

No place in the house holds more memories for Nilsson than the tiny second-floor bedroom tucked under the eaves, where she now led me. "It was cozy up here, but it was rather cold," she said as we stood together at the half-moon window through which she used to look out at the world. "We had to warm the bed with a heated brick. I'd watch the snow falling. The storms were tremendous; and the wind—we're almost living in the Atlantic! I'd watch the elegant cars going along the road in the distance and wonder if I would ever have one. I'd look out at the fields—it was said that elves would gather lost tools there and return them to their owners. Our neighbor—a fine woman—swore that she had seen a hay wagon drawn by two mice. People made fun of her, but I thought it was *wonderful*. Bertil will always offer a rational explanation. I tell him that I don't want to hear it. There's a saying: You don't need to be crazy to become a singer—but it helps."

Much can be imagined through a half-moon window. Over the past few days, Nilsson had been telling me the improbable story of how a farm girl had, in fact, become a singer.

"I'm sure I inherited my voice from my mother," Nilsson had said. "Hers was exceptionally high and clear. She had even hoped to study music, but, at eighteen, she lost her mother and had to stay home to care for her father and two brothers. She was constantly singing in our household. When she was in her sixties, and I couldn't get the high C very well, she said, 'Oh, that's no problem'—and showed me how easy it was."

Birgit sang before she could walk, sang for guests throughout her childhood, and sometimes sang in her sleep. One day when she was four, Nils Svensson came home with a second-hand harmonium on top of his horse-drawn wagon. Nilsson remembers, "I threw myself down on the sofa with my eyes closed and asked, Is it true? Can it be true? I was quite a lonely child. For years afterwards, I'd go to my harmonium, pick out melodies that I could sing to, and dream away for hours and hours."

Birgit taught herself to read music, and was surprised when a school teacher told her that her perfect pitch was an uncommon gift. Although Nils Svensson was not musical, he enjoyed his daughter's singing, and, when she was fifteen, borrowed money from the bank to buy her a piano—an Ekström upright that still stands in the parlor. "He didn't dare tell my mother about the loan," Nilsson says. "She never wanted us to have any debts. When she found out, years later, she was furious.

"I began to dream of becoming a singer—and how! I hoped I might become a soloist in churches, but I wasn't sure if I had the ability. When I was seventeen, I applied for a place in an excellent choir in the nearby town of Båstad, directed by Ragnar Blennow, a well-known concert singer. I was told that there was no opening, especially as I was from another parish. I kept my fingers crossed. All of a sudden, I got a call that a singer had fallen ill, and I could audition for Mr. Blennow. I had been listening to singers with big, shaky vibratos, and I assumed that this was the way one should sing. But my voice was very steady, and whenever I tried to vibrate like the others, I didn't succeed very well. In any case, I took courage and sang for him. It was the first time I had sung for a professional musician. When I finished, he told me, 'Miss Nilsson, you are going to become a very great singer.' That day changed my life."

Blennow began to cultivate Nilsson's voice. "He didn't know if I was a mezzo or a soprano," Nilsson recalls. "My voice had a darker color then, and my high notes didn't come naturally; they were rather hard and edgy. I always hoped that he would praise me again as he had on that first day—but he never did."

After a few weeks, Blennow fell seriously ill. Five years would elapse before Nilsson had another voice lesson. "I became despondent about my singing," she said. "I didn't dare think of going on my own to Stockholm to study music. It was far, far away; no member of my family had ever been there. It's hard now to say what I did during all those years. I went for a while to a school for domestic crafts. I worked on the farm, sang here and there, and took over many of my mother's chores. I remember that on my twentieth birthday I was almost out of my mind because I didn't know what to do with my life. I began to think of becoming a school teacher. But my mother had faith that one day I'd become a singer."

When Nilsson was twenty-two, Blennow was able to hear her again. He asked her, "How long are you going to be uncertain about yourself? I'm sure you have possibilities." He offered to recommend her to the Royal Academy of Music in Stockholm and promised her regular lessons for six months to prepare her for the audition. "I owe him everything," Nilsson says. "I've never forgotten him—never in my life."

Blennow's offer precipitated a crisis in the Svensson household. Nilsson's father opposed the plan and refused to support it in any way. "He could not help being possessive," she told me. "I was an only child, and that is always difficult. He was proud of my singing so long as I stayed in the surroundings where he could go and hear me. He also doubted that I would succeed in the audition, because there were only two places free for forty-eight applicants. He told my mother, 'If she goes to Stockholm, God knows what might happen to her.' My mother was caught between the two of us, and suffered greatly on my account. She had inherited a sum of money from her aunt, and she gave it to me—enough to support me for a year. The night before my departure, our farmhands were gone, so I had to milk all the cows. The next morning my father wouldn't leave his room— he was crying—and didn't see me off. I was very hurt, but I remember thinking, as I rode on the bus to the railway station, that a new life was beginning: If it's good or bad, I'll not return home. I'll stay in Stockholm and study singing."

The twenty-three-year old Birgit Nilsson arrived in Stockholm on a hot, late-summer afternoon, carrying three suitcases (one with a broken handle), holding her winter coat, and wearing her large felt hat. She took lodging with the only people she knew in the city, a kindly professor and his wife to whom Nils Svensson had offered shelter when they were caught in a rainstorm while cycling through Skåne.

At the audition, Nilsson sang "Black Roses" by Sibelius and Elisabeth's Prayer from "Tannhäuser." "While we waited for the results, some of the other candidates talked about how they had studied in Paris or Berlin," she remembers. "I thought I didn't have a chance. When the list of winners was posted, I was astonished to see my name. The letters danced before my eyes."

That very day, however, she received a forewarning of things to come. A stage director from the Royal Swedish Opera, who had attended the audition, stopped her in the street, told her that her singing had moved him—an old theatre fox—to tears, and advised her against studying voice with any of the teachers at the Academy. But Nilsson had no choice; she needed the comprehensive music and language courses the Academy offered and couldn't afford to study privately.

She has not forgotten her first lesson with the Scottish tenor Joseph Hislop with whom she was to work for three years: "When he heard about my background, he exclaimed, 'The daughter of a common farmer! Have you graduated from high school?' I said that I hadn't. He asked me, 'If you put Kreisler's violin in the hands of the café musician, do you think the instrument will sound the same?' 'No, of course not,' I replied. He went on, 'Well then, even if you have the best voice in the world but have nothing here (he tapped his forehead) it will come to nothing. Believe me, it's not for farmers to become singers.' I ran out, crying. Later I learned that he himself had come from a poor family. Perhaps I reminded him of his own past. Eventually he began to work with me enthusiastically—but that was just the problem, because, although he had once had a fine voice, he had no idea how to teach.

"I had been singing in a natural, unconstricted way. My voice was rich in overtones; it was big and wild with lots of hoo-hoo in it. When I'd begin to sing, Hislop would remark, 'Now we hear the boat leaving.' He rightly wanted me to get a more focussed tone—'Like a violin,' he'd say; he played the instrument himself. But in order to achieve this he had me sing directly on the vocal cords. In time, I lost my overtones completely and even began to sing flat. I thought it was my fault for not understanding, and worked all the harder. Sometimes he forced the voice so much that I bled from my throat.

"When I went home during the summer to help out on the farm, I sang again for Blennow. 'It's no good,' he said. 'But you learned so much from me that I think you'll survive.' I did—but I had to work at least ten years to get rid of the vocal tension."

With the aid of a scholarship, Nilsson completed two more years at the Academy, meanwhile earning her keep by singing at weddings and funerals, and working as an extra on a film set. When she was twenty-six, she began a two-year course at the Royal Opera School. The saga of her voice studies continued. "I tried another professor who held down my Adam's apple while I sang in the high register," she told me. "I could hardly swallow for two weeks afterwards. Finally I turned to a teacher named Arne Sunnegård. He didn't try to put everything on my vocal cords. I got back my hooting sound. But he wanted me to sing very loudly and to darken my vowels. I had to sing one high C after another for twenty minutes. He also insisted that I make frequent use of the chest voice in the low register—and I was absolutely against this. I felt that one should take the quality of the upper voice downward as far as possible, perhaps mix it with a little chest voice, but avoid any break between registers. After every lesson I was hoarse. One day I tried to talk to him about my problems—that's the first thing you should do when working with a voice teacher. He slammed down the piano lid and declared that he had been teaching all over the world and knew what he was talking about. I told him, 'I agree that there's nothing to discuss,' said goodbye, and never went back.

"I was afraid to put myself in anyone else's hands. So I finally came to a decision. I realized that I had to look for my own way of singing—that it was up to me, and me alone, to succeed or fail—and that made me strong."

When tenacity and intuition enter into play, it's not unusual for chance to throw a card. In October 1946, a leading soprano at the Swedish Royal Opera fell ill, and Nilsson was asked, on three days' notice, to take over the role of Agathe in Weber's "Der Freischütz." "Aside from the main aria, I didn't know the part at all," she told me. "I studied it frantically. The conductor, Leo Blech, was a German of the old school who probably thought that everyone imbibed 'Der Freischütz' with their mother's milk. When I made a few mistakes at the piano rehearsal, he threw a fit and told me that I was completely unmusical. I cried so hard that I had to borrow a handkerchief from the stage director."

Nilsson was then living in an inexpensive apartment in Stockholm's old town. She remembers walking to the opera house on the night of her debut: "I paused on the bridge. I was very depressed, and thought, I've tried my best—I've struggled for all of these years—and it's led to nothing but disaster. The future looked hopeless; I stared into the water and thought about jumping in. Somehow—I don't know how—I found myself on stage. My knees were shaking so hard that I had to cover them with the cloth Agathe is supposed to be embroidering. I managed to do everything well, except for one passage in the aria where the violins are syncopated; I entered early. Blech jumped up while conducting as if he would murder me—oh, I can still feel it. Afterwards, when he came backstage, I hid from him."

The reviews were favorable, citing as Nilsson's one difficulty the production of a finely spun pianissimo. But Blech expressed his dissatisfaction, and Nilsson wasn't assigned any more roles.

An entire year passed. Then once again Nilsson was called upon to substitute for an ailing colleague. The opera was Verdi's "Macbeth," and the conductor was the eminent Fritz Busch. "Busch's presence made all the difference," Nilsson said. "He had faith in me. When he conducted, so calmly in control, you felt that nothing could go wrong. The last phrase in the sleepwalking scene goes up to a D-flat in piano. Busch assumed that the note was too difficult for me, and arranged for someone to sing the phrase in my stead from the wings as I went off stage—a clever trick. But at the rehearsal, the singer cracked. So I told Busch, 'If she cracks, I'll get the blame,' and convinced him to let me sing it myself. Lady Macbeth demands virtually three different voices: dramatic soprano, mezzo, and coloratura. It was an exciting challenge. We had ten performances, and suddenly I loved being on the opera stage.

"I was beginning to realize that the stage is the best voice teacher of all—to feel how much you can give and how the voice projects. One learns too from good coaches and conductors. They listen in a better way than most voice teachers because they are concerned with the shape of the phrase. When you think of the musical line, the voice travels there more easily."

At Busch's invitation, Nilsson sang her first engagement abroad—at Glyndebourne in the summer of 1951, where she portrayed Elettra in Mozart's "Idomeneo." While in England, she heard the legendary Kirsten Flagstad, then fifty-five, in her farewell appearances at Covent Garden. Nilsson, who had only recently begun to sing Wagner roles, did not then suspect that by the end of the decade she would inherit Flagstad's mantle as the world's leading Wagnerian soprano. "I had heard Flagstad once before, in Stockholm in 1947," she told me. "She was nervous and unhappy and didn't sing at her best. Poor woman—people had persecuted her, saying she was a Nazi. It was her husband who had been involved; she herself was completely innocent. But now in London when she sang Isolde, it was marvelous."

I asked Nilsson if Flagstad had influenced her in any way. "Could be—could be that I tried in my way," she replied somewhat enigmatically. "She was the first person I bought on records. Her voice was an incredible organ; it had a darker color than mine. Everything was so beautifully phrased." (The two sopranos met in person one time only, in 1958 outside the Imperial Hotel in Vienna. "I was almost speechless in admiration," Nilsson recalls. "The first thing that struck me was how wonderful she looked—so healthy, an unbelievable complexion. She compared my Donna Anna, which she had heard at the Opera, to Elisabeth Rethberg's. This was truly great praise. I was touched that she could be so generous. She was very much down-to-earth and had no pretensions at all.")

In all our talks about her career, I found that Nilsson was drawn less to the triumphs than to the challenges. One of these came with her first Aida, in Stockholm. "I loved the role very much and learned a lot from it, especially in scaling down my big voice to piano and pianissimo," she said. "Verdi's shadings are extremely subtle. Italian music is quite another world for us northerners. It has a special warmth and softness of texture. In Stockholm we didn't have a single Italian coach. But, later, at La Scala I worked with Antonio Tonini, who taught me about the expressive use of the language, the rubato, and the art of the portamento: a slide from one note to another can sound exaggerated and even crude unless prepared by a diminuendo to pianissimo. I worked for years to assimilate the Italian style."

In 1952 Nilsson declined an offer from La Scala. It was an unusual decision for a thirty-four-year-old singer who had by then become the star of the Royal Stockholm Opera. She told me, "I felt that the offer came too early. There's a risk in leaping too far too soon, and forgetting all the development that's necessary in between. Young singers must start inwardly. Many think of the glamour and want to skim the cream off the top, rather than dig down and know what it's all about."

Even after Nilsson developed her international career, she continued to sing most of her major roles for the first time in Stockholm. The steady stream of her work was interrupted in May 1952 when tuberculosis was diagnosed (there was a strain of consumption on her mother's side of the family). After convalescing for several months on the farm at Svenstad, she was back on stage, albeit in considerable pain, singing Tosca.

Three experiences—all in 1954—had a decisive impact on her vocal development. The first was "Salome." "Up until then, I'd been portraying queens and princesses who walk slowly," she told me. "My high notes still had a tendency to tighten. But now I had to run, bend, and loosen up my body. And, as I did so, the voice became more supple. Six weeks later, while I was in Brussels for a performance of the Verdi Requiem, I came down with a terrible cold. I locked myself into a practice room and swore that I wouldn't leave before finding a way to cope with it. I thought, The front of my head is a vibrating chamber like the violin. The throat must be completely relaxed; the strength has to come from deep down—that is, from the muscles you feel when you ride a horse. I found a connection. Incredibly, no teacher had spoken to me about the importance of support. All of a sudden, the high notes started to bloom in a new way. It's simpler than anyone thinks: the higher you go with your voice the lower you feel the strength in your body. Often, afterwards, I lost the support when I got nervous, but I began to use it more and more. What I learned that day was a basis for me.

"During the summer I was scheduled to make my operatic debut at Bayreuth, as Elsa in 'Lohengrin.' When I woke up three days before the general rehearsal I found—for the only time in my life—that I had virtually no voice; I'd probably been over-rehearsing. I was desperate. I had to find a way to sing that was gentle to my vocal cords. I concentrated as never before: *every* note had to be as if played on a violin—not just every third or fourth note. I used only a very slender tone, as if I were singing Mozart, and, by the end of the rehearsal, not only had I regained my voice, but it sounded better than ever. If you start with a slender voice and get that ping in it, then it grows by itself. This discovery of the slender voice was related to the revelation I'd had in Brussels. Later, in Vienna, when a critic wrote that I sang Isolde like Donna Anna, I took it as a big compliment. Wagner himself wrote that German singers should study Italian vocal art. It's ideal if you can alternate Wagner with Verdi or Mozart because they help keep the voice flexible."

The period 1954–57 marked the expansion of Nilsson's international career, with Vienna, Buenos Aires, San Francisco, and London following in turn. With this growth in her activity came the influence of powerful musical personalities. One of these was Herman Weigert, a *répétiteur* at Bayreuth, whom Nilsson remembers as being "a wellspring of knowledge—for instance, about pacing: when to use the whole voice, when to save it because the orchestra is so loud that you can't be heard anyway. He stressed how important it is that the singer should anticipate the orchestra in feeling the expressive impulse appropriate to the phrase. This brings an immediate vitality. One heard that in the singing of his wife, Astrid Varnay."

Then there was Georg Solti, whose work with Nilsson in Chicago in 1956 initiated eighteen years of artistic relationship. "I'd never met anyone so true to the values of the written score," she said. "He insisted on absolute rhythmic precision and would never let you get away with anything. Many well-known singers who came to him learned for the first time what it was to be truly accurate."

A different sort of inspiration was provided by Hans Knappertsbusch, doyen of Wagner conductors: "Knappertsbusch conveyed enormous authority and held the orchestra in his hand like a magician. He could take incredibly broad tempos, but—unlike those conductors who tried to copy him—his performances were full of life and feeling. Beyond any conductor I've worked with, he believed in the inspiration of the moment, and hated to rehearse. The result was that—in Munich in 1955—when I sang Brünnhilde in German for the first time in the complete "Ring" (my previous performances had been in Swedish), I had no orchestra rehearsal whatever. Five minutes before the performance he introduced himself and said, 'So here is that courageous lady.' I told him that I didn't feel so courageous."

It was with Knappertsbusch and the Vienna Philharmonic, in 1959, that Nilsson was to make her first studio recording: two excerpts from "Tristan und Isolde," which reveal the full measure of artistry she had attained by that time and the way she could respond to a great conductor. Singer and instrumentalists enter into a chamber-music relationship, the voice merging into the orchestral texture with an un-canny sense of belonging. In the "Liebestod" the voice seems to glide on waves and, in its ease and repose, to be transformed into liquid matter. It rides the breakers with majesty and passion. Whether float-ing full-bodied in piano or rising brilliant and resplendent in forte, it is possessed of a mysterious quality that transcends considerations of vocal technique. Its substance is like an unblemished pearl, illumi-nated by a deep luster at its core.

In 1958, when Nilsson finally sang at La Scala, her unprece-dented command of the high tessitura in "Turandot" created near-pandemonium among the public. The following year, her debut at the Metropolitan Opera in "Tristan und Isolde" was featured on the front page of both the *New York Times* and *Herald Tribune*. Ten days later, when Rudolf Bing was unable to find a Heldentenor in good-enough vocal health to last through the whole opera, he provided her with three different Tristans, one for each act. She appeared for twenty seasons at the Met, sixteen at Bayreuth, twenty-eight at the Vienna State Opera (where the seventy-five curtain-calls after one "Elektra" lasted almost as long as the opera itself). Among her many recordings was the historic first complete Ring Cycle, made with Solti in the mid-1960s.

"I never thought I'd go as far as I did," Nilsson had told me. "But if one has self-determination one can absolutely move *rocks*." As she said the words, she thrust forth her arm, striking an imaginary wall with her fist. "I just wanted to focus on my work and do it really well. If I had another profession, I'd do the same."

An enlarged photo of Nils Svensson listening to his daughter re-hearse at the Royal Opera in Stockholm hangs above the Ek-ström upright in the Svenstad farmhouse parlor. During the twenty-six years that elapsed between Birgit's debut and his own death at the age of eighty-three, he went to the opera to hear her sing on only two occasions. (Justina Svensson had the satisfaction of hearing her daughter in 1949 as Senta in "The Flying Dutchman"; six months later she was killed in an automobile accident.) Nils Svensson would never admit to Birgit that she had done well to leave the farm. One of her friends expressed a view shared by many who know her: "Birgit could do anything on this earth except be a son, so she became the strongest woman-singer in the history of singing."

Nilsson herself put it this way to me: "In the early years of my career, it would have meant a great deal to me to have my father's encouragement. But in retrospect I can understand how he felt. It was a completely different world. He thought that because he was happy on the farm, I should also be happy there. He never got over his hurt that I hadn't obeyed him. But in his heart of hearts he was proud of me. He had his own way of making it known. He once heard me in 'Tosca.' Jussi Björling was the tenor, and I was inspired to do my best. After I had finished 'Vissi d'Arte,' my father told the person sitting next to him, 'Don't applaud *her*—she's only my daughter.' "

The more relevant consideration is not the extent to which Nilsson suffered from her father's lack of encouragement, but the way his patrimony of hardheaded vigor worked within her to energize her creativity and self-reliance.

"I have to decide things for myself," she would say. "No one can decide for me." Throughout her career, Nilsson never had an entourage, never employed a secretary, and rarely used agents. She preferred to negotiate directly with theatre managements, and would note her engagements in a little black book. From 1960 she commanded the top fee in the operatic world. She explained, "When I had those difficult roles—working hard and trying to be reliable—I didn't think it fair that others should have higher fees. Equal—okay—but not more." She summed up her attitude: "Know your own worth and be humble toward your art." On an income-tax form she declared Rudolf Bing as a dependent.

She often waited until the last moment to sign a contract—a habit that Rudolf Bing found unnerving—meanwhile offering her firm assurance that My Word is My Word. A gallstone attack did not prevent her from opening the 1963 Met season as Aida; a dislocated shoulder—resulting from a fall at a Met rehearsal—did not deter her from appearing as Brünnhilde with her arm in a sling. Shortly before her fiftieth birthday, she underwent major surgery for cancer. "Only my husband knew the truth," she told me. "I couldn't face people who might feel sorry for me." Eight weeks later she was singing "Götterdämmering" in Vienna.

"In my private life I don't think I'm very strong," Nilsson told me. "Bertil says that I am. But if it's something to do with my job, then I'm strong. I ask a great deal of myself, but I also ask very much of others."

"It wasn't just a heroic voice; it was a heroic personality," says one of Nilsson's colleagues. "Birgit managed to be patient and generous with most of the people she worked with. If she wanted to take on somebody, it was always a person on her level—another giant, like Herbert von Karajan." It is to be regretted that Karajan and Nilsson, often kept apart by conflicting recording commitments, worked together only intermittently. Karajan's Wagner performances were unsurpassed in architectural grandeur, expressive continuity, and orchestral transparency. He knew how to exercise personal power to attain his artistic ends, and expected unquestioning compliance from everyone with whom he worked. He met his match in Nils Svensson's daughter.

"When Karajan was there as a musician with his soul and nothing else was disturbing him, he was wonderful—really, really wonderful," Nilsson told me. "But he wanted to master everything, and his efforts at staging and lighting were absolutely amateurish. When we did 'Die Walküre' together at the Met, I was left in total darkness while Wotan sang his monologue to me in the second act. It's crucial that the audience see Brünnhilde's reactions. Sometimes it was so dark that the singers would just stumble around the stage. A Met staff member gave me a lighted miner's helmet to wear, but Karajan wasn't amused; he had very little sense of humor." When Karajan complained to the press of Nilsson's discontent, she told a reporter: "It seems clear that Maestro von Karajan has such a great talent for staging that he should give up conducting and become a stage director, just as everyone has told me, since I sang Salome, that I should give up singing and become a dancer."

Nilsson recalls: "Once, in Vienna, Karajan was on stage, directing 'Siegfried.' At the end of the love-duet, just as Wolfgang Windgassen and I were moving toward our embrace, he interrupted us and cried out, 'That's just cold coffee.' He told Windgassen to stand aside, and demonstrated his version of Siegfried's passion. He thought his sex-appeal was irresistible and expected me to fall into a swoon. "*Now* did you feel something?' he asked. I just looked at him innocently and shook my head 'No.' He muttered, 'These cold Swedish women are really pitiful.' "

A typical Nilsson day before a performance: A brisk two-hour walk—in winter without a scarf; she'd never worn one on the farm. Shopping and cooking in readiness for a late-night dinner party. Complete mental review of the evening's role. ("I always say, 'Sing less and think more.' When I learned 'Elektra' I put the score under my pillow at night. A colleague in Stockholm says, 'Anything Birgit knows, she learned in bed.' ") Arrival at the theatre two hours in advance, score in hand—no detail to be overlooked. A hand-made sign posted on her dressing-room door: ENTER AT YOUR OWN RISK. Stage fright with no real remedy. ("All my life I've been doubtful about myself. I'd ask myself, Do I really sing as well as the critics say?") The presence of Curlytop, a knitted bull kept in the Swedish railway-worker's lunch box that serves as a makeup case. ("Tebaldi had to kiss the madonna before going on stage. Franco Corelli had to touch holy water. I only had my Curlytop.") Vocalizing for no more than a quarter of an hour: a penetrating nasal hum progressing to a piercing cat yowl until the voice was ringing in the forehead. The fine line of "Porgi Amor" from "The Marriage of Figaro" as a preparation for Brünnhilde. After the performance: a cold beer, and hosting a Swedish supper for her friends.

Among singers, the adulation of the public is not commonly known to be an incentive to artistic growth. Yet, at the end of the nineteen-fifties, when Nilsson had reached the height of acclaim, she did precisely that which we most hope for from the famous, but least expect: she turned inward to explore those sides of her artistry that were least developed. She realized that barriers still existed between her heroic style and the feminine vulnerability of an Aida, a Tosca, a Sieglinde, Isolde or Brunnhilde. The more she crossed over into their imaginative world, the more she drew forth from herself a new range of expression: her voice increasingly became multi-colored, multinuanced. Nowhere did her womanly depth settle upon her more fully than in the final scene of "Siegfried," which Nilsson describes as Brünnhilde's most challenging moment dramatically.

Here, she is awakened to her mortality by Siegfried, who has penetrated the ring of magic fire Wotan had built around his disobedient daughter. "There are three main stages—all within a half hour," Nilsson told me. "When I first see Siegfried, I believe I'm still a goddess. Then I develop a motherly feeling toward him—I know the story of his origins that he himself couldn't know—and then I suddenly fall in love. All the changes have to be interpreted through the music and your inner feelings." When Nilsson sang "Ewig war ich" —the haunting "Siegfried Idyll" melody—it was like a Schubert Lied; and when she exhorted Siegfried: "As my eyes devour you, are you not blinded?" —her voice took on a stifled, incredulous astonishment that he should doubt her willingness to surrender herself to him. Georg Solti recalled, "Birgit never stopped growing in depth of interpretation. One often talks of Nilsson and Flagstad. Two wonderful singers. But Birgit developed a sensibility, a flexibility, a dynamic range, a temperament that Flagstad didn't have in that measure."

Nilsson's acting could not escape the shaping forces now unleashed. Leonie Rysanek, who often partnered her as Elektra's sister Chrysothemis, told me, "Birgit was not born a great actress, but she had a great personality—an unmistakable personality. She was always very shy. Some say she could be cold; I never felt that. She had an inner fire. Over the years there was an enormous growth in her expression on stage. Her Recognition Scene brought tears to my eyes, and not only because of the singing. She had a true feeling for the part: Elektra is a princess, a great woman underneath—not hysterical. We sang it together under Wieland Wagner's direction. He liberated her, brought out her deepest feelings."

Nilsson often speaks of Wieland Wagner, the composer's grandson, one of the most gifted opera directors of our century. When, together with his brother Wolfgang, he assumed the direction of Bayreuth in 1951, he initiated a revolutionary approach to the staging of Wagner's operas in which realistic settings were replaced by symbolic images and "acting" became intensely internalized. His art continually deepened until his untimely death in 1966 at the age of forty-nine. He attained what he considered the fruition of his work in his 1962 production of "Tristan" with Nilsson as Isolde. But the paths of these two artists did not come together easily.

"I first met Wieland in 1953 when I auditioned for him in Bayreuth," Nilsson told me. "After I had sung, he knelt before me—I couldn't believe my eyes—and offered me any role I wanted, but advised me never to touch Brünnhilde or Isolde because he thought they were too dramatic for my voice. I told him that I was going to sing Isolde in Stockholm two months later. I didn't hear from him for some time; a beautiful lady had come into his life and he had given her all the roles. Meanwhile, Wolfgang engaged me to sing at Bayreuth under his direction the following year and from 1957 onwards. There was a degree of rivalry between the brothers, and Wieland's attitude towards me became nearly hostile. When he decided to do a new production of 'Tristan' he looked everywhere else for an Isolde. Finally, he asked me. I swallowed my pride, and accepted.

"At the first rehearsal, I said, 'Mr. Wagner, I've sung Isolde eighty-seven times.' He interrupted: 'Oh, I already know about all your successes, Madame Nilsson," and laughed in his peculiar, nervous way with his shoulders shaking. 'But let me finish,' I went on. 'I'll forget all those performances and start from the beginning with you.' He found that very nice, but clearly didn't believe me. After we had worked together for an hour he realized that I meant what I'd said.

"By training Wieland was a sculptor and painter. His sets for 'Tristan'—based on the rough-hewn megaliths found in Cornwall—were truly atmospheric. He didn't ignore a singer's individuality as most stage directors do. He brought out what you had to offer. In a press interview he once described Astrid Varnay as "the revenge-seeking Isolde," Martha Mödl as "an Isolde compelled by fate," and Birgit Nilsson as "the impetuous and loving Isolde." Earlier, my Isolde had been more black and white. But now we worked on all the feelings in between. Isolde often says one thing and means something else. Love and hate are closely linked; you find that in Strindberg. In the first-act narration I tell of how I was about to kill Tristan, when suddenly 'He looked into my eyes'—'Er sah mir in die Augen.' I saw his love for me—there's a wonderful modulation in the musical line. In only a second or two an incredible transformation takes place within Isolde's body and soul. That's the turning point—oh, God, just thinking of it I start to get goose pimples! From then on until the end of the act, although Isolde fights against it, love shines through more and more. When I give him the death potion, it's not for revenge. It's to be united with him. We'll die together for love. I don't believe any role has so many facets or is so deep. You could never finish with it.

"Working with Wieland helped me in my other roles. Until then, I had more or less accepted what the stage directors were doing. I opened my eyes, and became more critical and questioning. Many directors today are such egotists. They want to display their special insights, but what they produce is just baloney. I've sung in a 'Masked Ball' where the king was supposed to be in love with his page boy; in an 'Elektra' where the sisters are supposed to have lesbian feelings. Ridiculous! I've seen a 'Don Giovanni' that was a sexual delirium from beginning to end: men dressed as women, Donna Anna pregnant and wanting to go to bed with Don Giovanni again. When you've lived into every part, you know it's so wrong. I got so upset—but people hardly react anymore.

"Some directors will ask you to drop to the floor twenty-eight times in twenty minutes. But Wieland would tell me, 'Birgit, you can't compete with Wagner's music. Too many gestures will just make you seem smaller. Less is more.' He felt that the expression should be apparent in the bearing, in the face, and in the projection of the text. He had a genius for lighting: the stage was dark but he lighted what was important. He captured every nuance, every mood. One of the most beautiful moments in his 'Tristan' came at the end. Wieland stressed that his grandfather never called the ending 'Liebestod': Love-death—but, 'Verklärung': transfiguration. That's why he asked me to remain standing and gradually raise my arms, as if drawn upwards. It should be unearthly. I felt I was sailing to heaven." As Nilsson spoke, her arms began to form an arc and her expression became radiant. I remembered the words of a Swedish friend, who has known her for three decades: "When Birgit speaks of the roles she's sung, she refers to Aida, Tosca, and Turandot as 'she'—and to Isolde, Brünnhilde, and Elektra as 'I.' "

In December 1974 Nilsson gave a concert performance of "Salome" with Solti and the Chicago Symphony. Afterwards, he told her, "It can't be sung better than that." "Then I don't have to sing it anymore," she said, and she didn't. At fifty-six she was still at the height of her powers. In the development of her singing and of her career she had—in the tradition of Nils Svensson—never been a slave to time. Now she benefitted from a remarkable preservation of voice. She sang her last Isolde at sixty and her last Elektra at sixty-four. In the later stages of her career she turned with increasing frequency to song recitals. She approached the repertoire with much understanding and sensitivity, although she never felt altogether comfortable when interpreting music on a small scale. She put it to me in one of her double-edged remarks: "Singing Lieder is like being a clock repairman; I was a house builder."

The final concert came in 1984. "The nervousness was with me throughout my career," she confessed. "But at the end it became almost unbearable. I'm a realistic person, and I said, Birgit; you're going to have to stop. I avoided giving any 'farewell' performances—no sentimentality. I did it little by little, so that I would just fade away, and no one would speak about it."

"When Birgit retired, I was really concerned," Bertil had told me. "I wondered what peril it would bring. But it worked out well, unbelievably well. She's often called upon to serve on juries of singing competitions—she's not ruled by preconceptions; she always speaks her mind—and she's given master classes. At first she lacked confidence that she could be a good teacher, but then she enjoyed herself enormously." Nilsson is not displeased when, honored in Bayreuth, Vienna, or at the Met, she still receives standing ovations. But she was, as Yeats expressed it, "bred to a harder thing than triumph." She partakes of a larger truth: her commitment to the flow of life, her identification with the task at hand, her satisfaction in doing "really well" whatever needs to be done.

"When I began to teach, the first thing I had to learn was to give up myself," Nilsson said during one of the master classes she gave at the Manhattan School of Music from 1983 to 1991. "It's not me any longer—how I did it, how I sang it. The young people couldn't care less; they care about their own future. I'm happy if I can give something back through the knowledge I've gained over the years."

The knowledge is profound; the means, simple and persuasive. "Before you begin to sing, imagine that you're smelling a rose," she told a young colleague. "All the cavities must be open; sense it even in your eyes. But the flower needs a root; that root is your support. Feel that you are grown together with the earth." She shepherded the students from phrase to phrase, sometimes from vowel to vowel, drawing attention to the least sign of vocal tension or any inadvertent change in tone color that compromised the musical line. Referring to the notes that bridge over from the middle to the high register, she said, "The art of singing in the *passagio* is to keep the voice slender and unforced. Then you'll have a long career." To an advanced artist: "Your voice is well placed, but you can make it a little rounder. I like to have a roof over every tone—a cupola." Technical advice was given in a musical context. To a soprano singing "Einsam in trüben Tagen" from "Lohengrin": "Elsa is a very young girl and shouldn't be sung with a Brünnhilde voice. Every tone must shine: it's mystic; you see him—he's coming in a marvelous light." To a tenor singing "Che gelida manina" from "La Bohème": "Don't begin an 'aria.' There's almost nothing in the orchestra; you are talking about her little hand. Think through the phrase to the end: float, float, float . . . The more simple, the more beautiful; the more simple, the more difficult." For a recitative in "Cosi fan tutte": "Bite more into the words; give variety to the expression. You're a good actress, but you should not only act with your gestures; act with your *voice*." To defuse nervous tension in Verdi's "Pace, pace, mio Dio": "It's tough to sing the high B-flat pianissimo. I can't. But I'm like a priest: don't do what I do; do what I say." And, as ever, a double-edged rapier: "Mozart is difficult; that's why I sang Wagner."

The Niklassons' main dwelling-place, near the town of Kristianstad, is a farm, dating from 1870, that Bertil inherited from his father. Its general plan is not unlike that of the Svenstad farm. One barn has been converted into a guest house, and there is a gracious garden and a well-kept lawn. The furnishings, more elegant than those at Svenstad but by no means ostentatious, consist, in part, of Georgian pieces, including a stately grandfather clock. There are several collections of eighteenth-century silver: salt spoons, button hooks, Spanish musicians. "I love old things," Nilsson says. "I love their shape and craftsmanship. I got that from my parents. When I didn't have to sing, I'd go to auctions. It was a hobby; it helped me when I was alone."

Upon my arrival, I had brought Nilsson two modest musical offerings. The first was a selection of recordings of Beniamino Gigli. "What an artist he was," she exclaimed. "I've never been so impressed by a tenor in all of my life. You know, I once slept in Gigli's bed. Unfortunately he had already died by that time. I had the privilege of singing with him—in 'Tosca'—in Stockholm when he was sixty-two. He brought his whole entourage—a secretary, hairdresser, and doctor—one older than the other. They seemed to require help rather than Gigli, but he didn't have the heart to put them on pension. When we sang, he felt that I needed encouragement, so at every opportunity he'd turn his back to the audience and tell me, 'Che bella voce.' There was never a thread of ugly tone in his voice, and it was so flexible—like rubber." She swayed her arms in an arabesque. "I wanted to try to do the same, but my voice was another material—more metallic—and it wasn't so easy to mold. Many years later I went to his grave, which was not very nicely kept; I put flowers on it."

She reminisced about her favorite Italian tenors and soon came to Franco Corelli. "Franco was *wonderful*," she exclaimed. "He had an incredible impact on stage. The public loved him, not least the women." The Nilsson/Corelli partnership was nowhere more memorable than in the 1961 Met revival of "Turandot." "Our 'Turandot' was like a bullfight," Nilsson went on. "The question was: Who will hold the high C longer? When we came to 'In questa reggia,' he was at the footlights, and I was upstage, perched on a staircase. When we sang the C together, I couldn't hear him at all, so I had to somehow see how long he kept his mouth open. In every performance, the C became longer, and I became bluer in the face. It got out of proportion. Before the curtain went up, Franco would worry that his voice wasn't going to function; he'd walk around like a caged lion. I was almost as nervous myself, but, to tease him, I'd pretend to be very calm, and sit reading the *New York Times*—although, God knows, it might have been upside down. Franco would hide sponges on stage and use them to keep his throat moist. Once, in the second act, when I was singing alone from my staircase, and he had nothing to do than to wait for his high C, he suddenly turned his back to the public, put his hand inside the front of his pants and began fooling around. I was very concerned as to what was going to happen. Finally, he drew out a sponge and began to suck it. Believe me, I could hardly go on singing."

My second gift for Nilsson was a facsimile edition of the autograph of the five songs Richard Wagner set to poems by Mathilde Wesendonck, the *femme inspiratrice* for his "Tristan und Isolde." She seemed pleased to have it, and said, "I think many of Wagner's affairs were just to keep him inspired. How lucky he was when he married Cosima. She understood him and always accepted him—even when he was interested in other women. Maybe Wagner was close to being crazy at times. But what he achieved! The will-power and inspiration were unbelievable."

I asked her by which means she first approached her Wagner roles: poetry, music, myth?

"I began with the music," she said. "I couldn't contain my excitement to sing it. Then it was easier for me to enter into the world of the poetry; it had to be as if it came from myself. I also read about Wagner the man, and about the myths and sagas. Wieland was fascinated with the mythological side—the timeless side. We talked and talked, and he helped shape my conceptions."

"You also happened to be raised in the land of myths," I said. "Might that have influenced you?"

She thought for a moment. "Could be—perhaps without my reflecting on it. Could be . . . "

She spoke of how late she had come to Wagner. I reminded her that she had once told a student, 'When I was twenty-one I couldn't even *spell* Wagner!' " "That's not far from the truth," she said, laughing. "In fact, the first Wagner opera I heard was 'Tannhäuser,' in Stockholm when I was twenty-three. But then I went to every single performance. My greatest dream was that I might sing Elisabeth one day. But when I finally did, I never thought I was very good in the role. Like Senta and Elsa, she is quite a passive girl. I think I did her more justice when, years later, I sang Venus and Elisabeth on the same evening. Wieland saw them as two aspects of one person—each fulfilling what the other lacks. Luckily for Tannhäuser the two women are never on stage at the same time."

Nilsson fetched a small box from which she took a silk handkerchief, almost as large as a scarf, decorated in a Persian design in red, black and ivory. "I was singing at Bayreuth and came down with an awful cold," she explained. "Wolfgang Wagner gave this to me; it belonged to his grandfather. Look—it's been mended." She held up a corner that had been carefully sewn. "Wagner used it when he sniffed tobacco. He'd hang it from a trouser pocket; it reached below his knee—he was such a short man."

"Supposing you were able to meet Wagner," I suggested. "What would you most like to ask him?"

"Oh boy, that's a good question," she exclaimed, and buried her head in her hands. After a long moment's reflection, she said, "I think I'd ask if he was *really* so secure within himself. Was he always the *Meister*? He had such a difficult life; so many people were against him. After seventy-seven rehearsals in Vienna they still couldn't perform 'Tristan.' It's one thing to show a brave face on the outside. But in his heart of hearts was he so confident? One sees in Cosima's diary: 'Richard cried again today,' and she cried with him.

"I'd also like to ask him why he composed 'Tristan' in such a way that Isolde sings during virtually the entire first act, lasting seventy-eight minutes—or with some conductors ninety-four minutes!—and then, after a short intermission, she continues singing for another fifty minutes. It takes so much out of you. Brünnhilde in 'Götterdämmerung' is even more taxing—but he paced it so well for the voice; I never failed."

It was now late afternoon in Svenstad, and Bertil was driving us up to the farm's highest point so that I could see the Ring of Judgment, the ancient circle of stones that Nils Svensson had so prized. We took a roundabout route, and stopped first at a large barn-like building that was devoted entirely to the making and selling of wooden shoes, hundreds of which were on display. Bertil needed replacements. "Mine last forever," Nilsson said. "I don't know why yours get worn out."

"I am working harder than you," he responded.

We drove along a precipitous and rocky coastline known as the "Italian road," occasionally fortified by bunkers built as defenses in 1942. A narrow cove stretched below, dotted with fishermen's huts painted in *faluröd*. Nilsson pointed to a house on a bluff overlooking the sea. "That was my grandparents' home," she said. "It has a splendid view, but it's difficult to live there; the wind is terrific. I used to go swimming here. We were the first ones in the water in April."

I asked Nilsson if she missed the stage, now so far distant in time. "I miss my colleagues," she said. "Leonie Rysanek—we were like sisters. As for the stage itself—I know too well what one has to put into it. It's strange, though: I often dream that I still have to sing—mostly parts I've never studied: Carmen or the Countess in 'Figaro.' I'm unprepared, and I become hysterical. When I awake, my husband tells me, 'That's nothing for you to worry about.' "

"You always knew your roles," Bertil affirmed.

"It's hard for him to understand," she went on; "he's never been on the stage. But he gets caught up in my worries anyway. Sometimes he has the same kind of nightmares about singing that I have. I feel sorry for him."

Our last stop en route was the Heritage Society Museum—a homestead of several buildings with steeply pitched, thatched roofs, devoted to regional folk life. A maypole from Midsummer Eve still stood in the field. Nils Svensson had contributed to the museum's founding and remains very much a part of it. A selection of his stone-age relics is on display, and the harmonium he once brought home for his daughter stands in one of the low-ceilinged rooms. The instrument, old-fashioned and charming in appearance, has a gracefully carved wooden crest; candlesticks are affixed on either side of the music rack. I played a few chords on it; it was somewhat out of tune, but still has a sweet and lovely tone.

Over tea, at the long oak table in the homestead's rustic kitchen, Bertil told me of the concerts Birgit has given to support the Heritage Society. "It's the least I could do," she added. "I want to help preserve the traditions of our village." I asked her how, in the face of so extraordinary a career, she had managed to stay connected to simple things. "When you work with only two small vocal cords, you shouldn't become overbearing," she answered. "When I sang well, it was almost as if someone else's instrument was being played upon. I took full responsibility only when I sang badly. I was very modest so long as I felt that people weren't taking advantage of me. I'm easy to get along with."

Bertil conspicuously cleared his throat.

"Well, I don't know what my husband thinks. But I've tried to remember what my mother used to tell me: 'Stay close to the earth. Then when you fall down it won't hurt so much.' I think it helped to have been born in the country. You don't make things too complicated; you don't make problems along the way. You see things more naturally."

We came at last to the hill of the Ring of Judgment, which surmounts a large cow pasture. Bertil parked at the foot of the slope and decided to wait for us in the car. Nilsson, still as energetic as when we had left the Baltic coast early that morning, led the way. She darted unceremoniously under an electrified fence. I followed rather awkwardly and with some trepidation as a dozen cows, their curiosity aroused, moved toward us. "I have my friends here," she remarked, patting one of the Holsteins. "Oh, they are so quiet and nice. Be careful not to step in the dung." As we climbed up the hillside, she said, "Rudolf Bing never understood why I didn't want to go on tour with the Met at the end of each season. He offered me high fees, but it wasn't a question of money. I wanted to come back to Sweden. I'd be sick if I ever missed the long sunlit nights."

We came upon a wide plateau, and there were the stones: six of them—sentinels planted in the earth, each three or four feet in height—laid out in a circle about eight yards in diameter. "These stones were placed here before there were any written laws," Nilsson said. "There was a grave in the middle where a chieftain was buried with his weapons. Villagers would meet here and judgments would be made. They had a view of the coast from three sides, and could look out for invaders. I remember it from the time when there weren't any trees here; it was even more beautiful then." Beyond a wide expanse of farmland, the sea was still largely visible. Far off, the church of Hov could be seen on the site where Odin was once worshipped.

"Like all the farmers at that time, my father needed every bit of land to grow crops on," Nilsson went on. "But he would never move these stones. He liked to come up here just to be by himself—even in his last years, when he was ill. And when he wasn't strong enough, he'd ask me to come in his stead, and then I'd tell him what it was like to be here."

A breeze had sprung up; the long twilight was beginning. "When I was a child, I used to play here with the children from the neighboring farms," Nilsson said. "We'd sit on the stones and pretend to be bishops, judges, and kings. Sometimes I'd come here alone." The cows began to wander into the Ring of Judgment as Nilsson stood there gazing over the fields. Suddenly she stretched her arms out wide. "These are my acres," she said. "My acres."

This interview was conducted in West Karup, Sweden, 25 June 1995.

About the Author

The late David Blum, distinguished conductor and writer, was born in Los Angeles and received his musical training in America and in Europe. In 1961 he founded New York's Esterhazy Orchestra with Pablo Casals as the Honorary President. His recordings of Haydn symphonies with that ensemble and of Mozart works with the English Chamber Orchestra have won international acclaim.

Blum resided in Switzerland from 1969 to 1989. He was appointed artistic director and conductor of both the Lausanne Symphony Orchestra and the Geneva Symphony Orchestra and guest conducted extensively throughout Europe.

David Blum's books, which have been translated into several languages, include *Casals and the Art of Interpretation; The Art of Quartet Playing: The Guarneri Quartet in Conversation with David Blum;* and *Paul Tortelier.* Blum's profiles on eminent musicians appeared in the *New Yorker;* his articles and essays were published regularly in the *New York Times,* the *Strad,* the *BBC Magazine,* and the *Musical Times.* His final work was a documentary introduced by Yo-Yo Ma and titled *Appointment with the Wise Old Dog: Dream Images in a Time of Crisis.*